POST-HOLOCAUST

JEWISH LITERATURE AND CULTURE

SERIES EDITOR, ALVIN H. ROSENFELD

POST-HOLOCAUST

Interpretation, Misinterpretation, and the Claims of History

Berel Lang

INDIANA UNIVERSITY PRESS

Bloomington and Indianapolis

This book is a publication of

INDIANA UNIVERSITY PRESS
601 North Morton Street
Bloomington, IN 47404-3797 USA

http://iupress.indiana.edu

Telephone orders   800-842-6796
Fax orders   812-855-7931
Orders by e-mail   iuporder@indiana.edu

The paper used in this publication meets the minimum requirements of American National Standard for Information Sciences—Permanence of Paper for Printed Library Materials, ANSI Z39.48-1984.

Manufactured in the United States of America

Library of Congress Cataloging-in-Publication Data

Lang, Berel.
Post-Holocaust : interpretation, misinterpretation, and the claims of history / Berel Lang.
p. cm. — (Jewish literature and culture)
Includes index.
ISBN 0-253-34501-4 (cloth : alk. paper) — ISBN 0-253-21728-8 (pbk. : alk. paper)
1. Holocaust, Jewish (1939–1945)—Historiography. 2. Holocaust, Jewish (1939–1945)—Influence. 3. Holocaust, Jewish (1939–1945)—Moral and ethical aspects. 4. Antisemitism—History. I. Title. II. Series.
D804.348.L36 2004 2005
940.53'18'072—dc22

2004010948

1 2 3 4 5   10 09 08 07 06 05

FOR ARIELLA AND ALEX,
JESSICA AND JÖRG—
JOINING THE PAST TO THE FUTURE
(AND BOTH TO EACH OTHER)

CONTENTS

ACKNOWLEDGMENTS

The chapters of this book were written during the past four years, most of them occasioned as texts for symposia, lectures, or anthologies, but with a common focus on some of the many issues that have arisen in what now claims its own period and title—the "Post-Holocaust." Nobody writing about these issues can be unaware of the criticism directed against the "surplus" of talk—companion to the surfeit of memory—that has been alleged in the aftermath of the Holocaust. Objections to the "Shoah Business" which criticize the exploitation of the Holocaust for purposes that have little to do with that event, continue to increase, at times with good reason—and few of its students would now deny that the "Post-Holocaust," the period of almost sixty years since the end of the Holocaust itself, has, beyond (or perhaps as part of) its contribution to understanding that event, also become institutionalized. Here, too, representations of the Holocaust have at times been moved by extraneous social or political or religious purposes in ways that skew or distort that event's historical and moral boundaries. The importance and the extent of interest in the Holocaust that make such "deformations" (in Robert Alter's term) virtually inevitable may or may not compensate for them (this issue is itself a pressing concern for the Post-Holocaust); but it is equally clear that even the severest critics of those excesses have little to say about how they can be avoided without, by the same measures, risking a blanket silence or erasure of the Holocaust itself.

What emerges from this mixture of imperatives and cautions is the sense of a special responsibility for anyone writing about the Holocaust—and now also, it might be supposed, for anyone writing, at one remove, about the Post-Holocaust. As *all* writing has a moral dimension—the author acting on (that is, doing something to) both the subject and the reader—the author's responsibility as "agent" increases in both directions in proportion to the moral weight of the subject itself. In this way, literary agency poses at once an ideal and a challenge to Holocaust writing, given that subject's moral import. And then, too, as Holocaust writing shares its very first principle with all other writing—cued on the warning in the opening lines of Aesculapius's Creed: "Do no harm"—the question beyond that of how much *good* a given representation of that event does, becomes more pressing than for most subjects. To be sure, the risks in writing about the Holocaust because of its moral weight are balanced—arguably, overridden—by the consequences of *not* writing about it. But however one judges this balance, it has the effect for those writing about the Holocaust or Post-Holocaust of posing at once a standard of measurement and a test. The way in which these converge is concise and severe: might it not be better not to have written at all? All Holocaust writing seems to me required to begin and conclude with that question. I hope it will be clear from the pages that follow here that signing my name to them does not mean that I take an answer to this question for granted.

* * *

I am grateful to the editors of the journals or volumes in which the following chapters first appeared for permission to elaborate on them here: " 'Not Enough' and 'Plenty': What Pius XII Did and Didn't," *Judaism*; "Self-Ascription and the Antisemite: Who Decides?" *Annual Report 1998* (Sassoon International Center for the Study of Antisemitism); " 'A Few Cheap Tears': Novick on 'The Holocaust in American Life,' " *Jewish Social Studies;* "Philosophy's Contribution to Holocaust Studies," in E. Garard and F. F. Scarre, eds., *Philosophy and the Holocaust* (London: Ashgate, 2001); "Misinterpretation and the Author's Responsibility," in J. Golomb and R. Wistrich, eds., *Nietzsche: Godfather of Fascism?* (Princeton, N.J.: Princeton University Press, 2001).

I welcome the opportunity to thank a number of friends, colleagues, and readers—often overlapping—for their advice, encouragement and (almost always) for their criticism: John Alcorn, Omer Bartov, Judith Baskin, Murray Baumgarten, Hedva Ben-Israel, Temma Berg, Warren Ginsberg, Jacob Golomb, Claire Kahane, Samuel Kassow, Joel Kraemer, Herbert Lindenberger, Michael Morgan, Gabi Motzkin, Dalia Ofer, F. F. Scarre, Richard Stamelman, Robert Wistrich, James Young, Anna Ziebinska, Steven Zipperstein, Susan Zuccotti. Leslie Morris has contributed largely and generously in these and many other ways. I also express my appreciation to the Remarque Institute at New York University and its Director, Tony Judt, for the semester I was able to spend at the Institute in Spring 2000—and to the United States Holocaust Memorial Museum for the opportunity given me through the Ina Levine Senior Scholar Fellowship to spend the year 2001–2002 at the Center for Advanced Holocaust Studies (CAHS) at the Museum. Thanks especially there to Paul Shapiro, Director of the CAHS, Wendy Lower, Director of the Visiting Scholars Program, and to Gerhard Weinberg and Simone Gigliotti, fellow Fellows.

My daughters, Ariella Lang Kornfeld and Jessica Lang Riegel, have provided a strong incentive for my study of the Holocaust from its beginning, and they now contribute more directly to that work, as to so much else that is close to me. Alex Kornfeld and Jörg Riegel, through their own histories and still more, through their design of the present, have put their mark on this book as well. To the two couples, then, Ariella and Alex, Jessica and Jörg, the book is dedicated: with love, with admiration, and with pleasure.

West Hartford, Conn.
September 2004

INTRODUCTION

On the one hand, to speak about *interpretations* of the Holocaust may seem a provocation or offensive. Surely, for that event if for any, the facts speak for themselves in the enormity of systematic genocide, leaving nothing over to interpret, nothing to ponder or contest. What could be more explicit, *plainer*, than the "Final Solution of the Jewish Question"—as that was first imagined and then enacted by the Nazis, and then, in the end, as it was also bequeathed to Germany's future generations in Hitler's Last Will as, speaking from the ruins of his truncated "thousand-year Reich," he would even then urge the continuing war against the Jews? Could there be more than one way of understanding—that is, interpreting—Himmler's declaration in his 1943 speech at Poznan that "this people must be made to disappear from the earth" (at a time when four million of them had already been "made to disappear")? If ever plain speech left its mark—determinate meaning: clear, unequivocal, unambiguous—here, one might say, it is.

And yet it has become no less evident in the period of sixty years since the end of the Holocaust—a span long enough to acquire its own title of "Post-Holocaust"—that if the essential facts of the Holocaust and that term's basic referent have spoken, much else has also been said about and around them that is not at all obvious or self-evident, but has had to be inferred or constructed or interpreted—all in the interests of elaborating or explaining but also, perhaps inevitably, at times losing the way and, worse still, misleading others. The search for *connections* among facts in the effort to trace them to their origins and then to push forward to their consequences unavoidably establishes a distance from history's surface. This becomes most evident in the simplest questions that have been and continue to be asked about the Holocaust: "Why the Jews?" or—no less puzzling—"Why the Germans?" And always, of course, "How was 'it' possible?" In the space surrounding such questions, the process of interpretation—and thus also the possibility of misinterpretation—become unavoidable, for here the question of what *did* happen evokes the necessarily related, and no less historical questions of what did *not* happen or what *might have* happened—and also, of course, for each of them, the further question of "Why." Nothing more is required to set this self- (and other-) critical process in motion than the possibility of alternative accounts: no one interpretation unless there are two—and *always* interpretation whenever two or more accounts appear. As they often do—and always do whenever spaces are seen as separating the facts from each other. At that point, the need for further scrutiny becomes part of the observation itself, testing the possibility of possibilities, and then too, one hopes, of detecting their limits—not necessarily with the expectation of forcing agreement on *one* interpretation, but at least of ruling certain ones out. Certainly, the recognition of alternate possible readings does not itself give them equal standing—a principle all the more urgent for measuring accounts of an event with the weight of the Holocaust.

Variant, even contradictory, interpretations among explanations of the Holocaust that track causes and effects are predictable. Nobody is surprised to come upon disputes among historical accounts of the causal processes of the French Revolution or the American Civil War; why, then, would more be expected for the at least equally large scale of the Holocaust? That certain aspects of the Holocaust seem—I should claim, *are*—"self-interpreting" clearly does not extend to others. Counting is one thing: even approximate numbers or dates and any disagreements that occur around them acknowledge the status of their limits *as* facts. But the processes leading up to or away from those numbers or dates are much less readily determinable; motives, intentions, circumstances, causes—all the contingencies of the human condition—are unavoidable, and unavoidably demanding of interpretation. The extent of the Holocaust's events is too large and inclusive, and the pressures too complex, to hope for a single overarching theory or explanation that could avoid competing with another no less serious or detailed one that views the same array of "data," but in a different explanatory order or proportion. It is understandable, then, that there should be differences in accounts (not in the outcome, but in the tracing of its origins and process) of the "Final Solution"—in registering the balance and character of ideological vs. economic causes, the role of individual agency (and psychology) vs. that of the "group mind" and its etiology. Similarly, the Post-Holocaust itself faces a continuing identity crisis: what exactly are its—that is, our—obligations to the event at its center; where do we, as observers, scholars, persons, station ourselves? "Remember!" after all, even for those who place that imperative at the center of their view, is empty of detail. Should that ideal be realized in political action? Religious observance? Monuments or museums? Memory and even mourning, we thus recognize, require limits and measure as a means, the design of a logic.

And then too, of course, the limited focus of study or analysis as it emerged in Post-Holocaust reflection has moved in a number of different directions. These can be variously categorized, but a set of four rubrics in particular seems germane to the corporate labor of Post-Holocaust studies: the Archival, Explanatory, Testimonial, and Representational modes—not as autonomous or independent of each other, but as reflecting different emphases.

By the "Archival" work of the Post-Holocaust, I refer to the attempt to record or recover or reconstruct empirical or physical evidence of conditions, plans, and actions during the Holocaust—such conditions having been initiated by or directed at anyone involved in that event. The material basis for this type

Introduction

of study dates from the Holocaust itself, with some of the Archival work—of writing for historical purposes, or more commonly, of preserving material for that end—having begun during that period as well. Such Archival recovery is epitomized in Raul Hilberg's *The Destruction of the European Jews* and his reconstruction there (among other things) of the railway organization required and achieved by the Nazis for the "re-settlement" of Jews across Europe in the ghettoes and camps of Eastern Europe. The debate that sprang up in the 1980s (the "Historikerstreit") between "Intentionalist" and "Functionalist" historians which revolved around the initial question of whether Hitler did or did not issue an order mandating the "Final Solution" is also an Archival question in the sense of the term used here. Archival work thus extends from the most rudimentary elements of Holocaust historiography and explanation—the "factoids"—to more elaborate patterns of those same elements that may at times seem to bear only tangentially on the Holocaust itself (for example, in the system of taxation imposed by the Nazi government on Germans during the war years—described by Reimer Voss, in his *Steuern im Dritten Reich*—as this points to the economic structure and motivation during the period).

This first category or mode of analysis is closely linked to the second one of "Explanatory" design—since for the Holocaust, as also for other less complex or consequential events, the search for Archival materials typically reflects a teleological concern for an understanding of why or how certain outcomes in an historical sequence occurred. But if the first, Archival mode principally involves the work of historians or political scientists, the second category spreads more broadly, expanding into the other social sciences—sociology, psychology —and also to theology, philosophy, linguistics, and literary analysis, as questions of the relation between individual and corporate "mentality" and decision-making (reasons and causes) come to the fore. The variety of work realized here is proportionately extensive, including books that are Archival in their ostensible emphasis (like Davidowicz's *The War against the Jews*), others in which the Explanatory design openly overpowers the Archival element (as in Goldhagen's *Hitler's Willing Executioners*), and others in which those two elements are explicitly joined (as in Arendt's *The Origins of Totalitarianism* and Adorno and Horkheimer's *The Dialectic of Enlightenment*). The Explanatory design of such accounts is meant to present a causal explanation, however abstract or ramified, of the phenomenon of the Nazi Genocide against the Jews. The way is opened here to accounts that question the standard "causal" model of historical explanation (in the instance of the Holocaust and/or more generally); so, for example, Götz Aly's "functionalist" *"Final Solution": Nazi Population Policy and the Murder of the European Jews*, in which the agency of individual decision-making is presented as so diffuse as to bring into question the historical importance of personal agency altogether. A similar range in Explanatory efforts comes from other directions—from theological or religious attempts to confront the phenomenon of the Holocaust in God's world (e.g.,

Richard Rubenstein's *After Auschwitz*), philosophical efforts like those of Emil Fackenheim in *To Mend a World,* analyses by way of linguistic or rhetorical analysis as in Victor Klemperer's *LTI,* and literary and stylistic studies, like James Young's *Writing and Re-Writing the Holocaust*—all of them directed, through different means and idioms, at the question of the "Why?" of what happened in the Holocaust. Such efforts thus propose accounts in disciplinary terms or by developing cross-disciplinary categories, on the shared premise that the results of Archival "gathering" may indeed yield explanations—as revealing for the events of the Holocaust as for any other complex historical occurrence.

These first two "modes" of Post-Holocaust expression need not take the form of impersonal scholarly discourse, although they often do. That stylistic register may in fact be misleading, since although the voice of the author appears neutral in them, the "disinterested search for knowledge" in respect to the Holocaust—as for all historical studies—typically reflects a highly "interested" concern with not only the historical subject but with the means and the outcome of the analysis. A notable example of this conjunction figures in Hilberg's *Destruction,* which joins the Archival and Explanatory modes in an authorial voice so terse and void of emotive reference that the stylistic force of "objectivity" is an essential element of the text—the "medium" in this way at once reflecting and reinforcing the "message."

The heading of "Testimonial" expression subsumes expressive forms extending from monuments or memorials (national, group, individual) to testimony, whether entered at legal proceedings or as "witness" to memory (as in the numerous archives of individual videotapes) or in the genre of the literary memoir. So, also, Holocaust Museums (or museum-like structures—e.g., the concentration camps that have been preserved) and communal and religious or quasi-religious ceremonies such as the observance of Yom HaShoah come under this mode of expression. Autobiographical novels like Elie Wiesel's *Night,* like many other examples of Post-Holocaust expression, elide two or more of the categories proposed here; Holocaust diaries—which are not, strictly speaking, "*Post*-Holocaust"—compound the difficulties of categorization: although clearly Testimonial in one sense, they are also, often if not always, Archival (for example, as in the Ringelblum or the Kruk diaries).

The "Representational" mode of Post-Holocaust discourse may seem too broad a category to be useful, since it seems clear that historical accounts intended as Explanatory or Archival will also be Representational. Without excluding such cross-references, there clearly are also works in which aesthetically representational features are of primary significance—and these are the principal exemplars under this rubric. Thus, works in any of the arts (painting, sculpture, film, music, poetry, drama, fiction) where medium and form, not historical or theoretical assertion and verification, are the focus of expression and reception in this mode. The formulation here is necessarily crude, dependent on a makeshift—"ostensive"—definition of art (arguably, its only possible definition). Crucial to the conception of Holocaust art, in any event, is its character as indeed Representational—a claim with implications for the general theory of art but also and more immediately impinging on the analysis and evaluation of Holocaust art in particular.

This claim of a representational ground for Holocaust art seems to me not stipulative but descriptive of that art in both its inception and its reception. The very fact that disagreements have arisen over whether Spiegelman's *Maus*, or Kenneally's *Schindler's List*, or Wilkomirski's *Memoirs* are to count as fiction or non-fiction implies that the same issue does not arise for other "representations"; and surely, in Paul Celan's poetry or Anselm Kiefer's paintings or the novels of Aharon Appelfeld and Gunther Grass, the Representational emphasis on "the Holocaust" is not in doubt as an intentional and significant factor for their audiences. One has only to imagine encounters with the works of those artists without reference to the Holocaust. As few would question or doubt the imaginative core of that work, so too, there could hardly be any doubt of such reference—and with that a link and accompanying responsibility to the historical event and its conditions. This connection between Representational expression, on the one hand, and the Explanatory and Archival modes, on the other, poses certain difficult theoretical problems—but then the question of the representational status of art as a form of knowledge had been longstanding and contentious in aesthetic theory quite apart from issues raised by the question of Holocaust representation.

* * *

I do not in this volume attempt to "box the compass" of Post-Holocaust studies or analysis. More time will have to pass, it seems to me, for that to be adequately attempted, not only because of the work it requires, but even more basically, to allow the Post-Holocaust to articulate itself more fully. To be sure, the boundaries of historical periods are largely a matter of convention wherever they are set; but it also seems clear that when we speak of the Post-Holocaust, we find ourselves so fully in its midst, so conscious of how what I have referred to elsewhere as "the future of the Holocaust" is likely to affect our present and past understanding of that event and ourselves in relation to it, that any account of themes or prospects based on the sixty-year period since the formal end of the Holocaust in 1945 can be at most provisional. What I attempt in this book, then, is an account ad hoc—and even then, partial in its reference. Thus, I consider a sequence of aspects of the Post-Holocaust that, under this collective heading, appear in terms of individual and at one level relatively independent issues. The larger project of weaving these issues into a single whole thus remains; but the questions posed in and by the Post-Holocaust are at this point so fragmented and various that it seems fair, and in some sense unavoidable, to address them in a form that itself reflects that fact.

Introduction

I do not mean to imply that the period of the Post-Holocaust will have to be "*over*" before a fuller account of it is possible (exactly when, it might be asked, will that be and how would it be recognized?)—but that the Post-Holocaust is yet too much with us to permit any summing up that could be more than only another partial engagement.

In Part One, then, "In the Matter of Justice," I consider questions raised in the Post-Holocaust about the retrospective legal and moral judgment of the principals in the Holocaust and their actions: about the Nazis, who—as I argue in Chapter 1—can be understood only insofar as their criminality outside the Holocaust is viewed together with their criminality within it; about the Jewish victims and survivors of the genocide who still, even now, face the acts of those perpetrators in judging (as Chapter 2 proposes) the possibilities of forgiveness and, at the opposite extreme, the more often covert impulse for revenge. Chapter 3, "Evil, Suffering, and the Holocaust," considers the reaction within traditional categories of Jewish ethical thought to the events—and, more explicitly, to the evil of the Holocaust. Chapter 4 addresses the more general issue of quantifying wrongdoing or evil on the scale of the Holocaust—a problem that arises not because of the Holocaust's uniqueness (itself a debatable claim) but for a contrary reason: because murder on the scale of genocide in the twentieth century became such a commonplace that moral comparisons, including comparisons of genocide itself, seem unavoidable if relevant legal and moral categories are to be sustained. Indeed, I argue here that however unsettling the comparative weighing or even "ranking" of wrongdoing is, the fact of moral comparison, although always invidious, is intrinsic to even the simplest moral judgment. It has thus been a constant if often tacit feature of moral judgment, and however prominent its recent appearance, there is nothing either novel or disabling in the problems it poses. To compare individual acts of genocide, in other words, although that concept itself adds a new entry to the legal and moral categories of wrongdoing, requires no formal innovation: the practice itself has been assumed. This does not mean that viewing the Holocaust retrospectively through the Post-Holocaust presupposes *only* recently articulated principles like "genocide" or "group rights" (relevant as those have become), but that the conceptual framework of which they too are now part brings into sharper focus a continuing "moral history" largely neglected in most previous standard historical or analytical accounts.

In Part Two, "Language and Lessons," I take up the daunting and presumptuous question of what there is to be learned from the Holocaust. Thus, Chapter 5 speaks of "The Grammar of Antisemitism"—the ways in which certain linguistic usage is ideologically implicated in the antisemitic expression that figured causally, not exclusively but largely, in the Holocaust. Chapter 6 takes up the claims of the "unspeakability" or incomprehensibility of the Holocaust —claims that so often appear side-by-side (and against themselves) with full and ambitious statements about the Holocaust itself. *Unspeakability* itself, then, warrants—indeed requires—its own exposition, as do such other presumptive terms of Post-Holocaust discourse as *trauma* and *testimony*. Such terms are, to be sure, relevant—but the points at which they are directed can easily be misrepresented or misunderstood (and have been); what is involved in such confusion is invariably more than only a dispute about semantics. This contention reappears with even greater emphasis in Chapter 7, which offers a critique of certain "mischievous" questions that have recurred about the Holocaust. Those questions are, I argue, *mischievous* because—like the question, "Why didn't they resist?"—they reflect not only mistaken but thoughtless premises which, taken at face value and left to themselves (as they often have been), skew the understanding of the Holocaust. The resulting "mischief" has led to misplaced praise and blame for actions or roles assumed in the Holocaust (to some extent, in the Post-Holocaust as well)—and what is at stake in such errors is obviously more than only the importance of setting the record straight. A prominent instance of such gratuitous and misleading representations of the Holocaust has occurred in the continuing argument between authors who insist on the Holocaust's particularity or uniqueness and others for whom such claims fly in the face of its universality—the Holocaust as evidence of the *human* capacity for inhumanity. Chapter 8 proposes a third way between these conflicting claims, linking the two in what I suggest is a form of moral judgment that recognizes their respective bases without admitting their apparent contradiction—a lesson of the Holocaust that points toward the future as well as backward to the past.

Part Three, "For and Against Interpretation," brings together a number of specific instances of interpretation and misinterpretation bearing on aspects of the Holocaust, raising also certain more general questions about the concept of interpretation itself. Thus, there is discussion in the five chapters of this section of the problem of objectivity in historical writing (as seen through the lens of Oskar Rosenfeld's Lodz diaries); of the "lachrymose view of Jewish history" on the basis of which Peter Novick has, I argue, misread the role of the Holocaust in American life; of the misdirected question of whether Pius XII's efforts on behalf of Europe's Jewish communities during the Holocaust were sufficient or not; of the particular wrong that marks off genocide (and so also the Holocaust) from other instances of moral and political evil; and finally of the character of misinterpretation itself—and who bears responsibility for that, as in the case of Nietzsche who has so often and (as I argue) mistakenly been viewed as an advocate for fascism.

In the Afterword, "Philosophy and/of the Holocaust," I consider the role that philosophical reflection and analysis has so far had in studying the Holocaust: miniscule, in my view, in comparison with the role that it should or might yet have. But any such change can be achieved only insofar as philosophy proves willing to learn from history; that is, from history outside it (including, of course, the Holocaust), as well, closer to home, from its own history. To be sure, whether historians or anyone else in the public who may be concerned with history would then pay more attention to philosophy than they do now depends as much on the willingness of an audience to listen as on what philosophers have to say; but to the extent that it does depend on the latter, there is nothing mysterious or obscure about what philosophers and philosophy need to do in order to contribute to historical understanding in general or to an understanding of the Holocaust in particular—beginning with an effort to take history seriously, both in itself and as grist for philosophy's own work as that necessarily originates and concludes in the everyday world, even (or perhaps especially) when that world includes an enormity like the Holocaust.

A constant question in my own thinking and writing about both the Holocaust and the Post-Holocaust has asked what philosophy can contribute to understanding these events or phenomena that other sources do not provide as well or even better. The limited and fragmentary answers I propose to this question here and in other of my writings do not derive from a view that philosophy is only a method or form of inquiry. It does, I should argue, also have a content: substantive questions—and, in the event, answers—of its own. But it is also a feature of that substance that it discloses itself only in fragments and through glimpses that are set in the particular context of its expression. To be sure, some fragments or glimpses are more suggestive than others, more coherent in themselves, and more readily leading beyond themselves: thus, the constant aspiration of philosophical discourse—but only to be actualized, in my view, as it looks first and seriously at its own historical context.

It thus seems to me that the answer to the question of what philosophy is or can hope to accomplish will be found only in viewing particular responses to specific philosophical queries about particular subjects—at once bound to that place and time, but linked also to philosophical thought in its history. Even to find such partial or possible solutions, however—the effect of which may be no more than to rule out certain others: a negative advance—would be useful. A common charge against the work of philosophy is that it seems to begin at the "same" place again and again, as though the most it can accomplish is to succeed at running in place: perhaps not even keeping up—and in any event not getting ahead. But the principal achievements of philosophy and philosophers have demonstrated that the "same" place from which they have allegedly set out over the centuries is not the same at all—any more than it would be warranted to direct that charge at painters of different centuries and schools who, after all, may have started in common from the "same" blank canvas. Philosophy undoubtedly has the capacity to reach beyond the historical moment—but only, as I hope to show in the discussions that follow, after it has acknowledged and understood that moment. And among the contemporary starting points that pose a challenge for such understanding, the continuing presence of the Holocaust and now also of the Post-Holocaust cannot, or at the very least, *should* not be avoided.

POST-HOLOCAUST

Part One

In the Matter of Justice

ONE

The Nazi as Criminal
Inside and Outside the Holocaust

Before discussing what I refer to as Nazi criminality, I feel obliged to raise certain objections to what I have to say about that subject. This means of proceeding may seem out of order, and certainly it makes for an unusual preface. But starting points come in various shapes, and the reasons for venturing a critique of a discussion yet to come will be quickly evident. Although I am not a historian, I propose to consider aspects of the history as well as the theory of Nazism and the Holocaust; furthermore, the psychology of the Nazis as well as their motives and reasons, will have a place in the discussion, although again, I am not a psychologist. I also apply the logic of explanation to Nazi policies and actions, but *the* logic of explanation, historical or philosophical, is itself a much contested (on some accounts, improbable) means of analysis. Certain ethical criteria, moreover, will figure here in relation to events and interpretations of the Holocaust—although it is generally conceded now that where moral decisions or judgments are at issue, nobody can speak with special authority; indeed, it is a serious question whether anyone speaks on that subject with authority at all.

Furthermore: the first part of this chapter's title—"The Nazi as Criminal"—is likely to sound, and fall, quite flat. With all that we have learned about the "Final Solution of the Jewish Question"—that innocuous code name that the Nazis attached to the act of systematic genocide—are we to use the same bland term that is applied to burglars and white-collar embezzlers for its perpetrators? However inadequate our vocabulary for conveying the enormity of the Holocaust, surely there must be apter labels for its perpetrators (more apt, one might hope, even than "perpetrators"). And then, too, more strongly still: the specific thesis asserted here, on the place of the Holocaust in the overall Nazi "Project," may seem not only questionable but dangerous. For what I propose runs contrary to the received reading of the policies and actions of Nazism during its twelve-year rule—a reading that finds the Holocaust at once distinctive in its own terms and central to the Nazi Weltanschauung as a whole, with the latter worldview animated foremost by antisemitism: "eliminationist anti-Semitism" (in Goldhagen's version) or "redemptive anti-Semitism" (in Friedländer's) or the more traditional, garden variety of antisemitism pushed to an extreme: Contrary to the accounts that build on these and that in effect equate the Nazi project with their declaration of war against the Jews, the claim argued here characterizes the "Final Solution" as one—prominent, but nonetheless, one—among a number of Nazi policies and programs that, understood as a group, aimed at a goal of racial and nationalist purification to be realized in the German "*Volk*," thus only to be understood individually against a broader background of Nazi policies in general and the atrocities, including the Holocaust, for which the Nazis were responsible.

This more extensive and inclusive goal also encompasses an ideal of transgression or criminality for its own sake—with criminality appearing, then, not in its usual "utilitarian" role as a means of furthering one's own self-interest, but as an ideal, in effect an end in itself. Especially this last feature gives an unusual edge to what then becomes the no longer bland term of *criminal* as it applies to the Nazis—both outside and inside the Holocaust. In doing this, it reinscribes as a marker or signature for Nazi history itself the moral standard of criminality that the Nazis had ostensibly sought to empty of meaning. In these terms, transgression, the will to violation as intrinsic to their project, appears as a significant, even necessary condition for clearing the space (moral, political, instrumental) within which the act and idea of national and racial, that is, biological transcendence and, within that, the genocide against the Jews, became first possible and then actual. Conversely, then, this account represents the Holocaust as explicable only within the framework of a larger causal and conceptual pattern—a framework to which the Holocaust clearly and even decisively contributed, but which was impelled by broader sources and goals than the Holocaust alone and which thus makes consideration of these others a requirement for understanding the Holocaust.

The dangers in this thesis, thus also the likely objections to it, will be readily apparent. For at first glance, the thesis may seem no more than a variant of familiar Holocaust revisionism: not Holocaust denial, but the subtler, more challenging effort to redistribute causes and effects in a way that so diffuses the roles of both agent and victim in the Holocaust that at some point they seem virtually to merge. One recalls here, for example, Ernst Nolte's various claims for the unexceptional character of the Holocaust, turning principally on his contention that both historical precedents and contemporary threats (mainly from Soviet Russia) caused or arguably (in his judgment) justified the response it provoked.[1] To be sure, Nolte acknowledges that the Nazi reaction in the form of the "Final Solution" to the threat posed by Russia was extreme; but even so, the reaction appears to him still as falling within the "normal" range—to use a benign medical designation for this far from benign conclusion. But would not categorizing the Holocaust as one of a number of acts by the Nazis in pursuit of a more extensive or fundamental ideal also "normalize" the Holocaust by a similar leveling, bringing it into line with other policies or actions of the Nazi regime that are, however, qualitatively quite different? Surely, it might be argued, this dilution of the Holocaust's distinctiveness challenges the claims of that event's historical and moral weight—with this shift in turn diminishing the burden of moral responsibility that is so crucial an element in any account, historical or moral, of the Holocaust. There has been, after all, widespread acknowledgment, since and because of the Holocaust, of genocide as the most serious violation in the already large and imaginative inventory of human wrongdoing. The twofold murder that genocide entails—of individuals and the group, of the former because of their membership, however involuntary, in the latter—seems to reach as far as the human imagination has yet gone ("progressed," one might say) in conceiving the ways and means of wrongdoing, with the Holocaust a paradigm instance. Is this—genocide in general or the Holocaust in particular—now to be re-presented as only a means to another, more notable end?

Well, *No* and *Yes*—those contradictory judgments to be asserted and defended here with equal emphasis. For "*No*," the account here is not meant to contest the place of genocide (or the Holocaust) in either the historical or moral order of wrongdoing: the evidence for that is clear. But "*Yes*": I will be suggesting that, ingredient in its numerous specific expressions including the very large one of the Holocaust, the criminality for which the Nazis were responsible involved certain factors that were, however, unrelated to the (specifically) "Jewish Question" at all—factors that require consideration in their generality if the Nazis' individual acts, including the Holocaust, are to be understood. The Holocaust, in other words, is on this view part—a large part, but still—of a more fundamental historical and also moral framework. We are obliged, then, to consider whether and how these apparently conflicting claims—the "*No*" and the "*Yes*"—can be reconciled.

NAZI CRIMINALITY

I outline here five events or acts that occurred during the period of Nazi rule from 1933–45, a period when that regime, through the Wehrmacht, its regular army, and the SS, its "state within a state," controlled all large-scale actions undertaken by the government's branches or agencies. The acts described are well known—some more than others, but none of them in dispute on the questions of what took place or who, in the main, was responsible for ordering them or carrying them out. Uncertainty remains in respect to some of them about the exact numbers or identities of the people involved, agents or victims, but this is a common problem for many large-scale historical events. Although the actions described vary in scope and detail, they share certain essential features. And there, on that point, I ask the reader to take an active part in the discussion—so that, in following the descriptions of the five events, readers should name for themselves the common properties they find among the descriptions, properties which thus, in their view, apply to the five as a group. (The examples are given out of chronological order, since for this structural discussion, chronology should not be a consideration.) So:

1. *Lidice:* On June 4, 1942, Reinhard Heydrich, head of the Gestapo and second-in-command in the SS to Himmler, died—a week after being severely wounded in an attack by two members of the Czech underground on the outskirts of Prague. On June 9, the village of Lidice, ten miles west of Prague, was surrounded by German security police and SD [Security Service] men. A group of women and children from the village were separated from the men; about 200 women were then sent to the women's concentration camp at Ravensbruck, and 90 of the children, separated from their mothers, were sent to a camp in the Wartheland (Polish territory annexed by Germany). The men of the village—183 in all—and about 70 women were shot on the spot (15 relatives of Czech legionnaires, who were already in custody, were also shot). A short time afterward, the village was razed; not a building was left standing. On October 24 of the same year, 252 Czechs, some relatives and friends of the inhabitants of Lidice but who had not themselves lived there, some who only had the same family names as Lidice residents but who were unrelated to anyone there, were killed in a single day in the concentration camp at Mauthausen. No evidence was ever presented that Heydrich's assassination could be traced to residents of Lidice or, geographically, to the village itself.[2]

2. *The T-4 Program:* Beginning in October 1939, a program was initiated within Germany, designed to kill certain individuals by a *Gnadenstod,* a "mercy death." In this Program (known as *T-4* after the Berlin address of its headquarters at Tiergarten 4), persons living what was judged to be a "life unworthy of life" would be killed: these were, first, children and, then, adults of any background or class judged to be incurably ill, mentally or physically (old age was included among these debilities), and thus a burden on the nation's resources. The selection of those to be killed was made by physicians who also signed falsified death certificates that were then sent to the victims' next-of-kin. The program itself was meant to be kept secret; certainly it was involuntary—for the victims who might have been capable of making decisions as well as for those who were not. Six main centers in Germany were put in operation for carrying out the murders; the victims were transported to those centers from other parts of the country, and the method of killing them at the centers was mainly by gassing. In August, 1941, following protests within Germany from families of victims and several religious officials who gradually became aware of what was happening, the program was officially halted (this cessation coincided—and not accidentally—with the German inva-

sion of Russia); the program continued informally, however, up to the war's end, nearly four years later. The methods of execution in this later period were mainly starvation and chemical injection. Estimates of the number of persons killed in the T-4 Program in Germany prior to its formal abolition range between 75,000 and 125,000 (remember that the program originated before any of the "death camps" were established, indeed before the "Final Solution" had been adopted as policy). There is ample evidence that the program was continued informally throughout the war, with the number of victims during the almost four-year period after its declared conclusion estimated at another 100,000.[3]

3. Massacre in Greece: At the end of July 1943, Mussolini was toppled from power in Italy, and in September, his successor, Marshal Badoglio, surrendered to the Allies. Greece had been occupied by both Italian and German troops (the Germans having entered Greece in order to rescue and complete the Italian invasion). When word of the Italian surrender reached the occupying forces in Greece, the Germans ordered the Italians there either to place themselves under German command or to disarm. Some groups of Italian soldiers refused to accept those terms, and on the Ionian island of Kefalonia, the Italians actively resisted, fighting against the Germans until being overpowered. After the Italians surrendered on September 24, German firing squads shot and killed the surviving Italian troops: 4750 men and 155 officers.[4]

4. The Commando Order: In an order dated October 18, 1942, Hitler stipulated that soldiers of the Allied armies captured by the German army while participating in commando raids on German-occupied territory should be turned over to the Security Police (of the SS) for summary execution. The order was issued after a number of commando raids originating in Great Britain had been directed at the coast of occupied Europe from Norway to southern France. The soldiers taking part in the raids were British commandos and volunteers from Commonwealth armies, together with members of the "Free" forces of some of the occupied countries. All were in uniform during the raids, and indeed Hitler's order recognized this: "From now on, all enemies on so-called commando missions in Europe or Africa, challenged by German troops, even if they are to all appearances soldiers in uniform, whether armed or unarmed, in battle or in flight, are to be slaughtered to the last man. . . . Even if these individuals when found should apparently seem to give themselves up, no pardon is to be granted them on principle."[5] Certain German commanding officers took this order as license to kill virtually all captives, whether involved in "commando" raids or not; this has made it impossible to determine how many captured Allied fighters were killed on the basis of this order itself, but the number is almost certainly in the thousands.

5. Russian Prisoners of War: Between the time that Germany attacked Russia in June 1941 and the War's end in May 1945, an estimated 5,000,000 Russian soldiers were captured by the German armed forces. Of that number, at least

2,500,000 and as many as 3,300,000 (between 45 percent and 60 percent) died in captivity; that is, as prisoners of war. No breakdown is available of these prisoners of war by age or physical condition, but they had evidently been fit enough to serve in the Soviet armed forces. (The latter point distinguishes the composition of this group from others incarcerated by the Nazis in the concentration and death camps.) "Normal" attrition, even under circumstances of hardship, could not account for this large number or percentage of deaths; and indeed, in addition to factors like contagious disease and inadequate medical care, two other factors contributed. The first of these, in the months just after the German invasion of the USSR, was the execution, mainly by shooting, of between 500,000 and 600,000 of the prisoners. The second was a plan of deliberate starvation adopted by the Nazis for the remaining prisoners, for whom the food distributed was known to be at starvation level: adequate on any given day for survival but insufficient over any period of time. By the fall of 1941, 2–3 percent of all Soviet prisoners were dying every day.[6] Unusual proof of the intention as well as the implementation of this policy emerges from the fact that when the Germans, having discovered by early 1942 that the conquest of Russia would require more time than they had anticipated—thus thinking forward to the use of the Russian prisoners as laborers—increased the prisoners' food rations, the death rate dropped immediately. (Even then it was not until 1944 that the rations for Russian POWs were brought up the level of other prisoners, for example, those taken on the Western front. A mocking reference to the early results of this policy appears in the Göring diaries, as Göring, Hitler's second-in-command, notes that "they [the Russian prisoners] are eating each other.")

THE COMMON FEATURES

The question was posed to the reader earlier on what common features characterize the five events described. No doubt, some differences will surface among individual reactions—but one common characteristic seems a virtual certainty, with a second only slightly less notable. The first of these is the unusual cruelty in all the acts, from the largest to the smallest; each is indeed an atrocity, on any ordinary understanding of that term. That is, even allowing for the differences in magnitude among the acts and the "provocations" to which they responded, each reflects a disproportion between what occasioned it and the extremity of the Nazi response. Even in assessing cruelty, after all, it is reasonable still to speak of degrees—and the fact of disproportion stands out in the events described. All the atrocities, furthermore, reflect not an impulsive act but planning and deliberation—a calculation that not only wills the extreme end, but also elaborates and even embellishes it. (So, for example, the razing of the houses of Lidice, the death by starvation, not by direct execution, of the Russian POWs.) In other words, there seems more than only a utilitarian or functional purpose at work here. At the very least, such "excess" establishes the character of these acts as intentional; at most, it has still stronger implications (to be considered below). For the moment, however, it suffices that the actions referred to should be recognized as atrocities, exceeding the limits of "normal" wrongdoing.

A second common feature looms large in the reactions to the descriptions of the five events—perhaps less fraught than the first but also significant and, against the background of the Holocaust, no less striking. This is the fact that none of the five atrocities or crimes described was directed at Jews; at least they were not directed at Jews as Jews. Quite the contrary, in fact: the actions were knowingly and deliberately directed against people who were (almost all) non-Jews. Admittedly, those victims were not killed because they were "not-Jews"; in respect to that distinction, the destruction of the Jews as Jews intrinsic to the "Final Solution" still holds its unusual place. But they were killed as non-Jews for possessing other supposed characteristics or dispositions which, in the Nazi view, warranted, or still more, required their destruction—because, we infer, that served the Nazi purpose as the Nazis saw it. Some of the acts mentioned (the case of the Soviet POWs) did in fact lead to the murder of Jews among others; also the T-4 program included among its victims Jews who would not have been killed had they not been Jews, but the proportion of these in the total number of T-4 victims is small. And also those killings were part of a broader intention than the specific focus that motivated the Holocaust itself. The principal intended victims of the five actions mentioned were variously non-Jewish Germans (in the T-4); non-Jewish civilians of countries occupied by the Nazis (the Czech inhabitants of Lidice); non-Jewish prisoners of war taken in combat and supposedly protected by the Geneva Conventions; non-Jewish Russians (the Germans did mention in respect to the Russian prisoners that the Soviet government had never signed the Geneva Conventions—but that was hardly to the point), Italians, Britons, Canadians, and Free French. Again, none of these was killed, for the instances mentioned, on the field of battle; they were killed, then, for some other reason than the pressure of battle.

Undoubted atrocities as they are, the actions mentioned yet had neither the scope nor the system associated with the "Final Solution." But the question raised here is not how the Holocaust differed from other Nazi atrocities, but what it had in common with them—and then how that common factor would bear on understanding the Holocaust itself. Here, it seems, we come to a crux in the process of explanation. For once the Holocaust is juxtaposed with other atrocities, two possible explanations emerge: either the atrocities directed against non-Jews were also a means for realizing the "Final Solution" (e.g., by demonstrating what the consequences would be for anyone opposing or seen as an obstacle to the principal Nazi goal of genocide); or the other atrocities and the Holocaust were parts of some more inclusive purpose, perhaps one on the order of that referred to here earlier as racial and nationalist redemptivism. In advancing that more general and comprehensive cause, members of many different groups, notably Jews but others as well and including non-Jewish Germans, would, as the Nazi regime's strategy evolved, forfeit their lives.

The former of these alternatives is not without evidence or advocates. That the Nazis pursued the "Final Solution" until the last days of the War and after their defeat was certain (and could have been known to be so for two years before, to anyone who cared to know), points in this direction. This position is reinforced, moreover, with recognition that Jewish slave labor was subordinated to the extermination process even after the potential usefulness of such labor in the failing German war effort became clear (there was disagreement in the Nazi hierarchy about the priorities here, with preference sometimes given to the need for laborers—but the general pattern moved in the other direction).[7] At least some of the Nazi hierarchy were thus willing to subordinate the general war effort—and ultimately their self-defense—to the purpose of annihilating the Jews in particular, with the latter goal then becoming an end, if not *the* end in itself.

On this view, however, also the five events described above, which have no immediate link to the "Final Solution" or the "Jewish Question," would have to be shown to be part of the struggle against the alleged Jewish "threat." No doubt, a case for this can be made—in the same way that any hypothesis can be made to serve a given body of evidence by adding a sufficiently large number of qualifications or disclaimers. But nothing short of such tendentiousness would suffice in this case. Furthermore, it would also have to be demonstrated that all the other ostensive purposes of the Nazis that seem either broader than or unrelated to the "Jewish Question"—for example, the strengthening of a master race (consider here Rudolf Hess's statement that "National Socialism was simply 'applied biology'"), or the goal of *Lebensraum* ["living space"] for German expansion eastward (what Hitler at one point called the "holiest mission of my life")—were not only linked to the war against the Jews, but subordinate to it. The latter is an especially difficult claim to sustain—with much counterevidence that would have to be explained and, in some cases, explained away.

Admittedly, the task of first determining and then comparing the weight of specific Nazi goals is complicated by ambiguity in the Nazis' articulation of their own goals: what the regime would have done if it had succeeded rather than failed in imposing its will—if, for example, it had conquered Russia and Great Britain rather than been defeated. It may seem odd that such a "final" vision of the world-according-to-Nazism should remain blurred and unclear even in authoritative Nazi sources, but so it is. Aside from a number of fragmentary projects within the setting of a *Judenrein* world—like the construction of a fortified line separating Europe from Asia, or the razing of Moscow and Leningrad, or the construction of a Museum of Extinct Cultures in Prague with a prominent place allocated in it for the Jews (a project initiated, we know, while the work of extinction was itself going on), or a projected campaign by Hitler on behalf of vegetarianism—aside from such piecemeal ideas, larger and more definitive ones remain to a considerable extent matters for conjecture.[8] To be sure, external speculation has conceived such apocalyptic predictions as Hannah Arendt's, that "extermination would not have come to an end when no Jew was left to be killed. . . . [E]xtermination per se is more important than anti-semitism or racism per se."[9] Or in the "vast medical vision" that Robert J. Lifton posits as a rationale for the Nazi project as a whole.[10] But these, and other inferred predictions like them, remain as speculative as the bases for them remain fragmentary; they are also diverse and uncoordinated and on certain points even contradictory. Viewed in retrospect, however, they agree that however large the "Final Solution" itself loomed in Nazi policy, it was but one part of that policy, an element of a more encompassing purpose. Few scholars now doubt that by early 1942 at the latest, the "Final Solution" did indeed become a goal of the Nazi government; few doubt that as the implementation of that goal went forward, it became a sufficiently strong commitment to foster acts or policies that were at times contrary to Nazi self-interest (in terms of winning the war). But the "Final Solution" did indeed *become* such a goal: it had not always been that, and even after reaching that status, its means and so its implications as a goal continued to evolve. Furthermore, even when its role as a factor became indisputable, it did not become the sole or, arguably, even the primary purpose of Nazi policy and planning. There is, in other words, no way to avoid considering the relationship among a number of individual Nazi goals and the more comprehensive goal of which they would be part if one is to understand the admittedly more restricted focus of the "Final Solution." The reverse of this is also true: that it would be difficult, even impossible, to articulate the ultimate design or goal of Nazism without taking into account the actions and their motives that constituted the Holocaust. But it is the latter sequence of events that has typically been given precedence, either to the neglect or denial of the former—and this, it seems clear, leads readily to disproportion or misrepresentation on all sides.

INSIDE

The discussion so far has focused on Nazi acts that were not directed at Jews, except incidentally; that is, on Nazism as it acted "Outside the Holocaust." And again, I have been arguing that only as we view the Holocaust in a framework that includes such evidence can we understand either Nazism in its general form or the Holocaust in particular (as a necessary, not a sufficient condition: there may be *no* sufficient condition for such understanding . . .). I propose now, however, to move back "Inside the Holocaust," and to suggest that just as the account of Nazi acts against non-Jews brings to light important features of the genocide against the Jews, so, also, aspects of the latter—"Inside the

Holocaust"—provide a key for understanding the events affecting non-Jews, thus also, then, for understanding the composite whole that the "inside" and the "outside" of the Holocaust comprise together. This key is not incidental or adventitious, since even if we assume that the view urged of the Nazi commitment to racial–nationalist purification or transcendence is an adequate "covering" explanation (so far as ideology goes) for both the world war as such and the Nazis' war against the Jews, it would yet leave what I take to be an important datum "uncovered." By this, I refer to the means applied by the Nazis in their effort to realize their goal (however that is construed). I refer here more specifically to the feature of excess or disproportion cited earlier in connection with the phenomenon of atrocity. For that was, in Nazi hands, a systemic, not an incidental feature: a role for excessive cruelty, expressed on occasions from large to small, and consistently present to such an extent that they require explanation as intrinsic to the actions and policies of the regime, not as incidental to them (as it is more commonly represented).

How, the question here asks, can we explain the recurrence, the persistence, of this feature in Nazi actions—again, both inside and outside the Holocaust. To be sure, instances of atrocity are known and plentiful before the twentieth century, and the Nazis' version of these shared many characteristics that appeared in that past. Furthermore, any theory of atrocity that begins by ascribing the purpose (for atrocity) of inflicting pain has also usually proceeded from that to various symbolic functions: setting an example (and so serving as a deterrent), taking revenge, instilling fear of authority, demonstrating the reach of power. All these functions conduce to excess: the more, the better—or at least, there is no reason for imposing limits. All were no doubt factors in the earlier history of atrocity, furthermore, as well as in the instances cited here. Even in excess, however, various means may be employed, and a clue to understanding Nazi atrocities can be found in certain aspects of the "Final Solution" that then carry over and illuminate those which occur "outside" it. Primo Levi introduces the phrase "useless ['inutile'] violence" as characterizing certain incidents in his experience that served no apparent practical purpose, not even the symbolic ones that have been mentioned. He refers with this to violent acts that seemed purposeless, at least as measured against what he took the Nazis' purpose to be in the context about which he was writing: the annihilation of the Jews. Why, he poses the question, the violence and cruelty which did nothing to further that purpose and yet recurred and appeared to hold an important place in Nazi practice even under the stress of an all-out war?[11] Levi himself, after posing this question, turns to the explanation given that question by Franz Stangl, the Treblinka Commandant, when Gitta Sereny posed it to him: that such acts, gratuitous as they might seem, accustomed the soldiers committing such violence to the larger—and, in Nazi terms, useful—violence that would soon follow it.[12] Levi's acceptance of the latter explanation—which makes what he had himself judged "useless" violence useful—seems to me to come too readily. In any event, I believe that an alternate, no less plausible explanation more clearly illuminates the larger, corporate Nazi project.

"Violence," as Levi conceives it in his account, needs to be understood on a broad spectrum, with at least some of its "useless" instances violent psychologically rather than physically, although with consequences that may be equally or even more severe. Consider, for examples (some of these are cited by Levi, some not) such arrangements in the Nazi design as the organization of musical bands in concentration camps; the strict regulations in the camps on how the tiers of bunk beds, each holding two or three often dying prisoners, were to be neatly made up on penalty of "the most severe punishment"; the slogans emblazoned at the entrances of certain camps (the best-known, "Arbeit Macht Frei" ["Work makes one free"] at Auschwitz, but others as well, for example, the Prussian motto, "Jedem das Seine" ["To Each His Own"] at an entrance to Buchenwald); or the use of Red Cross ambulances to deliver canisters of the gas Zyklon-B to the gas chambers. On the one hand, there is no overt violence in any of these; on the other hand, there is in them an excess close in kind to what figures in the more flagrant atrocities referred to earlier; indeed, these non-violent expressions in some ways provide evidence that points more clearly to an explanation than do the instances of open violence. The self-conscious "refinement" that shapes the examples cited approximates the means and contrivance of art, that deliberate refiguration which leads to individual style as the artist creates and deploys the means of expression. On both sides of this comparison, there is deliberation and intention; on both, there appears also the willful transgression of norms—although where the artist challenges aesthetic conventions (the norms of beauty), the Nazis' efforts were directed against moral norms, disputing both their individual prescription and their role as norms. In both cases, the agent responsible for them—artist on the one hand, criminal on the other—acts with an awareness of what is being transgressed, and wills the act not only nonetheless but, in part at least, because of it.

The Nazis knew as well as anyone could that work would not make the inmates of Auschwitz free; they knew as well as anyone that a band playing when prisoners who could barely stand were marched out to labor on tasks from which a certain number of them would probably not return clashed— violently—with the associations of musical pleasure; they knew well that rules requiring that a bed that was no more than a pallet be made up neatly and to rigid specifications when its two or more occupants barely had the strength to get up in the morning (and often failed to) mocked any rationale for tidiness; and they unquestionably knew that the use of Red Cross ambulances to deliver the canisters of gas crystals used to kill people was more than only a deception (and they had alternate means of transporting the canisters). Yet all these transgressions and many others like them were imagined and practiced. One cannot, it seems, explain them as private jokes among the Germans themselves (since they were not private) or as collective sadism (there is no reason to suppose sadism to have been a typical feature of the German army or of the SS men and women). And if one understands such expressions of violence, more plausibly, as the application of irony, perhaps designed to invite a will of iron—well, that entails just the kind of self-consciousness indicated in the suggestion posed here. That is, a moral awareness of the particular practice in its wrongfulness, its transgression of a norm—with the will to do it anyway and thus, quite consistently, also to elaborate or embellish the wrong, as artists do in their medium: a consciousness of the violation being committed, together with its affirmation. An intention of such actions thus becomes the process of transgression itself and the assertion of power accompanying it.

This last proposal warrants more evidence and argument than can be given here, but its relation to the need suggested earlier for a framework within which the Holocaust and the other Nazi atrocities are viewed together should be evident. The excess of atrocity figures in common among those acts, for all their other differences—and this carries over into the examples of useless violence as well. To be sure, any claim of a consciousness on the part of the Nazis of their own wrongdoing has a large burden of proof to make good on, and there clearly are alternate explanations for what my interpretation has cited as evidence. The signs at the camp entrances, for example, like much else within the camps, undoubtedly were meant also to deceive, to discourage resistance inside the camps and publicity outside them. Related explanations have been given for the many other Nazi efforts at secrecy that extended from elaborate language rules about what could or could not be said publicly (the very term *"Endlösung"* ["Final Solution"], for example, which was a code word for the annihilation of the Jews was itself forbidden for public use) to the unsuccessful cover-up used for the T-4 program, to the attempts at obliterating the death camps themselves and the evidence of their one-time existence. But secrecy itself may have various motives, and efforts to prevent the discovery of certain acts that have been committed may not be only prudential. Shame or a sense of guilt also lead to the same outcome, and however strained or unlikely it may seem to ascribe any such consciousness or conscience to the Nazis whose policies and actions typically appeared extraordinarily single-minded and assured, some evidence, of the sort mentioned, points in that direction. At the very least, the possibility of this explanation appears as an alternate interpretation competing with that of prudence or self-interest: each is an interpretation. I am not arguing here for an understanding of the "Final Solution" exclusively in terms of an "ideal" of criminality or of the will to power. The choice of the Jews as the object of the "Final Solution," for example—that is, "Why the Jews?"—evidently stemmed from a different (although, I should claim, related) source. But that ideal converges in certain common themes on the Nazi efforts against non-Jews as well, and it is the combination of these acts which in the end requires explanation and which must, as a means, provide whatever evidence such an explanation can draw on.

The Nazi as Criminal

In conclusion: I suggested earlier that after digging my way into this complex —and as it may seem, dangerous—thesis, I would hope then to dig my way out. And as I began with certain likely objections against the account given, let me close with a number of disclaimers that I hope are consistent both with what I objected to and what I have affirmed. Nothing proposed here seems to me to change, let alone diminish, the enormity of the Holocaust. Genocide differs, conceptually and morally, from individual murder; it differs also from mass murder. The phenomenon of genocide, however one construes its gene-alogy or occurrence, marks a distinctive stage in the history of evil or male-faction, and the Nazi Genocide against the Jews stands as a, arguably *the*, definitive instance of that act. But to agree on these several claims is not yet to explain the historical and conceptual framework within which the "Final Solution"—that cumulative series of policies and acts—was imagined and im-plemented. And it is this which seems to me to require the scrutiny of other acts of barbarism by the Nazis if we are to understand any of them—including what is arguably its most extreme instance.

I hope it is clear, furthermore, that I have not been assuming or implying here a single causal explanation for the diverse instances of Nazi criminality. Certainly, in principle there could be various reasons or bases for that phe-nomenon, conceivably as many as there were individual policies or acts. What is at issue in defining the goals that produced atrocities on the scale of the Holocaust and the other actions referred to here involves a process of interpre-tation, after all—and the interpretation of complex structures at that. The pos-sibility cannot be ruled out, moreover, that even the few examples cited here do not reflect a single motive or purpose—or that if they do, it differs from the genetic or national "cleansing" which I have proposed as a covering rationale for the Nazi project. A view of Nazi ideology as motivated primarily by anti-semitism is one such alternate hypothesis; others proposed along the same lines of "*Gesamtdarstellungen*" ("total representations") extend to versions of collec-tive insanity, to the heritage of the (allegedly) totalitarian rationalism of the Enlightenment, and to a historicized version of chaos theory. (According to "functionalism," the best-known version of the latter, individual departments or offices of the Third Reich, acting on their own and each for itself, yet con-verged to produce the single, unified effect that the Holocaust eventually had).

No doubt, discussion and arguments on the questions of exactly what the Nazi ideal or vision was, its "final cause," will continue. We probably should no more expect a consensus among responses to that question than we insist on one (or find it) for the causes or reasons or, for that matter, the consequences of the French Revolution or the American Civil War. To analyze Nazism and the Holocaust—historically, psychologically, morally—is surely no less diffi-cult than to deconstruct these other conglomerate historical events. But neither, I have been suggesting, is that analysis any more difficult to realize: if every understanding arrived at seems incomplete or inconclusive, that is as much due to the general relation between historical events and their explanations as it is to the character of the particular event of the Holocaust. Within the bounds of such understanding applied to the Nazi project, I have been arguing that criminality and the will to actualize it emerges as a recognizable category of explanation. When to this is added what is common to the character of individual Nazi atrocities (including the Holocaust)—as these point toward the goal of racial and cultural purification and domination through the "person" of the German *Volk*—we come as close as method permits to understanding the Holocaust in its convergence on the other sides of the Nazi project. As it did.

Forgiveness, Revenge, and the Limits of Holocaust Justice

So much has been said and written about the Holocaust in the more than half-century of the Post-Holocaust that it seems odd to call attention to issues that have gone *relatively* unnoticed—but certain of these are indeed the subject of this chapter. My reason for doing this is the importance, for anyone who looks back now at the Holocaust, of considering not only the issues commonly linked to that event—those principally responsible for giving it its name—but of inquiring also about other related topics that have been marginal to or even absent from the discourse. Depending on what it turns up, the explanation of such neglect may itself, after all, bring to light hardly less significant aspects of the Holocaust; silences, we know, are at times as expressive and informative as words. Such explanation would, furthermore, speak more broadly about the *concept* of the Post-Holocaust—a period, whether acknowledged or not, in which the contemporary world finds itself, including regions and people that were not, and in many cases could not have been, directly affected by the Holocaust at the time of its occurrence. Even the most extreme and extraordinary moments of experience take place, after all, inside history; thus, also the reactions to them—accommodation or denial, avoidance or transformation—are open to explanation as part of the historical and social processes in which they occur; that is, as indicators of the lives, and as it may happen, also the deaths of those directly affected by them.

To be sure, avoidance of a topic may reflect various causes—indifference as well as repression, exigency as well as ignorance. That there is no bottom or floor to historical explanation should not, however, deter us from reflecting on its probabilities or improbabilities—and I attempt such reflection here in relation to the two topics of revenge and forgiveness, as they, and the acts or inactions associated with them, figured in the events of the Holocaust. And as they have been largely if not entirely absent from the extensive discussions in the Post-Holocaust of so many other facets of the Holocaust itself. The relative silence about these two topics in the literature of the Post-Holocaust is the more notable insofar as the concepts themselves are, if not contradictory, certainly at odds with each other: where there is forgiveness, there will be little room for the expression of revenge—and conversely, where the impulse for revenge is present (still more, where it is acted upon), the option of forgiveness would have been rejected. The potential importance of these two impulses is underscored, furthermore, because both of them stand at, or arguably on the other side of, the boundaries of justice: Revenge as it is ordinarily understood moves outside the rule of law and so also of justice; and where laws have been applied—that is, as justice is done—forgiveness too is arguably extraneous. What more, after all, could be required, even in the face of extreme wrongdoing than that justice should rule?

But then there are also occasions, small or large, when justice either cannot or, in the way of the world, will not be done. And it seems likely that with respect to the enormity of the Holocaust, this limitation on the capacity of justice is an evident consequence of that enormity: that for what transpired in the Holocaust, in the Nazi Genocide against the Jews which claimed millions of lives solely because of their identification *as* Jews, no justice can be done, at least no justice that could balance or make good on the harm or wrong inflicted. Perhaps such inadequacy is intrinsic to the working of justice wherever it applies, even in much less fraught cases—if only because history can never be *fully* undone or overcome. The most generous compensation, after all, cannot "make whole" the victims of most terrible deeds, since the acts themselves have still been committed and their victims remain still (and always) victims. Whatever the biblical Job was given back after passing the test of God's wager with Satan, his children who had been killed in that test, and his flocks as well, were not *themselves* restored. Job himself was not the same person he had been, and this is all the more clearly true for the lives that had been ended.

It is, then, precisely because of these limitations on the reach of justice—the fact that in the imbalance between the victims and agents of the Holocaust, full justice cannot and so will not be done, now or ever—that the boundary concepts of forgiveness and revenge which characteristically stand just beyond the reach of justice become most pertinent. The analysis presented here about these boundary concepts does not argue for a particular judgment or course of action in relation to them, either as such or in specific reference to the Holocaust; my concern is with the dispositions themselves and what their significance is as they figure in our thinking about the Holocaust—most immediately, on what obstacles, real or imagined, have lead to their apparent avoidance and the silence that has surrounded them.

Nor do I mean to equate those two practices on the scale of moral dispositions. I propose rather that as the Post-Holocaust continually attempts to "rethink" the Holocaust and its consequences, it should consider the relevance of these two motifs as they even now extend beyond the Holocaust into the present. For although there was a sharper and more immediate pertinence in the context of the Holocaust itself for both the pursuit of revenge and for judging the possibility of forgiveness, it should be clear that this pertinence did not end in that context or its near aftermath. A distinctive feature of the Post-Holocaust is that in it certain unfinished questions bequeathed by the Holocaust persist, and it should be obvious that the justification for revenge and the desirability (or possible extent) of forgiveness remain live issues. To be sure, the burden of judging these has largely, if not entirely, shifted from the actual agents and victims of the Holocaust to their heirs, to that extent also altering the terms of the discussion (*how much* should be altered because of this becomes itself a pressing question for the Post-Holocaust). But the challenge of responding to the possibilities of revenge and forgiveness continues, since clearly there are means of expression that they might take today, even sixty years after the end of the events themselves. In this sense, the term "Post-Holocaust" would be misleading if taken to imply that the Holocaust as an event is even now fully "over"—and I should argue that readers of these words not only could but ought to press themselves to take positions on these continuing issues. As for so many moral issues, the avoidance of passing judgment here becomes itself a judgment, and not necessarily the most incisive or compelling one.

Consider first the question of the place of revenge as a reaction to the events of the Holocaust—and the virtual silence that has surrounded it. On the face of the matter, it seems that both in the immediate context of the Holocaust, during the years of its occurrence and directly afterward, and hardly less in the longer run of the Post-Holocaust period which continues now, if ever there were an occasion for acts or the potential for revenge, the brutality of Nazi policy and actions would have been, and even now remain, such an occasion, both in act and in discourse. Yet it seems clear that this has *not* been the case, that the phenomenon of revenge and the serious issues it raises have been largely avoided (at least "on the record") in practice as well as in reflection. There are, it seems to me, one quite general reason and two more specific ones for this resistance—what amounts to repression of this topic. The general reason reflects the morally problematic character of revenge itself—its place at or beyond the boundaries of justice. Revenge is typically personalized, impelled, and carried out by the same individuals or groups (or their advocates) who have suffered what they hold to be wrongs. Furthermore, revenge has in itself no natural or logical limits: it is the persons or groups who act who also decide, in the immediate context of their response, what the extent or nature of their revenge is to be. (Social and cultural conventions obviously play a role here, but they mainly underscore the limitlessness of revenge as a process.) Both these features of revenge conflict with the standard concept of justice, as we see "her" personified in the icons of justice, standing blindfolded in front of courthouses: blindfolded—signifying that everyone who comes before the court will be treated equally and disinterestedly, irrespective of social status, but also to represent the laws as limited in their reach, intended always to "fit the crime" rather than as subject to change or whimsy. Justice, in other words, must be both impersonal and measured—as revenge need not, indeed (by definition) cannot be. Revenge, then, is problematic precisely because it is open to arbitrariness and excess that laws and structures of justice are intended to avoid. This reason alone would work against making a place for acts of revenge in any social structure that rejects the legitimacy of taking the law "into one's own hands"—and would conduce, when such acts do occur, to a certain silence and embarrassment about them, whether from shame or prudence or both.

That silence or concealment may be understandable accompaniments to acts of revenge, however, does not mean that such acts did not occur (although by the same token, it does not mean that they *did*). There is, however, ample independent evidence that they did occur, and this fact becomes increasingly pertinent as the Post-Holocaust continues to find its way among the ruins left by the Holocaust. Some of those acts were overtly (that is, physically) vengeful; some were indirect or symbolic—displacements of more explicit reactions. But that there were instances of both of these, and that they point to motifs and motives in both the Holocaust and the Post-Holocaust that warrant more attention than they have received, and that suggest the likelihood of still other occurrences, is attested by the evidence itself.

· Thus, in the immediate aftermath of the liberation of the concentration and death camps, in the early months of 1945 before the War formally ended and then for several months afterwards, midst the understandable confusion of converging armies and of hundreds of thousands of displaced persons, there is no doubt that numerous instances of what might be called "personal revenge" occurred—that is, as individual survivors or soldiers in the victorious armies either sought out specific individuals or, more simply, struck at German soldiers or their collaborators. Some of these acts are on record—for example, from the liberation of certain of the concentration camps, as at Dachau, where upward of thirty of the camp guards were killed at the time of liberation by the *American* soldiers, not by the survivors who had been held prisoner there (the motives here might have been various, including but almost surely not confined to revenge for American losses in the War). Other acts of such immediate or direct revenge (some of it organized) are matters of record as based on what would usually be counted historically creditable sources; some are reported—however infrequently—in the video archives of testimonies taped by individual survivors. But the sum of such accounts remains minimal and sparse, and it seems clear that much of what might have served as evidence has been lost (and probably permanently). It is notable, furthermore, that notwithstanding the many different lines of research followed in Holocaust historiography, no systematic effort has yet been made to gather even the information or evidence that *might* be available about this phenomenon—an absence which seems to me due to something more than only the difficulty of locating it.[1]

Thus, we do not know, and probably never will, the extent of this impulse or the history of its expression: how widespread it was and what the identities of those involved were, whether as agents or victims. To be sure, the possibility remains that the silence around this phenomenon reflects no more than that there was little of it to speak *about*, that we find here an absence, not concealment. But there are documented records of attempts at more organized and explicit efforts, and one in particular warrants mention because of its unusual dimensions—also because the intensity of its design, in my view, underscores the probability that other, if lesser, attempts were also made, even if they remain unrecorded. This one large effort involved a small but determined group of former Jewish partisan fighters who, after having participated in Jewish resistance movement—in the ghettoes and forests of Lithuania and Poland—turned after the Russian liberation of those areas to plotting systematic revenge against the German people, since (in their view) the Germans had collectively been responsible for the Nazi Genocide. This group, under the leadership of Abba Kovner who later became a national cultural and social figure in Israel, took as its name the *Revenge Group*, or more formally, the transliterated acronym DIN—with the Hebrew meaning of that term, *Judgment*, and the acronym itself composed of the first letters of three words *Dam Yisrael Noter* ("The blood of Israel avenges"). This group developed two plans, both of which they began to set in motion, although only one was ever acted upon, and even that on a smaller scale than had been initially intended. The first plan proposed literally to take revenge against the German people as a people, exploiting the chaos in Germany during the closing months of the War and its immediate aftermath—by poisoning the drinking water of four major cities (Hamburg, Frankfurt, Munich, and Nuremberg). This plan advanced to the point where the poison itself had been obtained and where members of the group had gained access to the water delivery systems of those cities (by finding employment in relevant agencies). Various difficulties encountered by Kovner himself, however, together with both external opposition from sources in Palestine and a certain amount of internal opposition within the group, impeded the plan and it did not get beyond this stage. In contrast, the second plan, which targeted German prisoner-of-war camps set up by the Allied armies, was in part carried out. In the American zone of occupation, at an SS prisoner-of-war camp near Nuremberg, members of the Revenge group who had obtained employment in the camp bakery poisoned the bread distributed in the camp, with consequences that still remain disputed but that evidently did result in injuries and (probably) some deaths among the SS prisoners (this, in April 1946).

The story of how this Revenge group organized itself and of the aftermath of its efforts warrants a full account in its own right; only recently have the details of its history begun to be assembled, and there remain disputes (on the facts as well as on interpretation) within the Group itself.[2] The Group had initially taken a vow of silence and largely observed that vow over a considerable period of time; at least some of the reasons for this silence go beyond prudential considerations and bear on the discussion here: even more than individual revenge, collective revenge, like collective guilt, is a problematic and certainly contestable concept. It seems imperative, however, that both the concept and the phenomenon should be recognized as part of the aftermath of the Holocaust. For anyone who wonders at the extremity of the plans devised by the Revenge Group, the stark words that appeared in the testament of a member of the Dror movement (a Socialist-Zionist youth group) from Bialystok who was killed before the Revenge Group undertook its plan should be suggestive. Thus, the challenge of Zipporah Berman:

> With this I turn to you, comrades. . . . On you rests the absolute obligation to carry out our revenge. Let no one of you sleep at night or during the day: as we are in the shadow of death, let it also be so for you in revenging the blood that has been spilled. Cursed be whoever reads these words for whom it suffices to sigh and to return to their daily chores; cursed be he for whom cheap tears suffice. . . . We call you to revenge—revenge without pity, without feeling, without words about "good" Germans. For the good German—an easy death. . . . This is our demand. The scattered ashes from the ovens will not rest easy until this vengeance is exacted. Remember and fulfill our wish and your obligation.

It is difficult to hear or read these words without becoming aware of the destruction that would have occasioned them and the fearsomeness of the prospect they hold out. It is undoubtedly because of that fearsomeness that the impulse for revenge, even in relation to an event like the Holocaust, has more often appeared in other forms that might be referred to as symbolic or displaced, although still clearly rooted in the impulse for revenge. A few among the more familiar examples of these can be cited here—beginning with the so-called *Morgenthau Plan* (named after the Secretary of the Treasury in Roosevelt's World War II cabinet, who formulated it). In that Plan, post-war Germany would have been not only demilitarized but "de-industrialized," in effect turned into a pastoral country, partitioned into a number of smaller parts in such a way as to disable it from posing a future threat to the countries of Europe or the World. Morgenthau named his Plan a "Program to Prevent Germany from Starting a World War III"—a title that itself suggests a version of the symbolic or displaced revenge alluded to above. To be sure, a concern about preventing future wars might be interpreted as an expression of prudence rather than vengeance. But the details of the Plan make it difficult to avoid the conclusion that it was also—arguably, primarily—punitive, pointed toward the past no less than toward the future, and in facing that past, shaped by the motif of revenge. The division of Germany into East and West Germany that occurred as a function of the Cold War, after the USSR (on the one side), and France, Great Britain, and the United States, on the other, could not agree on a reunification plan to succeed their four-sector occupation of the conquered Germany, became in effect an "accidental" albeit incomplete version of the Morgenthau Plan; certainly, it came to be seen by many observers both within the Germanies and outside them as a form of symbolic revenge—and in certain ways, more than only symbolic. This interpretation came most clearly into the open in the resistance to the *re*unification of the Germanies after the tearing down of the Berlin Wall in 1989.

Again, on a smaller scale but more currently: the Israel Philharmonic Orchestra has only in the last several years included in its repertoire the music of Richard Strauss, who served as a censor of music under the Nazi regime before finding himself ostracized by it; the music of Wagner, who was an outspoken antisemite and published his views in what remains a relevant text for that movement (*Das Judentum in der Musik,* 1850), and whose musical works were a strong influence on Hitler himself (however one interprets the details in that lineage), is still excluded, although the subject of ongoing debate. To be sure, the "meaning" of such a boycott is itself open to interpretation, especially in the case of Wagner who was long dead at the time of the Nazi rise to power. But it seems unwarranted to deny a role here, as well as in other, more personal boycotts—the refusal to visit Germany or to buy goods "made in Germany"— for what I have been calling symbolic or displaced revenge.

As suggested, the purpose of citing these examples is less either to defend or to criticize them—important as it is to place oneself in respect to them, *to decide in the present on the past*—than to show how the past of the Holocaust is sustained in the Post-Holocaust both as historical fact and in forms more clearly defined now in certain ways than they were previously, with the role of revenge one such item. There are obviously limits admitted even in the saying, "Revenge is best served cold"—a point in time after which revenge, in its own terms, would seem *too* cold and thus irrelevant. But that point does not yet seem to have been reached for the many sides of response that the Holocaust has bequeathed to the Post-Holocaust. For anyone who now considers the future of the Post-Holocaust in addition to that of the Holocaust, the status of issues like the uneasy possibility and actual history of revenge points in two directions: on the one hand, bearing the hope that justice might yet be so fully realized as to obviate the need for such expressions as revenge that stand on the other side of the boundaries of justice; on the other hand, with a strong sense that the realization of justice—the ideal of "making whole"—is unlikely ever to be achieved in respect to an event with the dimensions of the Holocaust. This seems to be a fork in the path of the moral world that the prospect of revenge confronts *whenever* it occurs; as elsewhere, however, the extremity of the Holocaust adds weight to the tension.

The second and very different—and opposed—concept of forgiveness as it bears on the Holocaust has nonetheless had a similarly muted presence in the post-Holocaust period, although for different reasons. Here too, furthermore, there have been pressures on the concept in relation to the Holocaust from both directions—from the one side, the impulse, set at various levels, to invoke and/or to grant forgiveness; from the other side, to deny them. The tension between these two sides is understandable. In religious terms, the major Western traditions, and certainly Judaism among them, assign to forgiveness an important moral, social, and finally, religious role. In the relationship between man and God, as Judaism conceives it, man seeks God's forgiveness for wrongs committed against Him. This appears most notably on the Day of Atonement, in which God is represented as closing the books on personal destinies for the coming New Year, a judgment based on the person's past actions and present repentance. But a more immediate form of forgiveness is also mandated between man and man—a transaction that is a prerequisite for divine forgiveness which becomes possible only after the other has been sought. What often passes unnoticed in the practice of forgiveness "between man and man," however, is that this accounts finds an obligation not only to *seek* forgiveness from people whom one has wronged, but also an obligation to *grant* forgiveness on the part of those who have been wronged, at least for certain wrongs and under certain conditions.

This side of the process of forgiveness may seem skewed or odd. Why should anyone be *obligated* to forgive, when whether to do so or not seems clearly a matter of personal decision and a consequence of having been wronged oneself. Presumably the person wronged has the right to decide when or under which conditions he or she forgives someone else. But the counterargument here is precisely that forgiveness is not only a personal or subjective matter, that as a moral issue, it raises questions of principle and thus also comes finally within the domain of justice. So, for example, Maimonides stipulates that if a person publicly asks forgiveness of someone he has wronged on three separate occasions and has the request rejected each time, two consequences follow automatically: the wrong is in fact forgiven (as it were, by the community), and the person who refused to grant forgiveness is himself judged guilty of wrongdoing—in current idiom of being "unforgiving." In these terms, although forgiveness seems often to stand otherwise beyond the boundaries of justice—in philosophical terms, as supererogatory: an act or form of action desirable and praiseworthy but not obligatory—it is, in Maimonides's view, more than this, directly implicated in the search for justice. Seen in this light, forgiveness demands recognition as a moral value in its own right, one which by clearing the past of antagonisms and barriers fostered by wrongs committed among family or friends or even just within common humanity, revives the possibility of renewed human relationships, whether among small groups or large ones.

But what, it might be asked, do such general—and even bland—considerations have to do with forgiveness in the context of an event as extreme as the Holocaust and its innumerable cruel, individual acts? Is forgiveness *always* an obligation, irrespective of the nature of the wrong committed? And who is empowered to grant forgiveness, and under what circumstances?[3] A short book titled *The Sunflower*, written or composed by Simon Wiesenthal on the basis of an episode during the Holocaust when he was a captive in a labor camp in Poland, brings to the fore many of these issues in an unexpectedly dramatic form; it seems to me to underscore the complexity of issues surrounding the problem of forgiveness in relation to the Holocaust—but also, relatedly, to explain the relative silence that has cloaked the topic of forgiveness.[4]

Wiesenthal (as he relates the story) was one of a group of Jewish slave laborers delivering material to a hospital administered by nuns who served as nurses and in which wounded German soldiers were cared for. On one of his work days, one of the "Sisters" pulled Wiesenthal aside and ordered him to follow her to a room in the hospital in which an SS soldier, Hans, was evidently dying of his wounds—but had expressed a wish to speak to someone who was Jewish. Selected by chance in this way, Wiesenthal entered the room and then heard from Hans his story: that on the Eastern front, in a Russian town, he had taken part in an atrocity committed against the Jewish inhabitants who had been forced into a building which was then locked and set on fire. Hans, dying and with that act heavy on his conscience, wished to ask forgiveness for his part in it from someone who was Jewish—and it was to hear and respond to that request that Wiesenthal had been chosen. Wiesenthal reports that he listened carefully to Hans's account and to his request. Then he stood up and left the room—wordlessly, in silence, and so in effect rejecting the request: How could he, he recalls asking himself, forgive an act committed against others, others who now of course could not judge or speak for themselves. At the time, this seemed to Wiesenthal to be the just response. But he was later sufficiently troubled by his decision to take the episode and his reaction as the starting point of further discussion and of his book, *The Sunflower*. He then also asked a number of writers—theologians, philosophers, social critics—what they thought that he should have done under the circumstances and even more directly, what *they* would have done. The responses of those other writers make up the remaining, and indeed the larger part of the book.

As might be expected from such a varied group, their individual responses to Wiesenthal's question also varied, but beyond the differences they also divided along two principal lines: those who supported Wiesenthal in refusing to grant Hans's request—and those who said that he should have granted it, that not only had it been in Wiesenthal's power to do what Hans had asked, but that, in the circumstances and with Hans dying, he had an obligation to do so. At stake in this divided response is evidently something more than the particular circumstance: the issue turns largely on the different ways forgiveness is understood as a moral concept, for there *are* large differences in those ways. On the view of forgiveness running counter to Wiesenthal's decision, "vicarious" or third-person forgiveness is a clear option; that is, a person who did not himself suffer the wrong or injury may nonetheless grant forgiveness in the place of the victim who did. In other words, the person wronged has no special power or authority for forgiving or refusing to. Furthermore, it seems on this same view (although these two parts are not necessarily related) that no wrongs or injuries are in principle unforgivable—since, one assumes, there could hardly be greater wrongs for which forgiveness might be sought than the sort of act that Hans admitted to Wiesenthal he had taken part in.

On the other side, the writers who endorsed Wiesenthal's silence and his denial of Hans's request moved in the opposite direction on both these points. Their contention with respect to forgiveness was that nobody is empowered to grant forgiveness for wrongs suffered by a person other than the person himself, even if this means (as it would in *The Sunflower*) that some wrongs will remain perpetually unforgiven—or, differently but still more strongly, that certain wrongs are, quite simply, unforgivable (in *principle*). This is, it seems clear, a very different conception of the basis and rationale of forgiveness, and quite aside from the importance of analyzing and, if possible, overcoming the disagreement between the two views, the conflict between them itself explains to some extent the relative absence of discussions of forgiveness in the Post-Holocaust. For although the affirmation of many moral concepts (as in precepts against murder or robbery) seems always unexceptionable, where forgiveness is concerned—in this, again, resembling revenge—both those who urge it and those who oppose it cannot hope to ignore the force of counterarguments. Those critical of Wiesenthal's decision (they included such figures as Jacques Maritain, Martin Marty, and Leopold Senghor) would have been bound to recognize (and some of them also wrote of this) the danger in the view they advocated of so diluting the principle of forgiveness as to make its transaction trivial or empty. (On some expositions of this view, the person who has injured someone else need not even acknowledge wrongdoing or ask for forgiveness in order to be absolved.) And whether one finally accepts this view or not, the alternative to it, which would insist that someone who has done wrong must at least admit to wrongdoing before the slate can be wiped clean, can hardly be dismissed as irrelevant. From the other side (which included figures like A. J. Heschel, Primo Levi, and Cynthia Ozick), those who thought that Wiesenthal had acted properly—that is, as *they* would have acted, and some in more extreme forms than Wiesenthal—also recognize the gravity of denying the *possibility* of forgiveness, with the implication here that the person so denied would then live and die with the wrong that he had sincerely renounced nonetheless perpetually held against him. As those who have advocated or opposed revenge in relation to the Holocaust have been muted in their claims—on my explanation, because of the intense consequences that follow from either of those public positions—so here, in respect to forgiveness, it is the pressure exerted by the positions opposed to their own advocacy that seems to have held them back and to have muted their discussion. In the context of the extremity of the Holocaust, to be forgiving—for individual acts like Hans's or for the broader outline of that event as a whole—may seem too easy, even promiscuous; in the context of a common humanity which acknowledges a common fallibility, an ultimate or permanent denial of forgiveness may seem an expression of arrogance. This is not to say that a choice between the two cannot or should not be made, but that the terms and consequences of the choice have understandably hindered and limited its discussion. An additional contributory factor to that condition may have been a cautionary moral drawn from the issue irrespective of which of the two views of the respondents to Wiesenthal's narrative one favors. This would in effect be a warning—arguably a "commandment"—against committing acts that are, or perhaps even may be, unforgivable.

One aspect of the issue of forgiveness in relation to the Holocaust that has not been discussed needs at least to be mentioned. This aspect concerns the question of collective responsibility and, in the event, culpability—thus also, what would in response come to be something like collective forgiveness: forgiveness toward a group as that might be extended either by individuals or a group. An especially intense challenge to this possibility appears in Daniel Jonah Goldhagen's *Hitler's Willing Executioners: Ordinary Germans and the Holocaust*, as Goldhagen gives there what amounts to an indictment of Germany (and the Germans) as a nation with collective responsibility for the "Final Solution."[5] Goldhagen's contention is that the Nazi Genocide would have been impossible had the German people not participated as a whole—and that this participation was itself the result (also, the proof) of their common commitment to what he names "Eliminationist Antisemitism." Much has been written about (often against) Goldhagen's version of German antisemitism, and this does not need to be summarized here. But one issue raised by his account, relevant also to accounts of Nazi responsibility that are much less radical, needs yet to be addressed in relation to the discussion of forgiveness, irrespective of one's view of Goldhagen's position.

Suppose, for the sake of argument, that we accept as true that the German nation or state or people as a whole were indeed collectively responsible for the Holocaust, with certain leading figures having a larger role than others but with each individual German citizen also and, at that level, having a share in responsibility for the atrocities committed in the twelve years of Nazi rule. To be sure, a number of individual Nazi leaders centrally involved in conceiving and implementing that policy were indeed brought to trial in the years soon after the end of the War, through the International Military Tribunal in Nuremberg, but also elsewhere in Germany and in other countries occupied by Germany during the War. Furthermore, West Germany, once re-established as a government, acknowledged the responsibility of its predecessor German government's actions and recognized its own continuing responsibility in respect to the consequences of that government's actions. (One way in which the latter expressed itself was in the payment of reparations both to individuals who had been persecuted and to the newly founded State of Israel as a beneficiary of victims who could not be identified or who even if identified could not benefit.) Moreover, since the fall of the Berlin Wall in 1989 and the subsequent reunification of Germany, the denial of any responsibility for the Holocaust on the part of what had been East Germany has been displaced by the general policy of the one-Germany as recognition of the enormity of this period in German history. Thus, even if today a substantial number of Germans (in a country now of some 80,000,000 people) reject or are indifferent to any claims of individual or corporate responsibility for Nazi policies and actions during World War II, it seems nonetheless impossible not to recognize in the formal policies of Germany as a state both a continuing acknowledgment of the national wrong committed in Germany's past and a sense of continuing responsibility for that past.

And yet, on the other hand: it is now almost sixty years since the end of World War II. The youngest person alive in Germany today who was more than sixteen years old at the end of the War is now seventy-five years old; the percentage of Germans over that age who could possibly have had an active role in the "Final Solution" thus amounts to less than 10 percent of the German populace; ten years from now, that percentage will be well under 5 percent, and not very long after that will have decreased to zero. But if Goldhagen's thesis held for Germany's collective responsibility and guilt for the Holocaust in 1945—when the issue of forgiveness could hardly be raised as a possibility (even, there is evidence, among many Germans)—the question emerges with increasingly stronger relevance of what and how nations and peoples of the world should now, or if not now, in the future, address that charge. Obviously, the history of Nazi Germany and of its responsibility for the Holocaust does not and will not change; the record of the causes and means which figured in that history will no doubt be supplemented and in certain respects altered—but the basic structure, the roles and numbers of agents and victims, seems clearly fixed within certain parameters. There might be agreement, furthermore (or let us suppose this), that the process of judging individual agents of the Final Solution and of the corporate bodies who contributed to it and profited from it should continue as long as new evidence and those responsible continue to be identified. But when we are speaking, as has so constantly been the case both explicitly and tacitly, of *national* German responsibility and more than that, of German corporate guilt, it seems clear that at some point a choice will also have to be—*ought to be*—made between something like "corporate forgiveness" or, in a lesser version, a "Statute of Limitations": that is, a point after which Germany and its people, without at all effacing or obscuring the Holocaust in their national past, would be addressed in the present without invoking new obligations incurred by that past; that is, where the people and the nation would be judged by their actions in the present, at least to the extent that other peoples and nations are.

I do not claim that such a moment is overdue or that there has been injustice during the Post-Holocaust because that moment has not yet been recognized. Justification for any proposal of corporate forgiveness is necessarily *prospective*—and proposed as a matter of principle, based mainly on the consequences that follow if at some point, it is *not* carried through. For in that event, a commitment is implied to a principle that assigns the sins of one generation not only to some, but to all later ones; which in this case would assert that Nazi responsibility and guilt is heritable so long as there is a German nation at all— that whatever acts of contrition and compensation are offered in the future by individual Germans and/or by German governments, they would not suffice. Always something more than what had been done would yet need to be done in response to the fact of the Holocaust. A resentful consciousness within Germany that this is indeed the view of Germany's status as seen from the outside is not by itself sufficient reason for altering it; the grounds for doing so are simpler—namely, the implications of the *alternative*. Heritable guilt, like its metaphysical forebear, Original Sin, requires an argued defense that has rarely been forthcoming (or persuasive when it has been); in its political or moral consequences, it appears still less viable. Indeed, a version of the same claim itself was implicated in the history of the Holocaust with the Nazi assumption of inheritable responsibility and guilt on the part of its victims.[6]

To be sure, the proposal of what would what suffice as so dramatic a "Statute of Limitations" faces substantial difficulties of its own—the principal one among these in determining where the specific stopping point, the "moment" of forgiveness, should be. Any such point must finally appear arbitrary: why now and not later, why later and not earlier, and so on. That the same criticism applies to every statute of limitations hardly diminishes the objection in this case—and probably the less so because of the Holocaust's unusual moral status. There seems no obvious formula that could settle the matter; the closest I have come in this search for a figurative or symbolic ground is to transpose the Yiddish blessing for long life—"bis hundert un zwanzig" ("till a hundred and twenty [years]")—and to use that date, a hundred and twenty years after the Holocaust, as the line of demarcation. I know, of course, that this reference is without any larger ground—but again, what should be clear is that the specific date or number agreed to is less important than the recognition that at *some* time, a response of this sort will be required, even if there were agreement (as I believe there should be) that for a large number of the individual acts committed during the Holocaust, there simply is not, now or ever, the possibility of forgiveness.

Where then, more generally, does the discussion of revenge and forgiveness leave the possibility of the Holocaust-Justice invoked in this chapter's title? It seems clear, from what we know of events during the Post-Holocaust, as we find them originally set in motion by the events of the Holocaust itself, that for an occurrence of this enormity, the standard means and instruments of justice turn out to be inadequate for "making good" the wrongs and suffering inflicted during the Holocaust. It is difficult even to imagine, let alone to make actual, either punishment or compensation that comes close to righting those wrongs. So Primo Levi writes in a poem which he titles, "For Adolf Eichmann": "Oh son of death . . . / May you live longer than anyone every lived. / May you live sleepless five million nights, / And may you be visited each night by the suffering of everyone who saw . . . the air filled with death."[7] But even if *that* dream of Levi's were realized, it seems clear that the gap created and left by the Holocaust would not be filled. It is evidently because this seems so fully and demonstrably the case that impulses or practices on the boundary of justice— like those of revenge or forgiveness—become more pertinent and more pressing than they do in most other contexts.

But perhaps this conclusion, warranted in its own terms, should not be given quite the last word on the prospects of Holocaust justice in the present discussion, since there are at least indicators of movement in another direction as well. It may seem unduly optimistic, arguably even offensive, to suggest that one of the consequences of the Holocaust—to be sure, unintended and in any event beside the point of judging its evil—has been in effect to advance the cause of justice itself. But it is also undeniable that in the aftermath of the Nazi Genocide, not only the concept and term *genocide* came into existence, but the United Nations Convention on the Prevention and Punishment of the Crime of Genocide was formulated and adopted (in 1948); that cases are at present being tried which prosecute the crime of genocide under the auspices of the International War Crime Tribunal sponsored by the United Nations—all of this attesting that the crime of genocide, which if the Holocaust was arguably a flagrant and extreme occurrence, had occurred previously and has occurred since, is now registered in full view on the moral table of extreme violations. Nobody would claim that moral violations are "good" because their recognition and punishment expands the domain of the moral imagination—but the scope and detail of the moral imagination are indeed everyone's concern. Nobody would claim that this moral expansion overrides or compensates for any act of genocide itself. It might be argued that identifying and naming and even legislating against genocide in some ways foster such acts—and certainly it is a serious question as to why, in the aftermath of the Nazi Genocide and with that example so explicitly and fully in view, the world has found itself confronting more than a few subsequent acts of "ethnic cleansing" and group murder. Yet as the domain of moral right and wrong seems bound to include both of those "values," with instances of each shaping the character of the domain as a whole, the importance of the recognition of genocide as a crime and the translation of that recognition into international legislation, ratified by nations of the world, should not be underestimated. An accomplishment, to be sure that one would wish had not been necessary, but which, given the necessity, is itself an advance that we also know might not have occurred. Indeed, it *had not* previously occurred.

It may not be too harsh to claim that in a view of the moral history of mankind, the contribution of the twentieth century was a regression in that history rather than anything that might be construed as progress; that the twentieth century, in moral terms, was the century of genocide as the nineteenth century might be seen (again in moral terms and moving in the opposite direction) as the century of the ending of slavery. But if the twentieth century left as part of its heritage the phenomenon of genocide, we might hope also— and act to ensure—that this ominous heritage also marks the setting in motion of a legal and moral system capable of deterring genocide, and, as this proves necessary, of judging and punishing that act when it occurs. What would become, then, of the boundary concepts of revenge and forgiveness that marked the starting point of this discussion? So long as Holocaust justice (and its analogues in other instances of genocide) remain unrealized ideals, it will probably be impossible—and arguably, wrong—to exclude those boundary concepts from the moral landscape. Indeed, the pressure they exert on other moral concepts and the principles of justice may itself be a factor in the latter's actualization. If and when that does occur, we may then think of both revenge and forgiveness differently than we now do—as superseded or absorbed by the practice of justice. But then, it seems clear, is not yet.

THREE

Evil, Suffering, and the Holocaust

As far as human eyes can judge, the degree of evil might have been less without any impediment to good.

Samuel Johnson

The need to account for the appearance of evil in a world assumed to be ruled by goodness and justice provoked Jewish religious and philosophical reflection long before the Holocaust. The "problem" of evil, pointed most sharply in the phenomenon of human suffering and loss, figured in the very origins of Jewish philosophy (as in Saadya's commentary on Job [c. 935 C.E.]),[1] and Genesis itself provided an earlier view of the knowledge of good and evil in its synthesis of cosmology and genealogy—the entry into human nature of moral conscience which ensured that man would then make his own way across the grain of historical contingency *and* face divine judgment for his actions along that way. It was, then, this *second* nature that would impel the biblical narrative and subsequent Jewish ethical reflection.

Nothing in this history, however, suggests a distinctively Jewish representation of the "problem of evil" or of the connection it suggests between ontology and ethics—the substantive connection between the world as it is and the world as it ought to be. The common, and commonsensical, assumption of a relation between the *is* and the *ought* has figured prominently in theoretical and practical ethics for as long as records exist of either, and the twentieth century disclaimer of that relation in the "Naturalistic Fallacy" (and its empiricist predecessors)[2] should be viewed in the context of this larger, contrary tradition rather than the other way round. What, after all, would be a stronger incentive for moral analysis (also, admittedly, for *moralizing*) than to consider how badly human lives may fare under an allegedly beneficent and all-powerful ruler?

The skeptical reminder that righteous people suffer and wicked ones prosper is not universally true, but it does not have to be. Even a few local examples—

always available—underscore this imbalance, and it seems impossible to find a culture or age from which awareness of it is absent. An obvious reason for this widespread recognition is that illness and death are cultural as well as biological universals: however inventive a society's rationalized accounts of loss and suffering, those disruptions lodge in the social fabric and recur in its "thick" descriptions. Furthermore, the issue they pose dramatically in a divinely ordered world figures in other settings as well—for one example, in the problem of voluntary evildoing: how, or whether, a person can choose to do evil in full knowledge of what he or she is doing (human rationality as an analogue here to divine omniscience). The sophisticated debate reported in Job about the gap between divine justice and human suffering suggests a history in Jewish thought antedating that Book's composition (c. 500 B.C.E.); the "consolation" of his comforters as they urge Job to examine his own responsibility for his suffering rather than to dispute its justice—an early version of theodicy—is unlikely to have been invented for that occasion.

Motivation for philosophical and religious reflection on evil, then, is ample—and if that background presses no more urgently in Jewish thought than in other religious or philosophical traditions, it is no less evident there. On the one hand, the world was found "good" at each stage of the biblical creation, and except for scattered moments of mystical enthusiasm, subsequent Jewish commentary never disputed that judgment. On the other hand, a profusion of evidence attests to individual and group suffering in people who appear to deserve that condition no more (often much less) than contemporaries who fare better—often, *much* better. At least from the time of Rabbinic Judaism, in any event, the issue thus stated would recur in Jewish theological and philosophical discussion: how to reconcile misfortune, suffering or persecution, and exile with the goodness of creation and the authority of an all-powerful and beneficent creator. And if modern *pre*-Holocaust Jewish thinkers, from Spinoza to Hermann Cohen, seem less troubled than their ancient and medieval predecessors by the phenomenon of evil as a historical and then religious or metaphysical factor, this reflected new anxieties about primarily epistemological themes rather than the diminished significance of the ethical issues themselves.

The constancy in the conceptualization of evil is further underscored when compared to changes in other cultural themes. For in contrast to the variations in other traditional beliefs, few shifts occur in the constant idiom of "normal" representations of evil. This persistence appears also in the avoidance even among historical accounts of culture of anything like a "history of evil"—this, *against* the evidence that conceptions and practices of evil, like other ideas and practices, have altered over time (and might even, like those others, comprise a *progressive* history). Western ethical thinking, both within and outside Judaism, has emphasized the contrary view, treating evil rather as all-of-a-kind, effectively settled in its character and motivation from its first occurrence. Here the capacity for evildoing reflects an assumed constancy in human nature, appearing full-grown even in its first biblical appearance: the disobedi-ence in the Garden and its attempted cover-up seem, after all, quite effortless—if one did not know better, as if they came after long practice. However one understands the *Yetzer Ha-rah* ["evil impulse"] ascribed to man in the biblical account of Noah, furthermore, that impulse too remains unaltered in later sources as an aspect of human nature. In contrast to the varieties of its expres-sion, then, the *character* of evildoing—the evil in it—appears unchanging. If goodness and justice remain always goals to be realized, the option of evil seems always present and available.

Admittedly, except for the quasi-mythical Draconian law of a single and harsh punishment for all crimes, ethical violations and their corresponding punishments are typically distinguished by degrees of severity (again, both within and outside Judaism). The idea that "punishment ought to fit the crime" thus appears historically as a bedrock principle in systems of justice, notwith-standing other differences on *which* acts count as crimes or how to determine their relative severity.[3] The largest instances of suffering or affliction in group histories, furthermore, tend to appear as quantitatively, not qualitatively, dif-ferent from others: more or fewer victims, a longer or shorter period of perse-cution. What is typically *not* considered is the evil in the evildoing itself. (Stalin's responsibility for a larger number of murderous deaths than Hitler, for example, is often cited as if there were no differences in what led to those ends.)[4]

Divergent judgments of the same event, furthermore, often obscure ques-tions about the judging itself. A war that is catastrophic for the loser and thus (for that loser) challenges the claim of Providence, is to the victor additional evidence *for* that role. From the one side, then, evil and injustice; from the other, well and good—although both draw on the same evidence. Survivors of a massacre or catastrophe may thank God and cite that outcome as miraculous, but this reaction ignores the theological and ethical implications for the victims who did not survive. To see evildoing as part of an historical process already moves beyond the immediacy of personal agency or suffering, but even then the latter typically overshadow the structure and form of the acts involved. That people differ about which acts are unforgivable—one mark of evil at its extreme—is another indicator of the historicity of evildoing, but this implica-tion, too, often gives way to the conclusion that ultimately evildoing and its corollary, evil-suffering, are essentially all-of-a-kind. Differences in individual moral character have been generally recognized; evil itself has been viewed as constant and common.[5]

* * *

History, however, has a way of undoing the most conscientious expectations, and the Holocaust has had just that unsettling effect on moral history and theory. Evidence of this appears in the assembly of claims representing the

Holocaust as unique or as a *novum*, a breach or turning point in moral history generally and in Jewish history specifically.[6] Such characterizations start out from the systematic cruelty inflicted in the Holocaust—with that enormity also expressed in a related set of terms that call the Holocaust "indescribable," "beyond words," "ineffable."[7] Often, to be sure, such terms are figurative, hyperbolic; but even allowing for this rhetorical element, their literal core remains: the *fact* of the Holocaust, involving systematic cruelty on a scale that portends a rupture or paradigm shift in moral understanding generally and opens the issue for Jewish thought and consciousness in particular. The meta-historical implications thus noted evidently presuppose the historical ground—a dependence of moral or religious conclusions on historical premises, a dependence that although not unique to accounts of the Holocaust, requires closer than usual scrutiny because of the scale of the issues.

This requirement is not without its own difficulties, however, as even common references to the phenomenon of evil make clear. On the one hand, if evil were not apparent, there would be no moral "problem" at all to discuss. On the other hand, to speak of evil as real—e.g., without quotation marks—turns out, on inspection, to be tendentious, since a significant philosophical tradition has argued that evil is *only* apparent. On this account, any assumption that evil is more than that shows only a lack of understanding—since whatever else evil is, it is *not* real. In this way, the "problem" of evil itself proves to be a problem.

Even this deflationary conclusion, however, cannot obscure the occurrence of human suffering and loss—and it is these, after all, which on the scale of the Holocaust impel the claim of a breach or transformation in moral history, necessitating the revision and possibly the abandonment of traditional moral categories. Again, the prima facie grounds are clear for both the historical and the "meta"-historical sides of this thesis: the distinctive cruelty in the agents and the suffering in the victims impel the finding of a meta-historical breach in moral and religious history. Against that background, "Where was God in Auschwitz?" has become a formulaic question, recurring in Jewish and other religious reflections on the Holocaust (slightly altered, in secular accounts as well). With Auschwitz itself a metonymy for Nazism, furthermore, "*After* Auschwitz" also now designates a metonymic line of (chronological) demarcation—a transformative moment in moral and social and religious history.[8]

This line of reasoning underscores the need to assess the historical basis for the meta-historical conclusion that regards the Holocaust as having broken the traditional instruments of moral measurement. I can here only sketch this comparative historical critique—recognizing also that comparisons among such instances of suffering are necessarily invidious and themselves cruel. But the conception of the Holocaust as a moral turning point is (also necessarily) comparative—requiring that the event itself be scrutinized in similarly comparative terms, whether in relation to Jewish or to world history. Perhaps sur-

prisingly, the former—the Holocaust viewed in the context of Jewish history—
has been less often attempted than assessment of the Holocaust on a global
scale. Common to both views, however, has been the finding of rupture in the
post-Holocaust moral universe—a transformation in moral conscience and
consciousness. Thus, the need for testing the historical ground. For unless that
ground is substantiated, the *contrary* view would hold of continuity between
pre- and post-Holocaust consciousness in Jewish and/or world history, with the
Holocaust making no essential difference to the philosophical or theological
analysis of evil. That, too, remains a possibility, and indeed the burden of *proof*
seems to rest on the other side; that is, of demonstrating *dis*continuity—the
breach or revolution.

The turning points in Jewish history that suggest likely comparison to the
Holocaust are both few and evident: the destruction of the two Temples (586
B.C.E. and 70 C.E.); the destruction and disruption accompanying the Crusades
beginning in 1096 C.E.; the natural disaster of the Black Death (1348–1350 C.E.)
and the related massacres of Jews who were blamed for it; the expulsion of the
Jews from Spain and Portugal (1492 and 1497); the Chmielnicki "riots" (1648–
49) seem obvious, if not the only candidates. The numbers or percentages of
Jews killed in these catastrophes are not an exclusive measure of their significance, but they provide a starting place for the comparison required. So, for
example, the sweep of the First Crusade through Central Europe, which began
in 1096, caused the estimated deaths of 5000 Jews and corresponding communal disruption. But the communities evidently overcame the shock of those
events with "no substantial discontinuity in Franco-German [Jewish] society
as a whole. . . . The towns were quickly resettled, commerce and trade were
reconstructed."[9] The Jewish suicides in Mainz at this time (by those who chose
death rather than capture) made an enduring impression within and beyond the
local communities, and some contemporary accounts of the persecution understood it as a "trial of the righteous" rather than (as others did) a form of collective punishment. But both these explanations had precedents in Jewish history, and cruel as the pressures were, there seems no basis for regarding the
events themselves as a caesura or turning point in the collective moral consciousness (even taking into account the difficulty of any such assessment).[10]
Similarly, the expulsions from Spain and Portugal involved the dislocation of a
Jewish populace numbering in various estimates between 100,000 and 300,000,
with the deaths caused by the expulsion or otherwise by the Inquisition at the
time (at most) in the thousands. The communal upheaval and the crisis in the
flourishing "Golden Age" of Sephardic Jewry which ensued were evident; but
again, the survival through emigration of the largest part of that group allowed for continuity among those expelled and even enrichment for the Jewish
communities that absorbed them.

For its proportion of victims, the Black Death of 1348–50 arguably looms
larger than any other recorded natural catastrophe—having killed between a

quarter and half the populace of Europe and approximately the same proportion of Jews (250,000 of 500,000). To the latter figure must be added Jewish victims of related massacres—as Jews were variously held responsible for the Plague itself (e.g., through the libel of well poisoning). The number of victims in this related persecution was certainly in the thousands, possibly in the tens of thousands, and the period of recovery required by the Jewish communities was proportionately large. But in part because the plague affected *all* groups in its path, its impact, in terms of moral or religious upheaval, seems to have been relatively subdued; the Polish and Lithuanian Jewish communities, not very far off, were themselves relatively unaffected by the plague or the associated persecution. Estimates of the Chmielnicki Massacres of 1648–49 refer to victims in the tens of thousands, with a round figure of 100,000 sometimes cited (and up to 300 communities destroyed). The period was spoken of at the time by R. Shabbetai Sheftel Horowitz as the "Third Destruction" (after the First and Second Temples); but if the massacres seemed from within to warrant that label, it was also apparent, to some extent even at the time, that the Jewish communities in Western and other parts of Eastern Europe were relatively unaffected.

Even the admittedly vague numbers in these instances are unavailable for the conflicts that ensued in the destruction of the First and Second Temples and the periods of exile that followed them. What evidence there is suggests a minimal number of deaths—but it is also clear that in their communal and religious (and conceptual) consequences, the destruction of the Temples was at least equal to and probably greater than any of the later events mentioned. The religious prophecies prior to the first destruction and the ensuing exile that apparently validated them, effecting a revolution in religious thought and practice—the confluence threatening a breach in God's covenant with Israel—loom larger in their impact than any of the later events. This would include the Holocaust itself which in a number of ways allowed for regeneration and communal continuity (more about this below).

Such qualifications in relation to the breach caused by the Holocaust in *Jewish* history leave untouched, however, the analogous claim in world-historical terms. Here the argument has a sharper edge, as the Holocaust represents a paradigm (whether or not the first) instance of genocide: the intentional, state-sponsored, and systematic attempt to make "that" people "disappear" (Heinrich Himmler's wording in a 1943 speech to the SS at Poznan). To be sure, "uniqueness" claims for the Holocaust build to some extent on subordinate rather than on essential features of the Holocaust. That the Nazi Genocide against the Jews was initiated by a nation closely tied to both the Christian tradition and the Enlightenment; that it was carried on in full view of other countries with the same traditions; that it implemented a process of industrialized killing "invented" for the occasion; that aside from its principal purpose of annihilation, it constantly applied what Primo Levi chillingly calls "Useless

Violence"—these remarkable features do not alter the basic structure of the genocidal act itself.[11]

The same claim applies to the extreme consequences of the Holocaust *within* the Jewish community. The murder of two-thirds of the European Jews effectively ended the role of Eastern Europe as a primary source of Jewish communal existence; it was also a death sentence for Yiddish as a language and cultural means. Most basically, of course, it cut off the lives and futures of six million people. That the Nazis did not succeed in fully implementing their "Final Solution" is, furthermore, also "accidental"; they advanced sufficiently far on that goal, in any event, to mark their action as genocide (a conceptual feature of genocide—in contrast to homicide—is that it need not be "complete"). And it remains the phenomenon of genocide itself that ultimately distinguishes what the Nazis intended and did—and which also may render it more significant in moral history as such than specifically in Jewish history. It does not diminish the enormity of the Holocaust to acknowledge that it left certain centers of Jewish life physically untouched (in North and South America, to some extent in Great Britain, in Palestine, in the Islamic countries of Asia, and in North Africa); and that it thus subsequently allowed both for communal continuity there and for the valuable—arguably, decisive—contributions of those communities to Israel's founding. Certain commentators who emphasize the continuity of Jewish history as a whole, view that continuity as also a primary "lesson" of the Holocaust: another threat to Jewish existence as added to earlier ones that were *also* thwarted. Only on this basis could so measured a post-Holocaust writer as Eliezer Berkowitz conclude that "We [Jews] have had innumerable Auschwitzes. . . . Each generation had its Auschwitz problem."[12] Continuity indeed.

* * *

On the one hand, then, post-Holocaust Jewish ethical reflection faces the large-scale and systematic destruction caused by the Holocaust; on the other hand, the evidence remains of comparable or larger breaches in the moral and religious fabric of Jewish history and consciousness. In this sense, the claim for the Holocaust as indicating or demanding a moral transformation applies more clearly to world history; that the Jews were the principal victims of the Holocaust only intensifies the irony here. But this does not mean that post-Holocaust Jewish thinkers have not *claimed* that the Holocaust demands a transformative moral and religious response in Judaism itself. But although many such claims have been made, and with emphasis, they turn out on examination to represent a minority view, and one which arguably overstates its conclusions even in its own terms. Even if one grants this, of course, it would not follow that formulations which place the Holocaust on a continuum with prior events of Jewish history are by *that* fact adequate, but even the possibility that the enormity of the Holocaust might leave the status of evil in Jewish thought unaltered is significant.[13] Admittedly, the question would then arise of how far the meta-historical claim of continuity extends. But also a limited claim of continuity would bear directly on post-Holocaust Jewish thought—among other things, also providing a baseline for assessing accounts that emphasize *dis*continuity.

Thus: the conceptualization of the Holocaust "within the bounds of Jewish history" appears in various formulations, with several versions of the most common formulation revolving around a single thesis: that since whatever occurs in history reflects divine intention (at least, concurrence), all such events are also justified or good—*and* that this holds whether the rationale for such events is humanly intelligible or not. This "theodicy" (in Leibniz's coinage of 1710)[14]—"God-justice"—has itself appeared in philosophical and theological variants, but also with a constant basis: that God, himself outside history, nonetheless governs it through his qualities of goodness and omnipotence. *Apparent* evil is, in these terms, only that; in fact, whatever occurs is not evil, but justified, good—perhaps in direct response to previous events, but always, in any event, as part of a larger framework. Anything not so justified would, quite simply, not have occurred.

The most urgent application of this principle is to actions or events that ensue in suffering or loss and thus invite interpretation as punishment. Traditional claims in Judaism for such divine supervision have been widespread and substantial. So, for example, Maimonides writes in the *Guide* about "our" [the central Jewish] view: "It is in no way possible that He [God] should be unjust. . . . All the calamities that befall men and all the good things that come to men, be it a single individual or a group, are all of them determined according to the deserts of the men concerned through equitable judgment which is no injustice whatsoever."[15] An earlier, more specific formulation (cited by Maimonides in the same context) is R. Ammi's: "There is no death without sin and no suffering without transgression."[16] A prayer recited in the Jewish prayer for each "new month" and in the Holiday service points to the same principle in collective form: "*Mip'ne Chata'enu, Ga-linu Me'art̠enu*" ("Because of our sins, we have been exiled from our land").[17]

The implications of this "punishment–reward" model are evident. Also for the Holocaust, it implies that victims suffer only and always for reason—because of their own wrongdoing or because of someone else's for which they were responsible or because, on balance, the whole of which a particular event was part warranted its occurrence. As directed at the Holocaust, furthermore, this conclusion applies equally to the children and the aged among the victims, to the pious and the unbelievers, the criminal and the righteous—as for every other exemplar of religious or moral practice in the afflicted Jewish communities of Europe: all of them, now, justly punished.

The evident harshness of this judgment as applied to the Holocaust has provoked numerous objections, some of which extend the argument beyond that event; thus, for example, Berkowitz's sharp dissent: "That all suffering is due to [sin] is simply not true. The idea that the Jewish martyrology through the ages can be explained as divine judgment is obscene."[18] Yet, "obscene" as the interpretation may appear, it has recurred—and if its formulations seem marginal or problematic philosophically, their cultural and religious influence is undeniable. So, for example, Rabbi Yoel Teitlebaum, the then Satmar Rebi, finds Zionism the wrong that precipitated and so warranted the Holocaust: due punishment for its effort to pre-empt the Messiah's role in initiating the return to Zion. An analogous rendering is Rabbi Elhanan Wasserman's rhetorical tour de force: "In those [pre-Holocaust] days, the Jews chose for themselves two forms of idolatry . . . socialism and nationalism. . . . A miraculous event occurred: in Heaven the two idolatries were combined into one—National Socialism. A terrible staff of ire was created which extends harm to all the ends of the earth."[19] A more recent expression of the punishment-and-reward view was Rabbi Ovadiah Yosef's, in 2001, which finds in the Jewish victims of the Holocaust "reincarnations of earlier souls, who sinned and caused others to sin."[20] (The logic here is swift: the appeal to reincarnation anticipates the objection that apparent innocents—children and pious elders—were among the Holocaust's victims; there could be due cause from their prior existence also for *their* suffering.)[21]

Again, the severity of this position is clear: the cruelty and suffering inflicted in the Holocaust seem disproportionate to any possible wrongdoing by its victims. A further problematic implication is this view's representation of the perpetrators of such suffering (indeed, Hitler himself) as instruments of divine justice, doing, in effect, God's work. That consequence is unavoidable, however: if the punishment is just, whoever administers it must also, ultimately, be acting justly.[22] Yet, despite these implications, the view's persistence is in its own terms not arbitrary or groundless—as becomes evident in more nuanced explanations that hope to avoid the notion of suffering as divine justice by shifting responsibility for it from God to man, but that are in the end forced to revert to the same source: God's sanction for the events of world history.

The principal argument in this second variant of the punishment–reward model emphasizes man's free moral agency. Acting on his own, man rather than God becomes responsible for whatever evil occurs in human history, even on the scale of the Holocaust. It is not that the victims always bring their fate on themselves, but that *some* human agents act in such a way as to produce the harm to them. Again, the logic here is straightforward: Man has the freedom to do good or evil—a (arguably, *the*) distinctive human attribute. Given God's benevolence and omnipotence, evil when it does occur—inflicting suffering and loss on the innocent—expresses human and not divine character and choice. God *could* not have a role here if man's freedom is to be preserved—and the result of human agency and decision is what one would expect: human responsibility. So Berkowitz writes, "[Human] freedom must be respected by

God himself. God cannot as a rule intervene whenever man's use of freedom displeases him. It is true, if he did so, the perpetration of evil would be rendered impossible, but so would the possibility for good."[23]

The reason behind this effort to shift responsibility from God to man is evident. But the move also invites the charge of question-begging on the issue of whether man's freedom is worth the price of a world that includes the Holocaust—and of how to settle *that* question. The response of theodicy here would be certain: "Yes, of course: human freedom, whatever its consequences." And more generally: "Better the world as it is, *including* the Holocaust, than otherwise, or any other world." This version of the "Continuum" argument avoids finding fault in the specific victims, but the omission counts for little in distinguishing this from the earlier version because of its insistence in turn that *on the whole* whatever happens is justified. The question of who specifically provoked a certain punishment thus becomes irrelevant—in deference to the interest of justice "on the whole." All this, again, on the principle that whatever happens in history is warranted.

A third variant of the punishment–reward account of evil situates the Holocaust on a continuum of Jewish history within the framework of that history's redemptive features—most often citing the 1948 establishment of Israel as a central item of evidence. This assertion of the good that may come out of evil is sometimes set within a religious framework, but it also occurs in versions of secular redemption (for the establishment of Israel, on the principles of nationalism and self-determination). Both these lines of interpretation, however, find the Holocaust an important, arguably necessary, stage on the way to Israel's statehood, itself viewed as a consummatory moment in Jewish history. Thus the Holocaust is redeemed, whether partly or in full, by the creation of Israel which *would not* have occurred (this, as either a tacit or explicit assumption) had there been no Holocaust. The latter claim is itself a straightforward historical assertion, albeit with the problems of any counterfactual conditional. In strictly historical terms, the claim has often been disputed. But such objections do not, of course, address the "meta"-historical elements in the redemptive theory of Jewish history that finds hardship and suffering ultimately, and necessarily, transfigured. The significance claimed for the connection between the Holocaust and the establishment of the State of Israel is an especially dramatic application of this theory.

The fourth and last variation on the punishment–reward model invokes the concept of *"Hester Panim"*—[God's] "hiding of the face"—as a means of preserving God's justice and power and yet leaving room for (localized) injustice. The metaphor of "hiding" describes a divine withdrawal from history that allows events to occur which God would otherwise have prevented—the withdrawal occurring not because God wills the events but because he wills man's freedom more. So Norman Lamm writes: [In a period of *"Hester Panim"*] . . . we are given over to the uncertainties of nature and history where we can be raised . . . to the crest of the world's waves—or herded pitilessly into the fierce troughs of life."[24] And Berkowitz, with further emphasis on the role of human freedom, adds: "If man alone is the creator of value . . . then he must have freedom of choice and freedom of decision. . . . That man may be, God must absent himself. . . . He hides his presence."[25] This view has the (temporary) advantage of dividing history into divine and human parts: the former where God is active, the latter which moves by human decision. To be sure, God *could* control the human part if he chose to—but he chooses not to, in order to ensure man's freedom. "*Hester Panim*" thus intensifies the shift of evildoing (and evil-suffering) to man as initiator; also here (as in the second version above of the punishment–reward argument), the privileging of human freedom above other, possibly conflicting values is unquestioned. But once again, since also "*Hester Panim*" must acknowledge that God *chooses* to hide when he does (he could not, after all, be forced to do that), this "choice," too, emerges as a version of theodicy: whatever happens—including God's withdrawal—reflects a decision to do so, an *intention*. Thus, too, the claim, even for the prospect of the Holocaust, that what occurs must be "for the best."[26]

The "punishment–reward" interpretation of the Holocaust in these four versions is one of three formulations of the "Continuum" view that finds the Holocaust unexceptional in terms of traditional Jewish thought and texts—*and* justifications. The second formulation, also with a lengthy past, interprets apparently unwarranted suffering not as punishment, but as something quite different; thus it is a "Reductive" account. One version of this theory conceives of suffering as a test, with its "proof-text" in the biblical *Akedah*—the "binding" of Isaac—where God commands Abraham to sacrifice his son *as* a test. Other "tests" also appear in the Bible (for example, in Job), and indeed, conceptually, treating suffering or harm as a test has a dialectical advantage, since even a just ruler might reasonably test a blameless subject—in contrast to punishing him. But this conceptual looseness comes at a price, since unless there are limits to what counts as a test, what judgment is to be made about victims of the Holocaust who died in the "test" (in contrast to the survivors) would remain unclear.

A second variant of this "Reductive" interpretation views suffering as having positive value in itself. At times echoing Rabbi Akiba's statement that "suffering is precious,"[27] suffering on this account is accorded a justified place in the world—as it anticipates future reward, or as the price to be paid in the present for the goodness of the whole, or as proof of faith in the present, or (most basically) for the experience of suffering itself. Versions of this view range from a flat denial of suffering as a phenomenon (so, Reb Zusya of Anipol: "I don't understand why you ask me this question [about *my* suffering]. Ask it of someone who has known such evil. As for me, this does not apply, for nothing ill has ever happened to me")[28] to the near-utilitarian justification that Joseph Soloveitchik offers even in reference to the Holocaust: "Suffering occurs in the world in order to contribute something to man, in order that atonement be made for him, in order to redeem him from corruption, vulgarity, and depravity."[29]

The third formulation of the Continuum position, overarching the others, accounts for evil by *refusing* to account for it; that is, by falling back on the limits of human comprehension: for certain "difficult" events, human understanding finds *no* adequate ground—not because there is none, but because of its own incapacity. Such limits, if invoked for an event like the Holocaust, would, of course, apply more generally as well, and the arguments to this effect have a lengthy tradition both within and outside Judaism. Thus we hear that God's ways are not man's ways, that the difference between finite and infinite understanding makes access impossible from the one to the other—in short, that there *is* no way of comprehending the rationale for human history, whatever its turns, since that would require, per impossible, a human grasp of God's reasons.[30]

Superficially, this account might seem to replace theodicy with agnosticism—the view, for example, that "A certain event *appears* to have produced terrible injustice—but this is because our limited understanding cannot fathom the reasons." The implied directive here, however, is not agnostic at all—since its claim of incomprehensibility invariably surfaces as a means of justifying catastrophes, *not* of raising doubts about them: "There *are* reasons—if only we could grasp them." Admittedly, as Hugh Rice points out, consistency would require the tag of incomprehensibility applied here *also* for occasions of rejoicing—indeed, for all of God's actions, whatever their consequences.[31] But this common inconsistency should not be allowed to obscure its source. The unstated assumption of the Argument from Incomprehensibility is that there are reasons, and *good* ones, even for suffering and loss which seem senseless and unjustifiable to man's limited understanding. Far from putting God's supervision of history in question, this argument advocates its acceptance as just—attesting to human limits, not God's. Thus again, theodicy survives.

* * *

Despite their recognition of cruelty and suffering in the Holocaust, none of the accounts of evil noted so far finds in that a basis for reconceptualizing moral principle or religious commitment within the context of Judaism. Whatever the Continuum view judges to be demanded of moral conscience "after Auschwitz," the traditional principles and texts of Jewish thought remain adequate, in both explanation and justification. That the principal sources for this view come from religious "Orthodoxy" may not be surprising, but neither should it discount the response. Indeed, the Continuum position appears also in secular writers and in others who, although religiously committed, address the Holocaust in the context of ethical judgment as such. So, for example, Emmanuel Levinas acknowledges the Holocaust as a "paradigm" of suffering, but also finds it parallel to "the Gulag and all other places of suffering in our political century"—in other words, part of a broader, and in that sense, non-specific, historical tendency.[32] It is significant, furthermore, that most of the influential Jewish thinkers who have written after the Holocaust, wherever they place themselves in respect to the Jewish tradition and even when they allude (as all do) to the Holocaust, do not find that event as pivotal in their own rendering of Jewish history or thought. (I instance here such a range of figures as Martin Buber, A. J. Heschel, Mordechai Kaplan, Yeshayahu Leibowitz, Emmanuel Levinas, Nathan Rotenstreich, and Gershom Scholem.) Certain commentators, apart from any judgment on the character of evil in the Holocaust, call attention to the psychological or social grounds that, within the context of Jewish thought, influence responses to that aspect of the Holocaust. Thus, David Hartman writes, "For some, suffering is bearable if it results from the limitations of finite human beings, but it becomes terrifying and demonic if it is seen as part of the scheme of their all-powerful creator. Others would find life unbearably chaotic if they did *not* believe that suffering, tragedy, and death were part of God's plan for the world."[33] Undoubtedly, these ad hominem considerations affect responses to the Holocaust, and it would be valuable to have them systematically analyzed—but even if the difficulty of effectively carrying out such analysis were overcome, we would still have to consider the reasoning in the responses as reasoning. This would, in my view, bring us back to assessing the views of evil as they have been outlined here.

The Continuum position reflects a conception of evil in respect to which distinctions among its instances (in their explanation or justification) are finally irrelevant. And indeed, it seems to follow logically that the slightest occurrence of evil is as much a test of theodicy as any larger one, since for a just and all-powerful God, *no* evil or injustice could have a place. The Continuum position, drawing mainly on variations of theodicy, readily accommodates this implication—as in Berkowitz's summing-up: "As far as our faith in an absolutely just and merciful God is concerned, the suffering of a single innocent child poses no less a problem to faith than the undeserved suffering of millions."[34] That conclusion by itself is non-committal on whether evil *does* occur—but this point is then addressed in the several versions of the Continuum argument (and by Berkowitz) that displace or simply deny all such occurrence.

The claim of a rupture or caesura caused by the Holocaust in Jewish history must then argue against the Continuum position on grounds not of logic, but substance—asserting in both historical and moral terms that events are *not* all of a kind; that their differences may be qualitative as well as quantitative; and, in more specific reference, that the scope and scale of murder in the Holocaust marks a quantum jump from "ordinary" wrongdoing. On this account, the Holocaust is sufficiently distinctive to require new categories of moral understanding—in the context of Jewish history and arguably, for world history as well. On this view, too, variant accounts emerge concerning the nature and consequences of the breach alleged in moral consciousness. Thus, the dramatic thesis that even the extremity of the Holocaust makes no essential difference to moral understanding in the context of Jewish thought shifts to the drama of its opposite—which then faces the problem of showing how the Holocaust makes just such an essential difference, but without severing post-Holocaust Jewish thought from characteristic elements of its religious and philosophical past, however difficult or contentious the process of identifying them is.

The most extreme example of this response was as clear in anticipation as it has proved difficult to sustain. If the traditional view of evil in Jewish thought is obliged to confront God's role as omnipotent and benevolent, the most obvious break with the tradition would be to argue *against* that role—and this indeed is the direction taken by Richard Rubenstein, first in *After Auschwitz* and then in his later writings.[35] *After Auschwitz* itself appeared in a setting not specifically related to the Holocaust—through the "death of God" theme which, echoing Nietzsche's Zarathustra, was at the time circulating among non-Jewish theologians like Thomas Altizer, Harvey Cox, and William Hamilton.[36] Indeed, Rubenstein's own earlier "Reconstructionist" leanings laid the ground for this move in its Deweyan (by way of Mordechai Kaplan) denial of God's transcendence. But Rubenstein, arguing "*after Auschwitz*," believed there was now a still stronger case against Judaism's traditional conception of God—one that extended to what he regarded as the cultural and social liabilities to which that traditional belief contributed.

This meant also that there was (and in the event, would remain) a question about what Rubenstein could *affirm* in Jewish principle or thought, and his subsequent writings seem at once to have sought and to have avoided such affirmation. Their dominant theme has combined a view of truth and knowledge as functions of power (after Nietzsche and, latterly, Foucault) with a social or cultural definition of Judaism centered on the entry into history and power of the State of Israel. This emphasis on political rather than moral or religious factors offers a prescription for Jewish survival given the narrowed and shaken world articulated in the aftermath of the Holocaust; it says little about any specifically Jewish religious or social link to the past as an essential element. The lesson of the Holocaust disclosed for Rubenstein through the lens of powerlessness affords little positive basis for Jewish—indeed, for any religious or even ethnic—particularism, and little more for the institution of religion as such. The metaphor of *triage* to which Rubenstein later turns as a basis for political theory seems at once to epitomize the break he sees in Jewish history as caused by the Holocaust and the difficulty of finding a source of continuity for that tradition—other than force itself—that would enable it to overcome the breach.[37]

A less radical reaction against the traditional view of transcendence appears in Hans Jonas, who finds in a limitation rather than the denial of God's power as a means of accounting for the breach caused by the Holocaust. For Jonas, the Holocaust serves not as disproof of God's existence or of his justice but as evidence of certain constraints on him. It is not, on this view, that God could have acted in that history and chose not to—but that he could not act, however much he wished to. Jonas thus argues for a conception of God as limited by God's own earlier choices—if not to the same extent as man in *his* history, analogously. Admittedly, the logical limitations of omnipotence (as in the challenge of whether God could create a rock so heavy that he could not pick it up) had been long discussed, but for Jonas, the issue is directed at a particular context. It is not the priority of human freedom that motivates the shift of moral responsibility for the Holocaust away from God (although Jonas affirms such freedom), but that, given his own earlier decisions, God *could* not have intervened to deter or even to mitigate it.[38] On the terms of this account, evil becomes ingredient in existence, with the responsibility for its occurrence neither God's nor man's (exclusively), but shared between them and including constraints of history beyond the capacity of either of them to overcome. This view does not exonerate God any more than it does man—nor does it depict evil as an impersonal and independent force. Evil appears rather as friction that might in some circumstances be mitigated or redirected—but never entirely avoided, since its occurrence does not depend only on acts of will, human or divine; history itself accounts for its occurrence, with God himself inside as well as outside it.

Neither Rubenstein's nor Jonas's response to the Holocaust is rooted specifically in that event. Like other "death of God" pronouncements, Rubenstein's would apply retroactively, implying not that Judaism's transcendent God had suddenly died but that he had never actually lived. And for Jonas as well: the limits on God's power did not *originate* with the Holocaust. For both writers, however, it was the breach they find in the Holocaust that provoked the turn in their thinking about the status of evil.

A second version of the Holocaust viewed as transformative in Jewish thought and practice uses law or Halakhah as a bridge to the past that now, post-Holocaust, is elaborated or changed *because* of the Holocaust. The reason for considering this view as an example of "discontinuity" is its reference to the law which, immutable for subtraction *or* addition in Orthodox terms, retains that privileged position even when the Holocaust *compels* an addition to it. The most notable advocate of this position is Emil Fackenheim who proposed a 614th commandment—"not to give Hitler posthumous victories"—as a literal commandment, not a figurative expression.[39] The ground for Fackenheim's proposal was twofold: first, the extraordinary—for him, unique—evil that found expression in the Holocaust; and second, his understanding of Halakhah as having involved an historical or contextual dimension throughout its past. In other words, all the mitzvoth, in Fackenheim's view, have emerged in response to historical conditions that then also contributed to the shape they took; given this general feature, surely the extraordinary character of the Holocaust *ought* to be reflected in the law. To be sure, this principle would not itself determine what the 614th commandment must be; for that, Fackenheim draws on the distinctive goal of the Nazi Genocide to destroy the Jewish people. The fitting response to that, as he judges it, should then be a corresponding affirmation of Jewish existence: a commitment by its members to its (and their own) continuity. Sometimes charged by his critics with basing his apparently positive commitment on negative grounds—as reactive or ressentiment, part of a critical tradition that regards antisemitism as at once cause and reason for Jewish survival[40]—Fackenheim's basis is broader than that, encompassing other commandments and sources and indeed (as suggested) a general theory of Jewish law.

The starting point for Fackenheim's reflections on the Holocaust, again, is the "rupture in history" he finds in that event as an unparalleled example of evil committed for the sake of doing evil—unparalleled, as he sees it, either in Jewish or in world history.[41] As argued earlier in this chapter, the historical claim that thus serves as the basis for any such meta-historical claim would have to rely on its own historical evidence—as compared to other events in Jewish and world history. Fackenheim's contention that the evil in Nazism is unparalleled straddles the line between the historical and meta-historical—and is no easier either to demonstrate or to disprove because of that. Most notable about Fackenheim's account is the correspondence he affirms between the distinctive historical "moment" of the Holocaust and the addition he infers from that for Jewish law as serving at once as a breach and a bridge. The general question of who has the authority, and on what grounds, to add "laws" to precedent and generally acknowledged law, remains a question in Fackenheim's account.[42] His suggestion that the absolute evil which he finds evident in the Holocaust can only be shown, not explained, adds to the difficulty of assessing the premise itself.

A third position in the view of the Holocaust as a rupture or caesura—both historical *and* meta-historical—resembles the last position mentioned in connection with the Continuum model, in its reference to the Holocaust's "incomprehensibility." By contrast to the Continuum model version, however, this one offers no assurance of a positive outcome even in its conclusion. A compelling statement of this view appears in the work of Arthur A. Cohen, who, transposing Rudolf Otto's conception of the "tremendum" onto the Holocaust, finds the latter "beyond the discourse of morality and rational condemnation."[43] This stance might seem to bring Cohen back (full circle) to Rubenstein's skepticism about the possibility of a religious covenant—to say nothing about the unlikelihood of a living God. But Cohen rejects that rejection, although he acknowledges at least certain of its features. Thus, evil, as Cohen finds it in the Holocaust, *is* real—"no less than good." Yet God is also present and active—almost in partnership with man: " . . . God describes the limits but man sets them . . . God engenders possibilities but . . . man enacts them" (p. 93). One problem, of course, for any claim of incomprehensibility is that it must itself be articulated and explained—and Cohen, as he unpacks the concept, seems at times to make the Holocaust less incomprehensible than he otherwise would have it (for example, in the comparison he makes and defends between the impact of the Holocaust and that of the Jewish expulsion from Spain; or when he suggests that what the Jews find unique in the Holocaust is a feature of every group's response to *its* genocide). There is, then, a question of consistency here, together with a question of what the substance of Cohen's concluding affirmation is. The stark terms of the opposition with which Cohen both begins and concludes dramatize the issue posed by the Holocaust radically: on the one hand, the *tremendum*—in effect, atrocity that is outside history; on the other hand, the affirmation nonetheless not only of the Jewish people but of the God who did not prevent it and yet who, in Cohen's view, remains as a "source of hope."

* * *

The schematism of moral analysis presented here has been divided between responses linked to Jewish thought in which issues raised by the occurrence of the Holocaust are seen as continuous with issues raised by prior occurrences or instances of evil—and responses that have regarded the Holocaust as a genuine "novum": first, historically, and then, because of that, in its moral consequences. Undoubtedly the single most widely discussed analysis of evil in relation to the Holocaust remains that by Hannah Arendt in *Eichmann in Jerusalem: A Report on the Banality of Evil.*[44] There, Arendt also views the Holocaust as in some sense a novum—yet, in the conclusions she draws about the nature of its evil (through Eichmann himself), she also endorses a "Continuum" view that links up with elements of theodicy from which the present discussion set out. Arendt is rarely counted a "Jewish" philosopher (she rejected the designation of philosopher tout court), but the relevance of her work to both those characterizations can certainly be argued.[45] In any event, her book on Eichmann analyzes the trial in Jerusalem of an important agent of the Holocaust—and her conclusions on Eichmann's "evil" would thus be significant for reflections on the Holocaust even if it did not (as I would claim it does) bring out in sharp relief a basic crux in the understanding of evil that impinges both on Jewish thought and on moral conceptualization more generally. On the one hand, Arendt's view of Eichmann echoes in a shadowy way the aspect of the Continuum view that, in agreement with theodicy, disputes the depth and even the reality of evil. On the other hand, Arendt has no doubt, despite her procedural misgivings about the Eichmann trial itself, that Eichmann was criminally responsible and that he should have been, as he was, executed. If the tension between these claims is puzzling, that says as much about the issues at stake there as it does about her specific account of them.

The meaning of the phrase "*banality of evil*" has been often misrepresented, partly because it is sometimes confused with other issues in her account, and partly because of Arendt's own unsystematic development of her own concept. What is clear in her usage and her subsequent reflections on it, however, is that the phrase opens a question that goes to the heart of the analysis of evil. The first step in this progression is Arendt's rejection of the view of Eichmann as demonic or as an agent of "radical" evil. Compared to such stereotypic evil-doers as Iago or Richard III, she insists, Eichmann does not come close; he is, by contrast, "thoughtless," "a clown,"—dependent on clichés in his speaking and, still more fundamentally, in his thinking. This is, in fact, the source of his evildoing even in the monstrousness of the "Final Solution"; the agent himself was and remained "banal"—his actions not so much unintentional as "non-intentional"; he did not, in Arendt's depiction, *think* about what he was doing and its consequences.

This view of Eichmann was quickly contested by critics who did not accept the disproportion that she claims between source and effect in an event of such large dimensions. In the course of what thus turned into a heated aftermath, Arendt came to realize that a general theory of evildoing was at issue in the contrast she had at first only assumed between "radical" evil (as in Kant's rendering and in the conventional view of Nazism) and evil as banal. Perhaps in part as she noticed that her own examples of radical evil were drawn from literary, not historical sources, Arendt began to question whether historical (human) evil was *ever* "radical" in the sense of being intended or committed "thoughtfully"—that is, with true reflection or full knowledge of its character. The outcome of this deliberation was anti-climactic, and perhaps because of this was not much attended to in the critical response to it. But that outcome is also clear, and reveals itself as standing in a lengthy philosophical tradition—one initiated by Plato (then also in Platonism) and reappearing in modern rationalism (as in Spinoza and Leibniz). On this view, evil, whatever its scale, is not positive but a privation; those who commit it act not out of deliberation and choice—thoughtfully, knowledgeably—but precisely because they have *not* adequately considered or understood what they were doing. Certainly Eichmann, in Arendt's terms, did not know better; indeed, he hardly thought at all about what he was doing—with the crucial implication following from this description, that if he *had* been more thoughtful, had understood more or more adequately, he would not, and arguably could not, have done what he did.

The latter conclusion—itself "radical"—has precedent in the Platonic doctrine that "To know the good is to do the good" (in its contrapositive "Not to do the good means not to know the good"). Evildoing in this view reflects a failure of understanding—or, in Arendt's term, "banality." And this, it seems, would for her characterize not only the trivial wrongs commonly cited as "thoughtless" but extreme wrongs as well; it marks off what evil *is*. Thus, in a letter to Gershom Scholem (shortly before he stopped all communication with her *because* of the Eichmann book), Arendt wrote:

> It is indeed my opinion now that evil is never radical, that it is only extreme, and that it possesses neither depth nor any demonic dimension. It can overgrow and lay waste the whole world precisely because it spreads like a fungus. . . . It is "thought-defying" . . . because thought tries to reach some depth, to go to the roots, and the moment it concerns itself with evil, it is frustrated because there is nothing. That is its banality. Only the Good has depth and can be radical.[46]

Arendt adds certain nuances to this position in her subsequent writings, but the view thus indicated in the discussion around Eichmann remains essentially unchanged—as do its grave implications for the account of evil in or after the Holocaust. For if the charge against Eichmann—and, as it might be extrapolated, Nazism more generally: a large step, but implicit in Arendt's rendering—is one of "thoughtlessness," that such terrible wrongdoing has been committed mindlessly and without deliberation (and committed *because* of that), then the character of Holocaust-evil, together with related questions of moral responsibility for it, become quite different from what they would be as the outcome of meditated or deliberate intention and act. At issue here is not Nazi "pseudoscience" (as in their biological rationale for racism); it is a question of a failure to "think" in the face of atrocity. Arendt's analysis in these terms had begun more than twenty years earlier in her conception of totalitarianism as rendering the individual person "superfluous," as depriving him of all agency.[47] Compelling as that account is in political terms, however—arguably more dramatic even than Socrates's individual encounter with Protagoras in Plato's dialogue by that name—neither in that early work nor in her analysis of Eichmann does she provide an explanation of what happens to moral agency or responsibility under what now turns out to be the universal condition of evil as more or less but *always* "banal." Eichmann, she concludes, *should* have been hanged as he was, and the implication of this is that banality does not preclude that verdict; but the basis of the verdict, or before that, of the finding of guilt, is not itself explained in relation to the concept of banality.

The first phase of the circle traced in the present discussion of evil in the post-Holocaust—a beginning that also denied the possibility of radical or "real" evil—offered by contrast a solution to what, at the closing of the circle in Arendt, seems to become, and to remain, a problem. In those first discussions, human agency and responsibility were asserted as constant even in a divinely ordered world—and irrespective of the social conditions under which any particular individual person or agent lives. The *Yetzer ha-rah* introduced in Genesis had the function of asserting the lure of evil (not necessarily its triumph, but its presence) even in the presence of understanding and thinking

Evil, Suffering, and the Holocaust

that would *always* be options. The problem for this juxtaposition, we saw, concerned the imposed resolution of theodicy—that whatever happened in history, up to and including the Holocaust, was ultimately for the best, with God and man in some sense collaborative agents. Arendt would certainly reject this verdict on history—on world history, on Jewish history, *and* on Eichmann's history. But the terms that she herself sets for the problem of Holocaust evil by insisting at once on its banality and its extraordinary criminality afford her no ready way of reconciling the two sides of that tension. She was, of course, not alone in facing this difficulty, and no doubt Jewish thought in the Post-Holocaust will continue to wrestle with it.

FOUR

Comparative Evil

Measuring Numbers, Degrees, People

It is a truth universally acknowledged that some wrongful acts are more wrongful than others. Why is this? That is, why the universal acknowledgment, *and* (before that) why the "truth" itself? These are the first questions addressed here, since comparisons among specific instances of wrongdoing presuppose answers to these more general matters. How, after all, could we distinguish even wrongful from rightful acts without assurance from moral history (not the history of ethical *theory*, but the history of ethical *practice*) of a means and not only the fact of moral discrimination? Ideally, such assurance would establish not only the possibility but also the necessity of moral judgment through gradations of value (or, inverting the order, gradations of disvalue)—and we do indeed find this in the history of evaluation itself.

What are the specific steps in the gradation of wrongful acts, and how are those distinctions made? This second, in many ways more dramatic, set of issues bears on individual comparisons through the measurement of "evil"— for example, by counting the numbers of victims or by distinguishing manners or intensity or degrees of particular intention. The practical difficulties of making such specific comparisons are greater than those raised by the prior question of the status of those comparisons in principle—but this is due, I would argue, more to our excessive demands on the process of measurement than to the process itself. Aristotle's stipulation that we are entitled to require in a science or method only the precision of which it is capable can, of course, be used in a self-serving (or self-deceiving) way—but in this instance it seems a cogent response to the common objection that because moral comparisons seem in the end always imprecise (to some extent, indeterminate), even to attempt them is obscurantist or mystifying. But quite the contrary: comparison is at the very heart of moral judgment and assessment—no right without a wrong, no justice without injustice, no prohibition without (prior) violation.

The intrinsic vagueness of specific comparisons pales beside recognition of their *necessity*. (To be sure, all such comparisons are invidious—even when they conclude without finding for one side over another.)

Thus, to begin: some words about the claim of universal acknowledgment of the *principle* of discrimination among degrees or kinds of wrongdoing. This principle, put more concretely, holds that wrongs come in—certainly are known by—*degrees* of "wrong-ness" (that is, of what makes them wrong); and that the moral differences thus found are formally so clear and significant that the principle is generally (even, I would suggest, universally) recognized.

This claim of universal acknowledgment may seem exaggerated, but if it is overstated, it is not by much. The one historical counterexample that comes to mind is quasi-mythological and remains at best a solitary exception. This deviant case is the Code of Dracon, dated to 621 B.C.E., of which few details survive but which has nonetheless become emblematic of a rare (and rarified) ideal of justice. "Draconian" laws are now usually cited for their harshness, but a more notable feature structurally is their denial of any significant difference between lesser and greater transgressions. One punishment for all crimes was Dracon's rule—with the implication that wrongful acts provide no grounds, in themselves or their consequences, for distinguishing gradations or degrees of "criminality." The uniform punishment imposed, moreover, was harsh; namely, death. Hence the association of Draconian laws with severity—although, strictly speaking, this reference is less tied to the punishment imposed than to its extended range. By contrast, legal systems that sanction capital punishment more typically reserve it for only certain (that is, "capital") crimes, thus distinguishing these major offenses from lesser ones—itself a "fine" distinction rejected on the Draconian view. "Small offenses," Dracon is said to have observed, "deserve death, and I can think of no more severe penalty for larger ones."[1]

The theoretical grounds on which Dracon drew are unknown, but there might well have been a principle—a theory of justice—underlying his harsh table of laws. For if we think of justice (at the level of laws) or the good (in terms of moral obligations) as circumscribed domains, then every violation of them might be viewed as equivalent to every other one just insofar as it *is* a breach. To be sure, the grounds that determine prohibitions or norms are variously construed—as expressions of natural law, or of the rule of state or conscience, as the word of God or as social convention. But so long only as the norm invoked has *some* such authority, its violations would have the common character of transgressing what within the given community of discourse commands obedience. Since all violations are then equal as violations, there could arguably also be no basis for variations in punishment. (Determining what the specific uniform punishment should be is separate, of course, from the question of whether the punishment should be uniform.)

But again, there have been few, if any subsequent advocates of this view, whether among political theorists or rulers in fact. It might be argued that for consistency's sake, Kant should have been a Draconian, and certainly there is a kindred echo in Kant of Dracon's unflinching view of the inviolability of all moral law. But Kant did not in fact take that position, arguing instead for a proportionality or "fit" between crime and punishment rather than the one-size (of punishment)-fits-all model (of crime)[2]—and there are, it seems, no more likely successors to Dracon than he was. The distinctiveness of the Draconian Code, furthermore, emerges not only from the practices of individual rulers or thinkers: there seem to be no states or societies that have refused or failed to identify certain transgressions as more wrongful than others. The hierarchical ordering of moral and/or legal violations thus persists as a genuine, if rarely noted, instance of a "cultural universal," accepted and practiced without exception among otherwise very different cultures and traditions. Such universal acceptance of that principle does not mean, of course, that the *specific* hierarchy of values or prohibitions asserted in a given society applies generally; quite the contrary, of course. (So, for example, the death penalty is mandated biblically for a violation of the Sabbath such as picking up and moving a piece of wood from one place to another but not for serious bodily harm that stops short of murder—an order of judgment that would differ elsewhere, as would the more general definition of what even counts as a crime). Such *inter*-cultural differences, however, do not affect the claim of universality for the *intra*-cultural gradation of moral offenses.

The explanation of why this differential pattern is so widely held may seem self-evident: *of course*, there is a difference between murder and wounding, between telling a lie and ordering a campaign of extermination—moral differences that quickly translate into legal distinctions and then, on both counts, into gradations of punishment. But for the most basic ethical issues, there is (of course) no "of course"—and some explanation is thus required, with the most obvious place to look for an answer in a combination of the intentions and consequences of the actions judged. Thus, where human life is a fundamental good, murder would be a more serious offense than an assault that leaves the victim alive (even if the assault were an unsuccessful attempt at murder). Even punishment that involves the taking of life is held—however ironically—to reflect the high value attached to life; the thirty-eight states of the United States that have capital punishment on their books typically restrict that punishment to acts of murder (and not even for all of *its* varieties or degrees). Nowhere is capital punishment sanctioned as a punishment for speeding or illegal parking, although it seems certain that, in contrast to the non-deterrent effect of capital punishment for murder, were capital punishment mandated for instances of speeding or illegal parking, it would indeed reduce their occurrence.

The principle at work here—and indeed, the basis for any system of differential punishment—is some version of the maxim that "the punishment should fit the crime": a principle in effect of proportionality between the successive acts of crime and punishment. The latter principle itself depends on two assumptions: first, that punishments differ in severity (that is, in the degree to which they indeed do punish); and second, that crimes differ in *their* severity (that is, in respect to whatever makes the crime a crime, in moral and/or in legal terms). Fitting the punishment to the crime thus argues for a proportionality between the two hierarchical sides of that relation. It asserts this proportionality, moreover, not only as warranted but as required; that is, as itself a moral condition.

To be sure, the consequences of an act are not the only considerations affecting judgments of crime or punishment; intentions are also commonly recognized as a factor, at times a decisive one. In the distinction between murder and manslaughter, for instance, the consequences are identical: a death has been caused. It is the intentions (or their absence) underlying the acts that thus support distinctions in our judgments of an agent's action (and of the agent) and then, subsequently, of the punishment to be imposed. Philosophical views of the elements of moral judgment have typically been more "purist" than legal systems in defining those elements; thus, the Kantian's exclusion of consequences as relevant to moral assessment—balanced at the other end of the spectrum by the utilitarian's or consequentialist's counterclaim of the irrelevance of intentions. But quite apart from their other, often serious differences, these systems in common distinguish between more and less serious transgressions. On that point, they are at one; hence the claim I have made for the universality of that principle.

In this sense, comparative assessments seem intrinsic to moral judgment, and certainly they are its constant companion. Only consider a possible world without moral gradations, or even one with *only* the Manichaean dualism of good and evil—and we find what in practice becomes an unrecognizable and just as certainly an uninhabitable world. However compelling that dualism may seem dramatically or heuristically, it is quite underdetermined in practice; that is, in the all-too-familiar world of common moral experience where gray is a much more prominent color than black or white. In other words, the sub-branches of the tree of the knowledge of good and evil—the distinctions within those concepts—turn out to be as significant as the distinction itself; indeed, in the end, they arguably *comprise* the distinction. This holds, I should argue, not only for degrees of wrongdoing but also for gradations of the good, although the focus of moral and certainly legal analyses has been on the former. The category of "supererogatory" acts—heroic deeds that are not in moral principle required—marks a stage or degree in "right-doing" that goes beyond obligation and is yet highly esteemed.

It seems clear, however, that these same graded distinctions, however necessary in establishing and sustaining moral judgment, pose difficulties for moral comparisons in practice—especially where the wrongdoing at issue involves the irreparable harm to human life (and that, on a scale where more than one life is involved). The very formulation of any mass comparisons in the loss of human lives presupposes the possibility of ascribing responsibility for large-scale acts involving the murder, intentional or adventitious, of large numbers of people, and the twentieth century offers two remarkable examples of this in the policies and acts of Nazi Germany and the Soviet Union respectively, over the periods during which they were in power. (Other twentieth-century examples might be cited that bear comparison with these; for the moment, I wish to focus on the comparison between these for the sake of the comparison.) The structural—and moral—questions begin as soon as the juxtaposition is made: can we distinguish or compare those acts and agents in moral terms? Is numerical computation the key to such comparison?—a double murder counting as twice the wrong of a single one, two million twice that of one, and so on? And would the agent's guilt—or wrongdoing—be similarly tabulated? For the utilitarian or consequentialist, such a "felicific" calculus is not only all that a moral judge requires in order to answer such questions, but all that anyone can ever have. On the face of it, however, this computational view of ethical judgment is too crude to serve as a standard, at least as a moral standard. If this objection were not evident from examining comparative examples of murder, it becomes clearer where human lives are pitted against other social goods—as the consequentialist might require (supposedly, on moral grounds) that some lives *ought to* be sacrificed in order to increase the "well-being" or perhaps even pleasure of a larger number of others.

Is there an alternative to this that does not take numbers decisively into account? I should argue that we do not here have to concede an either/or, but that the two extreme alternatives (ethics by the numbers or ethics by pure form) themselves impel a third way. I would point here to a distinction in moral degrees, in contrast to measurement by numbers—a distinction alluded to earlier in my reference to the contrast between manslaughter and murder, which seems to me to suggest an analogy in the difference between mass murder and genocide. If we recognize Cain (even figuratively) as responsible for the first murder on record (and so also the inventor of the very idea), we find also that even in the brief course of biblical history, an extension was made to murder in larger numbers, although still, it seems, as groups of individuals. Like individual murder, mass murder, too, might be either premeditated or ensue as a consequence of what has been called double causality: the unintended, even unforeseen, consequence of another act.

Since the events of World War II, however, there has also been a second direction that might be followed—in effect, a quantum jump—in the phenomenology of murder; this, in the conceptualization of the crime of genocide as that crime involves what is in effect single causality but a double murder. Central to the issue here is not whether the formulation of the concept of genocide in 1944 by Raphael Lemkin attested to its *first* occurrence (with the Nazis as its agent), or whether it designated a practice that had occurred earlier but gone unnamed. But the concept does point to a distinction in kind or degree from other acts (or crimes) that fall under the heading of culpable killing—since for genocide it is not only individuals who are murdered, but the group of which they are members, with the killing of those individuals due to their membership *in* the group, membership which, in the clearest instances of genocide, was and would be at least to some extent involuntary.

The break or extension that genocide marks in the hierarchy of culpable killing requires more detailed analysis than I can provide here. But that it represents such a development (in a perverse sense, progress) seems evident. The conclusions I propose are thus more formal than substantive. At certain junctures of moral and/or legal judgment, the quantification of wrongdoing by numbers and not only by degrees is unavoidable—but where that is necessary, there seems no possible formula that can serve satisfactorily as a basis for comparative judgments. On the face of it, someone responsible for a million deaths has done something larger in moral enormity than the murderer of a single person—although, also on the face of it, the claim is compelling that nothing *could* be more wrongful than the murder of a person. Sentencing a serial killer to four or five "life terms" may serve some symbolic purpose, but it hardly answers to the moral issue that arises here—and the latter difficulty is of course compounded where mass murder or genocide is at issue. The conventional formulas by which damages for "wrongful death" are assessed in terms of economic loss do not pretend to (and do not in fact) provide a moral estimate of the criminality or evil attached to the act or the agent—and it seems even clearer that within the categories of kinds of crimes committed, numbers are an inadequate basis for further moral distinctions. The difference between the deaths of a million people and of ten people is surely significant in its consequences and usually also in terms of its design—but there seems to me to be no way of marking that difference in respect to the act of murder or the agent responsible by a contrast based on those numbers as also establishing a *moral* distinction. In this sense, within the categories or kinds of crimes committed, numbers do not resolve moral comparisons or, for that matter, moral dilemmas. Even the repetition of the same crime at different times—with the implication this might carry of a failed or rejected opportunity of change or repentance— does not provide a sufficient basis for additive computation.

On the other hand and by contrast: moral differences in terms of *degrees* of wrongdoing are both measurable and relevant to the judgment of morally significant acts. Here, too, the distinction between "degrees" and "numbers" becomes crucial. The number of victims of an act of mass murder may be larger than the number of victims of an act of genocide—as there may be more victims of an accident caused by a driver under the influence of alcohol (and so, guilty of manslaughter) than of a premeditated murder that claims a single victim. But in neither case does (or in my view, should) the difference in numbers override the differences in the moral quality of the two acts. That qualitative difference is crucial, it seems, for the larger-scale distinction between mass murder and genocide—not because of the absence of premeditation from the former (since intention may be present there as well), but because of one aspect of intention that is necessary for the latter—directed at the group—but is by definition absent in the former. Even within genocide, moreover, gradations are indicated that override the issue of numbers or of percentages: the forcible dispersion and assimilation of members of a group are no doubt a version of genocide (sometimes called *ethnocide*)—but it, too, is distinguishable from the act of genocide involving the physical murder of the members of a group because of that membership. Thus, within genocide itself, as well as between genocide and other forms of culpable killing, distinctions by degree emerge as markers, analogous to familiar distinctions of degree within the category of individual murder.

Where does this leave—or take—us on the question of the comparability of the acts of Soviet Russia and Nazi Germany? The comparative numbers of victims, I have suggested, can never be morally irrelevant—but neither, on the account here, are they by themselves decisive for rendering moral judgment. Unless, that is, everything else is equal, which it is almost invariably not—certainly not for measurements that involve degrees and kinds. The number of Soviet victims (even apart from the years of World War II) is generally recognized as larger than the number of victims for which Nazi policies and acts were responsible (and the number of victims of Mao in his rise to and exercise of power arguably larger than either). On the other hand, if one raises the admittedly difficult question of how to characterize the acts responsible for those two sets of consequences, there nonetheless appears to be a difference, conceptually and, as that leads farther, morally. Insofar as genocide represents a distinctive act (and crime), it is indisputable that Nazi Germany was responsible for genocide against the Jews and the Gypsies. That the Nazis failed in this attempt was due neither to their lack of will nor to deficiencies in their conceptualization of their goal. The argument has been made that the planned famine in the Ukraine initiated by the Soviets and claiming between one and five million lives was genocide, and that the dispersion of the Chechens to Kazakhstan and the oppression of the Tatars is at the very least a version of ethnocide. In both those cases, there are counterclaims, and I hesitate here to judge the categorial issue. Whatever its outcome, in any event, if the charge of genocide admits of degrees, there still would remain a significant difference between Nazi Germany and Soviet Russia in respect to those acts; that is, in respect to the totalizing will in the two cases that is an essential parameter of genocide. Such distinctions (and comparisons) are bound to appear invidious—indeed, offensive as they do also in marking differences of degree in individual murder, although it surely is also a consideration there. Yet for the latter, too, differences within the principal charge of murder turn out to be significant for judging the act, and this seems no less compellingly the case where the distinction between genocide and mass murder and distinctions within types or degrees of genocide are concerned.

What bearing if any this has in analyzing the comparative structures of the two systems or in articulating the concept of totalitarianism more generally is an important but separate question; I hope it also to be evident that what has been proposed here is not meant to cover over, much less to excuse the will to barbarism and brutality intrinsic to totalitarianism—part of its very definition. Nor do I mean to rule out the possibility that at some point in moral history—perhaps even now—a radically different system of measurement may be required. It is surely possible, as Jean-François Lyotard has suggested,[3] that the enormity of twentieth-century history (exemplified, for one, in the Holocaust) has broken and made unusable what had previously served adequately as instruments of moral measurement—or if this has not happened yet, that it may well occur as a consequence of some future event. There is, in any event, ample evidence that both the moral imagination and its counterpart in the immoral imagination "have" histories. But at least for the present, the graded distinctions of kind or degree seem the one means available—and, I have been proposing, necessary—for assessing comparative moral significance on the scale of the regimes of Soviet Russia and Nazi Germany. If that basis for judgment applies at all, surely it applies to those regimes, not because others are *in*comparable to them, but because their enormity challenges the process of assessment in a way that few others do. The two are, in fact, a principal reason both for seeking and for justifying a means of comparative moral assessment at a corporate level—sufficient for the purpose even if there were no other basis, and also necessary for that purpose first because of what they did but then also because of the differences between them.

Part Two

Language and Lessons

FIVE

The Grammar of Antisemitism

.ON THE "THE" IN "THE JEWS"

The several tongue-twisting "the's" in my title are less difficult to manage than the problem they conceal. For there is a conceptual, cultural, and, finally, moral issue that bears directly on antisemitism in the common linking of the definite article *the* and Jews—that is, in *the Jews*. I do not mean to claim that antisemitism would not have occurred or would now disappear if only its initiators or advocates paid more attention to grammar. But when a common and superficially innocent use of the definite article in statements about Jews turns out to be not innocent at all but antisemitic, we need to consider more closely how and why that happens. Whether the linguistic usage originated as a cause or only a symptom of antisemitism hardly matters; it has over time served both functions, and it has thus also, from both these sources, extended the reach of ideology to grammar. Since ideology flourishes, furthermore, mainly by concealment, bringing into the open this secret role of the "the," trivial as it seems, may also contribute to undermining the many-layered foundation of antisemitism.

The usage under suspicion here is the phrase "the Jews"—and if the particular use of the phrase that I criticize is not its only application, it is distinctive. As, for example—most famously—in "The Jews killed Jesus." Or, more currently, "The Jews control Hollywood"—or again, in the aftermath of the recent Holocaust-controversy about "neighbors" in the Polish town of Jedwabne: "In 1939, after the Russians entered [Jedwabne], the Jews took over all the offices, including the town hall."[1] The general intent behind these statements might be inferred, but for the moment—since we're talking first about grammar not psychology—I propose to put questions of motive aside in order to examine the difference between the statements themselves and what they would mean if they appeared *without* the definite article that all the statements cited include; that is, without their references to "*the* Jews."

Consider, for contrast, the shortened versions of those statements which omit the definite article: "Jews killed Jesus"; "Jews control Hollywood"; "In 1939, after the Russians entered [Jedwabne], Jews took over all the offices, including the town hall." The difference between the first and the second groups of statements is clear. Both assert that certain people "killed Jesus," "control Hollywood," and "took over all the [Jedwabne] offices"—*and* that those people were or are Jews. But the first group of statements goes a step farther, implying that not only were or are the people responsible for the acts described as Jews, but that they acted collectively or in concert, among themselves and as part of a larger whole. That is, they are referred to as "the" Jews—not merely as some Jews, but corporately, expressing a common purpose or will. To deny this last implication would make the definite article in the sentence quite misleading— since there would then be nothing definite for the "definite" article to refer to.

Admittedly, anyone making the statements in the first group is unlikely to believe that every Jew alive at the time played a part in the act or disposition mentioned. But the main point of the statements is that "*the* Jews" (as a group) are responsible for that action even if, at a practical level, it was the work of only a few of them. A collective will is thus presupposed, and so also, of course, a common responsibility, both of these now ascribed to "the" Jews. Not just "this one Jew" or "those several Jews," but the Jews as a group.

Each of the first set of statements, then, has two parts. The first is a straightforward claim that those responsible for a certain act are or were Jewish; the second is the implied claim of a collective purpose motivating the act. Neither of these assertions is itself necessarily antisemitic; each is subject to the test of truth or evidence that the speaker purports to have. To be sure, the second assertion echoes a well-worn antisemitic theme: the claim of a conspiracy among "the" Jews as a group. But that claim, too, is subject to proof or disproof, even if its best-known appearances have rarely troubled themselves with that issue or with the question of evidence altogether. (The forged *Protocols of the Elders of Zion* remains a paradigm representation for this view of "the" Jewish conspiracy.)

It might be objected to my characterization so far that the phrase, "the Jews," need not—indeed could not—mean *all* Jews. On a variant reading, "The Jews killed Jesus" might refer only to a sub-group within the larger one—perhaps to the Jews then living in Palestine, at a time when many Jews lived elsewhere. But even in this restrictive interpretation—which is not how the statement is typically understood—a common purpose would be posited among *those* Jews, with that claim then having to be demonstrated (as it rarely is). In this sense, Nazi antisemitism, for all its pseudo-science, had the systematic "advantage" of biologizing race. The conspiracies alleged by the Nazis (as, e.g., among Jewish Bolsheviks and/or Jewish capitalists) did not require specific evidence of covert meetings or documents, since the genetic features that in the Nazi view made Jewish character dangerous would also account for the nefarious ways in which that group purpose was to be realized. (That this "foundation" posed serious problems for a "scientific" genetic theory did not faze the Nazis who, from their earliest response to the question of "Who is a Jew?" relied on a social rather than a biological basis.) To be sure, in social and historical terms, anyone familiar with Jewish history and communal life would find implausible the claim of a single or even a common purpose there. The conceptual and practical difficulties in proving *any* reference to corporate "persons" or intentions are greater still for this particular case; indeed, since there has been no central or coordinated authority in the two thousand years post-exilic Judaism, it is difficult to understand what a claim which referred in this sense to "the Jews" would even mean.

The line of reasoning here may encounter the objection that "the Jews" does not necessarily designate a collective or corporate Jewish will at all. What sometimes serves as a collective or substantive noun is in others shorthand for a group of individuals as individuals—who may, for instance, share certain beliefs but not because of any prior collective design. "The Jews are monotheists," for example, implies not that every Jew believes in one God, but that biblical or traditional or "essential" Judaism claims that tenet. So also "The Jews in the U.S. have an average educational level of three years of college"— from which a certain characteristic can be inferred of a hypothetical individual, not a group plan or even a common feature of all individual Jews. Such references to "the Jews" are common enough—but they also differ from the use challenged here. With the second, "individualist" use, there is no gap in meaning between statements in which "*the* Jews" appears and versions of the same statements in which that "*the*" is omitted. And this is clearly not true for the first group. There is, I hope to have shown, a difference—in ideological terms, a large one—between saying that "The Jews killed Jesus" and its shortened counterpart, that "Jews killed Jesus."

* * *

A question remains of why any of the three pairs of statements cited as examples should have been asserted at all. And indeed, nothing said so far touches the question of their truth or falsity, whether in the first or the second versions. I have been trying to show only how ideology makes its way into an apparently innocuous phrase like "the Jews." But if "the" is the primary culprit here, it is not the only one. For there is a substantive question that goes beyond grammar in asking what basis there could be in such statements for even mentioning the Jews (or Jews) in the contexts cited. On the assumption that there is ordinarily a live connection between the subject and the predicate in a sentence, it is reasonable to ask why "Jews," let alone "*the* Jews," should appear in the statements noted. Is the assertion that "Jews control Hollywood" meant to explain the types of film that Hollywood produces? Hollywood's financial success? The popular culture of which Hollywood films are part? Any of these, and still other, meanings are possible—but a question to which they are all subject is what relevance the role of Jews (or "the Jews") has to whatever they assert: why the reference at all?

A standard Jewish joke traced to World War I makes the point here:

A: "The Jews are responsible for the War" (or, as extended, for the Crucifixion or the plague).
B: No, it is the Jews and the bicycle riders.
A: Why the bicycle riders?
B: Why the Jews?

The issue being pointed in this exchange is that in the pairs of statements cited, not only is no evidence offered for the roles ascribed to the Jews as Jews, but there is also no acknowledgement of the question itself as relevant. Even if it could be proven that the people responsible for the Crucifixion or who control Hollywood were (or are) Jews—and putting aside the dispute over who is to count as a Jew or not—the substantive question remains of what importance this "proof" would have: what difference does it make? This is to ask, why it would be relevant to know that the people who control Hollywood or who killed Jesus or who took control of the municipal offices of Jedwabne were Jews? Identifying them as Jews implies that this factor somehow contributes to understanding the act or disposition mentioned (perhaps also of other general social or cultural issues). But does it? To allege that members of a certain group have power disproportionate to their numbers, or that members of the group were responsible for a particular historical act, would warrant the identification only if a connection could be shown between the group identity and the event. But what, we ask, is the connection here?

It is probably true, for example—and let us for the moment assume—that the people who "killed Jesus" were less than six feet tall. Would that finding itself be worth reporting? It might, one supposes, have some interest as bearing on the average heights of people at the particular time and place—in contrast to the average heights of people at other places or times. But unless there was a reason to associate their heights with the act of killing Jesus, the conjunction would seem arbitrary—and trivial even if true: what difference could it make? The fact itself would have little to do with explaining the circumstances of Jesus' execution—unless, of course, one built on it a verdict of continuing guilt through subsequent generations of everyone less than six feet tall.

Nor, in the same way, do we learn very much about Hollywood in determining that the studio heads who shaped or now "control" it were (or are) Jews—except, again, as a kind of anthropological stereotype, with all the excesses and dangers that stereotypes inevitably convey. Does this information contribute to understanding film as a medium? the "entertainment" industry? Perhaps as much (but how much is that?) as the contention that the automobile industry, at approximately the same time, was developed by midwestern Protestants— except who has ever commented on that? This does not mean that something substantial *might* not be illuminated by the reference—for example (in the case of the Crucifixion), the evolving negative attitude towards capital punishment within Judaism as that figured in the trial and execution of Jesus as a co-religionist. Or, in the case of Jedwabne, that Polish Jews, because of their system of education, were either better or less qualified for certain types of work outside the community itself. Such connections might indeed turn out to be historically significant and would then justify the statements cited here as examples—but in fact no such connections have been demonstrated, and more importantly, the very issue of providing or testing evidence for or against them has typically been ignored.

In practice, of course, claims that "The Jews killed Jesus," even when reduced to only "Jews killed Jesus," have usually been cited not in historical studies of the relation between early Christianity and Rabbinic Judaism, but as the basis for a charge of deicide—and this, as a matter of corporate and thus continuing Jewish responsibility. That charge is intelligible, however, only if "the" Jews of Jesus' time, whether in Jerusalem or elsewhere, not only acted in concert with each other but also implicated future generations of Jews—a collective "the" on a large scale indeed. The claim that "the Jews" "took over" the municipal offices when the Russians arrived in Jedwabne may have fewer metaphysical implications than the charge of deicide, but neither is it meant to be part of an analysis of social class or municipal governance in Poland during World War II. The reference is clearly intended to explain if not to justify the massacre in Jedwabne of members of the Jewish populace by their non-Jewish Polish "neighbors" after the Nazis, in 1941, had driven out the occupying Russians with whom (it is claimed) "the" Jews collaborated. In this way, then, ideology embodied in the grammatical "the" links up with ideology in a much broader framework.

Again, no link to antisemitism is intrinsically entailed in any of the statements cited. As truth is the measure of all descriptive statements, so here too; thus, the claims remain questions rather than assertions until tested by the evidence. Furthermore, applying the phrase "the Jews" presupposes acceptance of the notion of a collective will (and responsibility)—first, in general, and then, in particular reference to Jews as a group. In point of fact, to be sure, we know that the "the" in "the Jews" has often been summoned to the cause of antisemitism. And even if the locution has at times been used spontaneously or unconsciously, this would not make that connotation insignificant—or, for that matter, unintentional. In this way, a slight grammatical gesture turns out to be no less weighted ideologically than many of ideology's more blatant pronouncements. Expressions of language or reasoning are sometimes regarded as "beyond ideology": neutral in respect to social causes or even personal interests, and perhaps certain uses of language warrant this exemption. But the connection between ideology and grammar in the "the" of "the Jews" is too evident—and dangerous—to be ignored.

ON THE "I" IN "I AM (NOT) AN ANTISEMITE"

In a review of what was widely acclaimed as a major work on the history of Europe, the reviewer alleged a number of serious distortions and/or mistakes in the book about *Jewish* European history—distortions or mistakes that echoed certain traditional antisemitic themes. The reviewer concluded, however, that since the author himself had on a number of occasions denied being antisemitic, the explanation for these flaws must lie elsewhere: "On that matter [the allegation of antisemitism], we have to accept the author's judgment."[2] The questions raised by this conclusion, however, go well beyond the particular book, author, and reviewer involved in the exchange. On the one hand, the conclusion raises the general question—much less often addressed than might be expected—of how the designation of "antisemite" or "antisemitic" is ever assigned; on the other hand, it raises the narrower question of whether, when it comes to judging any particular person's acceptance or rejection of anti-Semitism, the person himself or herself is the final arbiter.

Important as the first of these questions is, it is the second on which I focus here. For although there may be disagreements on the application of a general and impersonal criterion (or "test") for determining the presence or absence of antisemitism as the judgment is made from a "third-person" point of view, at least the principle itself seems straightforward. As an instance of bias or prejudice, antisemitism in others would be judged by the application of a principle of generalization or universalizability: Does the (alleged) antisemite act or speak about Jews in terms of the same criteria or standards that he or she applies to non-Jewish individuals or groups? Acts found to be antisemitic in these terms would range from obvious cases—the refusal to sell a house advertised on the open market to a Jewish person—to subtler ones, as, for example, in "The Jews control Hollywood." In the latter statement, it *seems* that what is being asserted is that the number and power of Jews in Hollywood is predominant—with the implication that this finding says something significant about either the Jews or Hollywood or both; and it also seems that the assertion, prima facie, accepts the "Universalizable" test since at least implicitly it would be comparing Jews to members of other groups in respect to the same set of characteristics. But the subtext of the assertion is not only that the people who control Hollywood are Jewish, but that their being Jewish has something to do with the fact of that control (and by innuendo, also the question of what they do with that control). And here the issue of universalizability becomes more significant, since whatever evidence may be presented for the second claim, it typically, and arguably invariably, falls short of that test.

The second question, then, of whether a person himself or herself is the best, and in any event, the final judge of whether that person is or is not antisemitic is more interesting and perhaps more puzzling than the first because there *is* a category of "self-ascriptive" statements that in philosophical analysis are regarded as "privileged." This is to say that speakers of such statements are acknowledged to be in position of privileged access to the statements' truth or falsity. If someone says, for example, "I feel warm," he might of course be lying and saying what he does in order to deceive the person he is speaking to; but putting that possibility aside (since it might be true of any statement whatever that any person might make at any time), we would not ordinarily consider responding to the person who claims to feel warm by saying, "No, you're mistaken, you don't feel warm." We would not say this, under ordinary circumstances, even if the room we were in with the speaker was notably cold, although we might well, in that circumstance, believe—and perhaps then say— that the person who "felt warm" under such conditions must be ill. Even here, however, we would not be challenging the statement itself: if someone says that he *feels* warm, we typically do not doubt that this is indeed how he feels; that is, how he *is*. We are not in a better position than he is of judging how he feels; in some sense, we are not in any position at all.

But does this sense of privileged access extend to the judgment by a person of whether he or she is antisemitic? It seems evident that there is no all-purpose litmus test for determining whether someone—including oneself—is an antisemite or not; it seems also true that for some people, even certain public figures about whom much is known, there may remain doubt as to whether they should indeed be characterized as antisemites or not. But it is also and no less clear in this sometimes confusing field of dispositions that the final decision on this question does not and should not rest with the person in question, certainly not entirely or finally. More concisely: whether or not someone is an antisemite is not solely a matter for the person charged to decide.

The reasons for this, once stated, are obvious. Namely, that antisemitism is not simply a matter of sentiment, of a feeling or disposition to act or speak in a certain way—but that it entails *actually* acting and speaking in certain ways. Insofar as this condition holds, the person who is doing the acting and speaking is not the only, and sometimes not the best judge of what those actions or words are or amount to. Common experience indicates that at times, other are better interpreters of our actions and statements than we are ourselves; and this general finding would be no less applicable to possible instances of antisemitic actions and statements than to any other. Indeed, the argument extends still further than this, since even at the level of disposition or intentions, the subject himself is not necessarily the only or best judge of what they are. Everyone is familiar with the statement, "But my intentions were good"—a claim most frequently heard when the intentions defended had either led to or been unable to prevent harmful results. But unless one believes either that people are invariably the best or only judges of their own intentions—or that everyone's intentions are *always* good—this statement too does not have the weight of privileged access.

The fact that intentions are always to some extent invisible and thus inferred does not mean that the person who "has" the intentions is the only knowledgeable judge of them: a person might well think, and claim, that his or her intentions were good when in fact, as others discover, they were not good at all. And if people can be mistaken in this way about their intentions, it should not be surprising to find that someone might deny being an antisemite, and yet, on the basis of his actions and words, be judged by others to be just that. That this is a matter of weighing external and objective evidence—however indefinite the criteria are, since the question of the criteria is a separate problem—comes clear in that most common of all clichés resorted to, as "proof" that the speaker is *not* antisemitic: "Some of my best friends are Jews." As the premise of an argument, of course, this is vacuous; nothing in the concept of antisemitism would prevent an antisemite from making exceptions for *some* Jews who might then be his friends. But what is more pertinent here is that the contention itself appeals to external evidence, not just to the subjective feelings of the person speaking. And this is, again, just the point. Being antisemitic is not only, and perhaps not even primarily, a state of mind or a psychological disposition. For one thing, no one has clear access to these (not even the person to whom they belong); and for another thing, by themselves, and as long as they do not manifest themselves in words or actions, they hardly count as anti- or pro-anything. Where antisemitism *matters*, where it becomes visible, is in its expressions, in the acts or statements (with statements, after all, very much a form of action) that bring feelings or mental dispositions (and prejudices) into the world. That is, into the open. In judging these occasions or moments, the source responsible for the actions or statements may well have an opinion or interpretation of what lies behind them, of what motivated them and what their "meaning" is. But that opinion or interpretation is one among others; there are too many ways for it to be mistaken or deceptive for it to be honored as decisive.

This view of how to analyze statements that take the form "I am not antisemitic" or "I am not an antisemite" has the strange—to some, it might seem perverse—consequence that someone might assert that "I *am* an antisemite"— and also be mistaken about *that*. That is, we might be able to show, on the basis of the speaker's other words or actions, that although he might have believed or felt himself to be antisemitic, that he was not or had not been that in fact. Obviously such instances are likely to be rare; given the history of antisemitism and its consequences, the possibility itself amounts to an ironic and bitter joke. But this distracting possibility should not obscure the analysis in what are the more common appearances of antisemitism—of which the antisemite himself may not be the best and surely not the final judge.

SIX

The Unspeakable vs. the Testimonial

Holocaust Trauma in Holocaust History

> I can see the time approach when we will no longer have to base modern
> history on reports . . . to say nothing of re-working the sources. Rather we
> will construct it from the accounts of eyewitnesses, and the most genuine
> and direct sources.
>
> Leopold von Ranke

> No one witnesses for the witness.
>
> Paul Celan

Few more portentous terms could be fitted into the space of this chapter's title,
and the only justification I venture for this is the interconnection among the
terms that do appear: History, Trauma, Testimony, and the inclusive issue of
Speakability—all of them converging and intertwined in the event of the Holocaust, observed now from the perspective of sixty years later, as that event
continues at once to evoke and to challenge all the expressive means or motives
available. To be sure, another common feature of those same rubrics is the
skepticism they have at times provoked because of their filtering or blurring
effect on the stark reality of the Holocaust itself. I am myself among the writers who have registered doubts about many of the claims made for interpretations or applications of all of these categories; in this sense, the position to be
outlined here on several of them might be understood as representing the
Devil's Advocate—with the difference, I hope, of providing both the questions
that I raise and the alternatives to the standard accounts that I propose a fair
trial. I do not, in any event (at least at the moment), mean to recant the reservations I have expressed about the extent or possibilities of Holocaust representation.[1] But partly in order to clarify those reservations, and partly to elaborate a different—although, I should argue, consistent—side of them, I shall be

emphasizing what Holocaust representation *can* do, in addition to what it seems to me that it can't; that is, where and how it might turn, given the limitations that history and ethics, affected by the enormity of the subject and the constraints of systematic reflection, impose.

The discussion here will focus sequentially on three issues—all of them through the demanding lens, that true camera obscura, of the Holocaust (or, as I've argued for calling it, in a continuing but losing struggle, the Nazi Genocide against the Jews). These issues are, first, the concept of the "unspeakable," a concept that in related variations has surfaced also in references to the "indescribable," "unimaginable," "unthinkable," or "incomprehensible." What, I ask, can we think or imagine or say about *these* terms as they in effect deny the possibility of just those activities—thinking or imagining or saying—in relation to the Holocaust? My second topic here involves the opposing concept of "testimony"—those first-person accounts of firsthand experience that are recounted after—sometimes, long after—the events described, with those representations typically assuming and being granted the privilege of first-person authority; that is, of *unquestionable* authority. I will be considering such testimony as a form of discourse—a contextualizing that makes unavoidable the issue of the status of its truth-claims and the question of the dependence of testimony on them. Lastly, I turn to the category of trauma as a means of uncovering the present view of the import, or more blandly the perception, of the Holocaust "as it really happened." The purpose of this turn is to address the problem of understanding the understanding of the Holocaust: hoping to identify the difference that the category of traumatic experience makes not only for memory to which, by their common silence, it is most obviously related, but to speakability or representation more generally. Trauma is deepest and most "traumatic" when it is least explicit or overt; in this sense, all the issues of the nature of representation—Holocaust representation or any other—reach a point zero in traumatic expression: the layers through which interpretation must make its way could hardly go any further down. And yet, of course, the dangers of misinterpretation here are proportionate: the greater the distance from landmarks, the more difficult it is to find one's way.

This limited discussion can hardly say very much about any one, or even all, of these large topics, and that liability is compounded by the conclusions I propose about them which may seem commonplace or dubious or both: almost, as it were, the worst of both worlds. But the alternatives to the conclusions asserted here seem to me more seriously objectionable than the arguments against them. That the conclusions drawn may be conventional or literal-minded, if that is not itself an argument in their favor, should not count against them either; the commonplace need not be discounted just because of that. Thus, I shall be proposing that the Holocaust *is* speakable (and imaginable and describable and comprehensible)—as much so, at any rate, as other historically complex and morally charged events; that testimony as a genre has no privileged authority in its historical claims, but does have distinctive, albeit limited, force in moral terms; and that psychological traumas, however impelled by or related to the Holocaust, disclose neither a specific Holocaust identity nor reveal anything distinctive about the Holocaust itself: overdetermined, they invariably exceed their symptoms. Thus, too, although emblematic of the Holocaust as a corporate act, the project of "working through" trauma will always leave an untouched residue—a remainder of silence. This remainder also has the function of completing the circle from which the present discussion sets out, initiated with the question of whether, and if so, how, talk about the Holocaust can advance farther than a contrasting silence would. Silence, we know, can be significant—in texts as in life; it is not, however, often applied or recognized as a standard of assessment. It survives, however, as a presence, and for an event with the dimensions and weight of the Holocaust, that silence has to be made explicit and known.

Thus, first:

1. *The Holocaust as "Unspeakable"* (often otherwise cited as "Unimaginable" or "Unthinkable" or "Incomprehensible" or "Indescribable"): Although clearly not synonymous, these terms have certain common features, one of which, itself historical and thus accidental, is also symptomatic. This is the frequency with which the terms cited have been associated with the Holocaust— in effect constituting a standard trope in the varieties of Holocaust writing. So we find in book titles: *Speaking the Unspeakable,*[2] *Thinking the Unthinkable,*[3] and *Voicing the Void.*[4] And although these particular formulas might be viewed as themselves vague or equivocal (more about this later), their intent is indeed to emphasize the unthinkable, the unspeakable, the void by which the Holocaust challenges its would-be representations—not only particular efforts at representation that the act of representation faces for any of its subjects, but the prospect of representation as such, based on the nature of *this* subject. This challenge has been formulated in more concrete and dramatic form—as in Elie Wiesel's contention that there *cannot* be a novel about Auschwitz: "If it's a novel, it's not about Auschwitz; if it's about Auschwitz, it's not a novel"—or at a farther extreme, in George Steiner's one-time proposal of silence itself as the only adequate representation of the Holocaust: a representation, in effect, by the absence of representation. Nor do such claims come only from those who speak in opposition, in the register of horror; so we hear Admiral Canaris, head of the Abwehr (the Wehrmacht Intelligence): "The Third Reich is such an unimaginable (*"unvorstellbare"*) phenomenon that when it is over nobody will believe it." The Holocaust, viewed in these terms, seems to carry the biblical commandment against making graven images to a still more radical extreme: of it, we hear, no one *can* create images, even if they wish and attempt to.

Again, the several terms thus grouped together are not synonymous: what is incomprehensible need not be indescribable (we describe things or events that we cannot understand, and so on). But the terms do in this context also share a basic internal feature: their assertion of a limit to the intelligibility and/or representability of the Holocaust, which is thus held to be beyond our (that is, human) capacity to describe and understand adequately or, perhaps, at all. The assertion of such limits, moreover, is meant to distinguish the Holocaust from other events or even atrocities—not because of the Holocaust's *historical* complexity (few commentators claim that mark of distinction), but for its moral enormity that is held to exceed ordinary, and perhaps any, means of representation.

For all their categorical tone, however, these claims themselves involve substantial ambiguities. Most importantly, they leave untouched the question of where or how they have drawn the line they assume *between* the speakable and the unspeakable, the thinkable and the unthinkable. Assuming that the distinction is more than only a manner of speaking, what exactly *is* it that separates the two sides of the divide, marking the place to which thinking and speaking cannot reach? One response to the latter challenge would be (and has been) a requirement of direct experience; that is, a stipulation that only those people who were personally, immediately, within the Holocaust could have access to thinking or comprehending or imagining it—first, at the time, but then also subsequently. A related but more severe gloss on the stipulation would be that the line thus drawn does not require having had such direct experience, but implies the impossibility of grasping or imagining what occurred for *anyone*—those who went through it as well as those who did not: human capacity is the issue here, not the difference between immediate or mediated experience.

The more insistently one analyzes such arguments, however, the more nebulous and unconvincing they become. The thesis that something—anything—cannot be understood without direct experience of it has been appealed to for a wide range of emotion and circumstance, from love to mystical ecstasy to nationalist or racial identity—all of these exemplifying the premise of classical empiricism (as in Locke or Hume) that it is impossible to have an idea of *anything* in the absence of a prior sensation. Far from distinguishing thinking-the-Holocaust from other ideas or manners of thinking, then, this stipulation draws thinking about that particular event *closer* to thought (or history) in general. (There are also important side issues here that can only be alluded to: the question, for example, of what is meant by "experiencing" or "facing" the Holocaust. For horrific as individual experience was within that event, it would not, because no individual experience could, take in the act of genocide as such. A second is the question of what *can* be represented of the Holocaust but has deliberately been avoided. So far as I know, for instance, no film yet has included a scene of what remains the crux or epitome of the Holocaust—that is, the gas chambers of the death camps in action. This is clearly a deliberate and self-imposed limit since the occurrence *is* an epitome and since its absence from filmed representation could not be due to technical difficulties; the staging might be managed easily enough.)

Even if the terms mentioned were interpreted as bearing on the moral rather than the epistemic incomprehensibility of the Holocaust, the questions behind the appeal to such terms also have a familiarly unsatisfactory ring. How can we explain or understand people who would commit such acts? Could anyone knowingly intend evil on that scale? Philosophical rationalists and religious deists alike must be hard-pressed to locate such an event in their presumably orderly or beneficent worlds. When the conventional answers to these questions—that even the greatest wrongdoers tend to *believe* that their actions are justified, or that in the end justice or reason will show apparent evil actually to be good—appear in the context of the Holocaust, they take on the character of insults rather than explanations. The difficulty of moral comprehension thus persists, and the fact that such efforts stumble in explaining slighter instances of evil as much as they do this larger one is no consolation. Consistency in these accounts virtually requires that wrongdoing be unintelligible, hence vacuous—more bluntly, unreal. But how, and why, would anyone accept that conclusion for an event whose consequences and "reality" have affected history as deeply as the Holocaust has?

These unsatisfactory foundations and rationales for the alleged unspeakability or incomprehensibility of the Holocaust suggest that such claims might not even be meant to be understood literally, but figuratively. One possibility along these lines would be a version of the literary figure *praeteritio*—in which a speaker professes to avoid saying or alluding to something but manages to bring the matter or subject up in describing the effort to *avoid* doing so. This figure is especially familiar in political rhetoric, where the speaker wishes to avoid responsibility for something he or she says—and yet wishes to say it: "I do not, of course, intend to make an issue of my opponent's personal life," etc., etc. Admittedly, to call something unspeakable or incomprehensible differs from common appearances of *praeteritio* since such designation does not detail *what* is unspeakable or incomprehensible. But then, it does not have to do this, because the "fact" of the event's incomprehensibility or unspeakability is itself proof (and so detail) of its distinctive cognitive or moral character: not literally, but as it were (that is, figuratively). Nobody would infer that when we call something "unspeakable" or "unthinkable," the connotation is intended to be favorable; and this is the case although similar or related characteristics are also features of the sublime as it exceeds the beautiful; "I can't tell you how much . . . " or "Words fail me" appear also on emotionally stirring occasions of great happiness—but *not* the terms *unspeakable* or *unthinkable* or *incomprehensible*.

Perhaps other figures of speech might be adduced here—for example, simple hyperbole. In any event, the indication that the terms mentioned are not meant to function literally has substantial external evidence as well, the most obvious instances of which are the numerous writings about the Holocaust—historical, literary, philosophical, psychological—that *have* attempted its representation and understanding and that have also, at least to some extent, succeeded in this effort. If none of these attempts, or even all together, has won agreement on the necessary and sufficient conditions of the Holocaust as those remain the ideal of scientific explanation, few historians claim to have met those conditions for *any* historical event; the attempt to apply the "covering law" model to historical explanation was an almost instant non-starter in the philosophy of history. (Daniel Goldhagen's claim of this status for his theory of "Eliminationist Antisemitism" was in this respect as unusual as it was also unfounded.)[5] The very assertions of the Holocaust's unspeakability or incomprehensibility, in fact, typically go on to describe at length just what is unspeakable or incomprehensible in that event. And although the objection thus formulated is ad hominem, what it refers to is symptomatic. Perhaps events do occur that are genuinely incomprehensible, notwithstanding the article of faith assumed in scientific analysis that for any physical occurrence, *some* causal explanation will always be possible. There are, we recognize, incomprehensible linguistic utterances (gibberish), but even their most severe critics have not claimed such characterization for the long and varied list of Holocaust writings. Are the terms being examined then merely means of emphasis, intended to reflect the Holocaust's magnitude or importance? As already suggested, we hear often, after all, in much slighter contexts, statements like "Words cannot express my feelings about *x* or *y* or . . . " But hyperbole or emphasis also admits of degrees, with some of those degrees greater than others, and even if we grant that the Holocaust as a subject would invite and warrant as much emphasis as language is capable of, this would still leave the question of what, if anything, remains at the literal core of references to the "unspeakable" or the "unthinkable." There would not be much disagreement about the claim that historical explanations never *fully* account for historical events. On the other hand, historical explanation—reaching into cultural practice, psychology, economics—*does* make intelligible aspects of events or acts, and this has unquestionably been the case also for the Holocaust. In both these respects, then, to refer to the Holocaust as "indescribable" or "incomprehensible" is to obscure the basic features of that event which, notwithstanding its moral enormity, are clearly—if anything, *too* clearly—recognizable and describable.

Again, little of what I have been saying will be startling, but then puncturing exaggerations can hardly be more than deflationary. All that such efforts add is already what other skeptics believed or took for granted in the first place. But there may be progress here nonetheless in the way of ground clearing—by showing that in the context of the Holocaust, attempts to intensify or enlarge on that event turn out to have precisely the contrary effect of diminution—as stimulants do in calming hyperactivity. No one who has seriously addressed the subject of the Holocaust can doubt the difficulty of working at it or in it: cognitively, morally, aesthetically. But to say this is far from moving that subject beyond the possibility of analysis and representation; if anything, such study demonstrates the place of the Holocaust *in* history: speakable, thinkable, comprehensible—at least as much as any complex historical event may be.

2. *Testimony:* Witness or Survivor Testimony has increasingly claimed a special place in the rolls of Holocaust discourse. Gathered in video archives and films or in recorded and transcribed interviews, such testimony conveys the possibility of immediate contact: the person speaking who sixty or sixty-five years before also lived the Holocaust, that "first person" whom we see or hear both was and is that person. Such testimony, delivered and heard if not in tranquility, certainly in retrospect, is typically neither fully spontaneous nor fully designed, but a mixture of the two. Typically the testimony is solicited—and even if certain marks of improvisation or spontaneity characterize the "text" delivered which are absent from intentional and thus deliberated memoirs or essays or even letters, the narrative form of testimony is recognizably generic. The absence of *all* design, in Lawrence Langer's view,[6] identifies testimony as a distinctive genre, unmediated, unaffected, *artless;* but that seems to me an exaggeration of features which in more minimal form are quite real.

There is an obvious justification for deference in respect to Holocaust testimony, even if such deference, as Henry Greenspan has pointed out, poses certain dangers as well.[7] It takes nothing away from the respect due to testimony and its speakers, however, to ask exactly what the basis of its force is. Consider the following response by Elie Wiesel to a doubt expressed by Alfred Kazin about the historical accuracy of a scene in Wiesel's *Night:* "How dare he [Kazin], an American Jew, who discovered the tragedy of our people very late, from other people's testimony, deny the validity of a survivor's testimony? . . . If Kazin says this, why should not others? . . . Why should all the deniers not simply say, 'We do not believe you?' Which they say."[8] The issue here is neither what basis Kazin had for questioning Wiesel's account in particular, nor the irrelevance of Wiesel's ad hominem attack; what is crucial is the implication in Wiesel's questions of the unimpeachability of survivor testimony. What could this mean? Is everything asserted in testimony true by virtue of its status as testimony? Wiesel himself, before the statement just quoted, mentions two survivors of Auschwitz who disagreed about the color of a belt they recalled seeing there. "Still," Wiesel concludes, the two contradictory witnesses "told the truth, and their truth had to do with something other than a simple visual statement" (p. 14).[9] How to characterize this conception of testimonial truth (in contrast to what—"*scientific*" truth?) is a deeper problem than the particular disagreements between Wiesel and Kazin or the two survivor witnesses—a problem familiar from better-known settings: from the Demjanjuk trial in Jerusalem, for example, where testimony identifying Demjanjuk as "Ivan the Terrible" was juridically found sufficiently problematic to require an embarrassing dismissal of the charges; or in the public reaction to Benjamin Wilkomirski's *Fragments,* which, published and much-honored as a memoir, was then revealed to be impossible as a history of the author and so, although no court could formally order this, was to be moved from the non-fiction to the fiction sections of libraries and bookstores.

What *is* the relation between history and testimony? If history sits in judgment on testimony, then testimony loses the privilege it typically asserts of first-person authority.[10] There seems to me to be no way to avoid this conclusion when, indeed, it is history alone that judges testimony. But it is also important to recognize that this is not the only measure of testimony—as certain analogies, pointed elsewhere, demonstrate. The diary is distinctive as a genre not because it is beyond the reach of historical assessment, but for the immediate contact it provides with the events described, in their contingency and with the person of their authors. At the time of writing, the diary's author has no way of knowing the outcome of the events described, or the fate of the diary, or—most urgently, for Holocaust-writing—even the future of the diarist.[11] This sense of contingency remains a factor in the reception of the work also for later readers, although they will usually, by the time they read the diary, be aware of the resolution of these contingencies. It is mainly in this connected tissue of features that the diary differs from the memoir that is written retrospectively—thus, with the survival of the author a given and the outcome of the one-time contingent events settled. The memoir is thus closer to testimony than to the diary; the memoir, too, depends on memory casting backward from the present. A diary discovered to have been revised retrospectively is arguably no longer a diary, since the defining immediacy has been displaced; at the very least, the fact of revision marks its status and should indeed also affect its reading.[12] Also in this schematism, then, testimony occupies a place between the other two.

All three of these genres, however—diary, memoir, testimony—depend on one common aspect of historical truth: the evidence that the apparent voice of the author is indeed his or her voice—which in turn presupposes that the author was indeed in a position to have experienced the events recounted. To find doubts registered about either of these premises (and for Wilkomirski's "memoir," both of them were doubted) is necessarily to alter the status of the work. Some commentators argued at the time that whether Wilkomirski actually experienced the events he depicted in his "memoir" does not matter: the decisive test is the force of the account itself—an issue of which the reader is judge (and not, presumably, the reader qua historian). This dispute cannot be settled prescriptively; but even if one looks to reader-response theory for resolution, the outcome is not beyond either prediction or criticism. Would (and should) it make no difference if we were to discover that Primo Levi had spent the year he claimed to have endured in Auschwitz in a northern Italian village—there composing the trust-inspiring "histories" he would later publish? The texts themselves, after all, would be no different. But if this historical difference makes no other difference, very little of any distinction would be left for testimony. Why would the words of Lear, maddened on the heath and with Cordelia dead in his arms, not *also* count as testimony—thus adding to what is already more powerful than almost any other representation of human despair because of the genius of an author who was, however, most definitely not King Lear himself?

A recent essay by Derrida calls attention to the lines in the Paul Celan poem cited as an epigraph at the beginning of this chapter: "There is no witness for the witness" ["Niemand / zeugt für den / Zeugen"], Celan writes—and Derrida takes these words to suggest that the power of testimony arises from the fact that it is *not*, and not to be judged *as*, history.[13] Surely there is a point to this claim (since otherwise, testimony would be simply written off as history-manqué). But the point's force, I should argue, is limited if, as I have proposed, historical verification, although not a sufficient condition of testimony, remains a necessary one, required in broad outline if not for each detail. (If Wilkomirski *had* been in the camps, few readers would have questioned whether he did in fact see other children gnawing at their own limbs from hunger). Judged only as history, some of what appears as testimony may be (has been) discredited—*both* as history and as testimony. Few historians or readers of history would find such an outcome especially noteworthy: historical discourse, like work in the natural sciences, *expects* revision. But this is precisely what testimony does not do—and remains a key both to its import and to its vulnerability. Unless one is willing to argue that testimony, by the fact that it is testimony, is unimpeachable, testimony by itself will not, and should not, have the last word—even about its own words.

With this shaky underpinning, the question of what the distinctive character of testimony *is* becomes ever more pressing. Derrida, in the essay cited above, does not stay for an answer to this question, and I suggest here only the outline of an account and a number of analogies. That the first-person voice is central to testimony seems evident; what remains unexplained is the force of that voice, and here, it seems to me, the status of the voice as such, not its particular assertions, are crucial. For again, those assertions individually cannot—*may* not—escape the test of historical disconfirmation. Admittedly, the same test applies to the voice itself—but once *that* test is passed (that the voice in the present is the authentic), a new phase opens in recognizing the voice that speaks now as the same voice that "spoke" or experienced at the time and place of the events recounted. Roland Barthes in *Camera Lucida* describes the distinctiveness of the photograph in the history of representation as not conceptual or aesthetic, but chemical: the same inscription made chemically on film at the time of the photograph now impinges on the viewer's eye.[14] Sight becomes here in effect a matter of touch—commonly judged a grosser sense but also more implacable: touching is *more* than believing. And so also, I suggest, sound or hearing function in conveying the voice of survivor testimony. Admittedly, the voice heard there is current, not past—and to that extent, then, not contemporary with the events it describes. Yet we know that the voice is the same: assurance we gain from the discovery that voice prints are as constant, as permanently expressive as fingerprints. In this case, too, the past physically enters the present.

Why or when this relation between past and present holds our attention are separate questions, related to the past recounted and the present from which the viewer views it. Individual testimony from the Holocaust conveyed to someone who knew nothing more of it than what the testimony told would indicate that something terrible had happened—but heard only by itself, surely the single voice would also, perhaps only, bewilder. "How?" "Why?" The more extraordinary what was recounted, the more urgent such questions would be—and for the combination of improbability and horror conveyed in testimony from the Nazi Genocide, this reaction would be as immediate and as basic as any other. More information is needed, then; the requirement of testimony for the filling in of background, both through other testimony and non-testimonial history, *especially* for such a "corporate" event as the Holocaust, is often overlooked. Yet once that background is confirmed, the single voice stands out from it, beyond that "more"—as it is the immediate contact, the past entering the present (in Barthes's description of the photograph, its "punctum") that compels the impression, sometimes not relying on words at all. (Although a Holocaust "witness" who several times addressed classes of mine held the students' attention as he spoke, when he rolled up his sleeve to show them the tattooed number on his arm, their attention moved to a different level. *That* writing was for them of a different order.)

Once again, we ask why or what the difference—and I suggest here what may seem an improbable group of analogies. Consider: the study preserved in Thomas Hardy's house in Dorchester; the shores of Walden Pond; Rembrandt's Self-Portraits; T. S. Eliot's recording of "The Wasteland"; the memoirs of Glückel of Hameln; Karl Marx's grave in Highgate Cemetery. What is it that draws observers to these "sites of memory"? Surely the particular sites could have been different (differently located, differently contrived). It is not, then, because they are exactly as they are that they exert the power they do— the sort of reasoning or explanation often appealed to for explaining the force or attraction of art. It seems rather to stem from the *fact* of the site as it conveys what *was,* and also *as* it was—with that actuality more than a function of historical truth. What observers or listeners come into contact with in these sites—through vision or hearing, thus through the senses, but still more by the mind—is the past itself: not just *any* past, of course, but one so enlarged by its role in the present as to come alive in itself. The actuality realized in this contact is palpable, cognitive—but its import is personal, moral, practical, with our own present vivified by instances of the past even when they speak of horror.

Testimony becomes in this way a connective thread, all the more important because the fabric in which it works to that effect has otherwise so many knots, gaps, loopholes, and unknowns: the elements of forgetfulness, of dissociation. Testimony is not the only means by which links or connections are marshaled against the lure of fragmentation (and forgetting), in relation to the Holocaust or to any other event; other forms of expression contribute to the same effect, which is, again, the encounter—beyond the fact—with a presence. Admittedly, even with the increased availability of recorded testimonies, it seems certain that the future for many of them is in the obscurity of archives; there we see, truly if unhappily, a surfeit of memory. But this may well be the only possible way of avoiding its alternative which is, after all, a deficit of memory or, still less, its erasure. History without testimony would not be empty, and testimony without history would not be blind—but it would, in both cases, be a near thing.

.3. *The Residue of Trauma:* I touch here on certain edges of the concept of trauma in relation to the Holocaust that, as a subject in itself, Cathy Caruth and Dominick LaCapra have focused on more systematically.[15] One of these "edges" involves the external or historical configuration of the concept of trauma, which seems to me underestimated in its applications to Holocaust memory and Holocaust writing. Historically, the primary usage of the term *trauma* referred to *physical* wounds that were both serious and evident, typically associated with assault or accident rather than nature. In technical medical terminology, before the use of X-rays became standard, the wounds had to be open. (A word search in classical texts places the first use of the Greek term—later appropriated in English—in Aeschylus's *Agamemnon*, as Clytemnestra foreshadows the wounds she would then inflict on Agamemnon.) Many hospitals currently have a "trauma unit" connected to their Emergency Room in which patients are treated only for wounds, and not for other, even life-threatening episodes (like heart attacks or strokes). This background note underscores the derivative and to some extent metaphoric extension of the term to psychological wounds, an extension that is evidently still in progress and thus changing. (Certain recent dictionaries and encyclopedias of psychology, for example, still do not have entries for *trauma* (e.g., *The Gale Dictionary of Psychology, The Concise Encyclopedia of Psychology*); the term itself sometimes appears as a plural noun, sometimes in the singular, sometimes as a substantive, much like the word *dogma* which is a linguistic parallel in the Greek).

Such etymological nuts and bolts would hardly matter if they were not also related to differences in the temporal parameters of the two types of wound that the term has now come to cover. For in respect to physical wounds, present (often, instant) recognition is assumed—in contrast to psychological trauma where evidence of a wound may manifest itself only long after the injury occurs; indeed, it is arguable that the more serious the psychic wound, the longer it may take to manifest itself. It is not that psychological wounds are undetectable when they occur or that their future expression cannot be predicted, but that often (and again, often for the most serious ones) the symptoms do not appear immediately, with the person wounded in no position either to recognize or respond to them, and possibly nobody else present or aware of their occurrence. The psychological wound itself, moreover, may be so severe that the analogue of physiological "shock" (which in physical terms has well-defined medical indicators, principally a sharp drop in blood pressure, sometimes producing unconsciousness) impedes or prevents awareness of the condition on the part of the person who suffers it. The complexity of the temporal dimensions of psychological trauma is exemplified in the language about it—as in the condition of "Post-Traumatic Stress Disorder" (PTSD), where "traumatic" refers to the initial occurrence of the wound(s) rather than to their later expression which is, however, often included in references to trauma in other—principally psychoanalytic—uses.[16]

The contribution of Freud and the psychoanalytic tradition in placing psychological trauma on a level with physical trauma has been extended more speculatively, beyond individual "wounds," to cultures or peoples. Thus, discussions of Holocaust representation in terms of trauma have considered how the Holocaust has affected *collective* Jewish identity and culture; more recently, such discussions have extended their purview to Holocaust trauma in Germany as well.[17] There is nothing new in the suggestion that the phenomenon of the twenty years of relative silence about the Holocaust that characterized its expressive aftermath among both those groups is explicable, at least in part, on a standard model of psychological trauma and the silence often accompanying it: repression shaped by shock and the elements of helplessness, shame, and most of all, injury.

One connection with earlier comments in this chapter may now become apparent: that allusions to the trope of unspeakability or unrepresentability of the Holocaust have *also* to be understood as a rendering of silence occasioned by the traumatic event, as that event was experienced directly (and so now, expressed by survivors) or indirectly, through what was projected as collective memory. In this sense, claims in respect to the Holocaust of unspeakability or even un*think*ability would be neither figurative nor problematic as literal—but literally referential (and verifiable) to the extent that any symptom can be. In respect to this interpretation of silence no less than for its figurative rendering, however, the condition itself is not only not fixed or permanent, but indeed evokes its opposite. Trauma, in the psychoanalytic tradition, can be brought into the open, moved to speak—this arguably being the only means by which trauma begin to heal, insofar as that is possible at all. The process here works not by erasing the wound but quite the contrary—only when its repression, its forced silence and its symptomatic expression in other forms, are broken into, identified, and raised to consciousness: directly thought, represented, parsed. In this way, the silence produced by traumatic experience would be overcome only as it is undone—which is not the tautology it might seem but a causal revision. Here again, the professed unspeakability of events occurring within the Holocaust would be confronted, and so disproven, by their speakability in fact.[18]

At least some of the discussion of trauma in relation to the Holocaust is caught, however, in what finally appears as a dilemma. On the one hand, analysis of the Holocaust and post-Holocaust in terms of trauma has been linked with a sense of the historical distinctiveness of that event, with that distinctiveness evident in its psychological consequences as well as in the historical character of that event. This would suggest that Holocaust trauma constitute a recognizable category—a type or modality of trauma within which individual personal histories are located and, in the event, interpreted. On the other hand, the most prominent and characteristic features of psychological trauma evidently cross the lines among "kinds" of trauma—both within the category of Holocaust trauma and as between that one and others (the latter caused, for examples, by childhood abuse or parental death). It is in fact difficult to imagine any of the conventional occurrences of psychological trauma that would *not* have also occurred in the Holocaust. And few psychological accounts of Holocaust survivors have claimed distinctive patterns (that is, distinctive to the Holocaust as an historical event—even, for that matter, the act of genocide) in the trauma identified among them.

Furthermore, a standard difficulty in conceptualizing psychological trauma persists in connection with Holocaust survivors as well—in determining the relation between symptoms or the expression of trauma and their specific origin: the problem, in other words, of recovered memory. The issue here is related to the distinction mentioned earlier between the historical truth (or falsity) of memory and the testimonial truth that may emerge in the same discourse, indeed in the same words. More than one defender of Wilkomirski's "memoir," for example, has claimed that since his account is authentic *emotionally,* that basis also certifies something akin or even identical to historical authenticity. Insofar as his actual childhood—the dislocation to an orphanage, then to a foster and later an adoptive home, even his imagined experience of the Holocaust—suffices for authenticity in *traumatic* expression (for the sake of argument, this might be granted, although it is not self-evident), it also on this account provides a sufficient ground for its historical representation. In other words, since Wilkomirski might *as well* have lived the history he laid claim to, having lived the experience imaginatively, why not then, also the reality of the related but also "imagined" trauma?

I have indicated above my reasons for skepticism about the conclusions drawn from this line of reasoning; but it does suggest the possibility that analysis of *types* of trauma may discover patterns sufficiently distinctive to constitute a schematism within which Holocaust trauma would be identifiable as a category. Even in the absence of such a typology, however, there is no reason to assume that expressions of trauma are interchangeable or neutral in respect to their individual historical causes. No doubt there are common features of traumatic effect—likenesses that occur as the consequences of quite different sources. So far as trauma are confronted by the recall of their supposed origins, moreover, the sources alleged in the "talking cure" may not be independently verifiable. (This is, to be sure, a version of the larger question of verification that has challenged the psychoanalytic method in general.) There are obviously instances in which the sources of trauma—the "facts" of the matter—remain inaccessible and in which the transactions of the discourse of discovery must themselves set the terms of reference (of what is recalled and its patterns). This broad limitation would, however, itself be limited in the case of Holocaust trauma. For the very enormity of the Holocaust, attested in its public record, provides a defense against such doubts—if not for every individual claim, certainly at large. The Holocaust thus provides uncommon assurance against those critics who dispute "recovered memory" as such—although at the same time and for the same reasons, it adds bitter confirmation (testimony) to the difficulty (more exactly, the impossibility) of "working through" the memory or trauma recovered. It is true that the claim is rarely made that the "talking cure" *erases* the past, allowing "survivors" to live in the present as if the past had not occurred; but it does claim that bringing past trauma into the present—in effect, opening, or more precisely, re-opening the wound—enables its victims to confront and cope with the trauma more fully or adequately. There is thus an intrinsic optimism in the discourse of trauma— and here, it seems to me, especially in relation to an event of the order of the Holocaust, a reverse course to the one I have defended earlier is indicated. Not that the Post-Holocaust should not look back into the Holocaust, in both collective and individual consciousness—but that it should not do this on the assumptions either that trauma, or anything else in the past, *can* be made fully present, or that what can be brought openly into the present will testify fully to itself. In this sense, the phenomenon of trauma indeed supports the claim of unspeakability and the judgment of silence.

* * *

I would hope to anticipate one objection among many possible reactions to the foregoing discussion. I am well aware that even at best, the issues addressed require fuller treatment than they have been given—and that one general effect of the discussion so far might be said to "normalize" the Holocaust, with all the pejorative implications of that phrase: to show that the Nazi Genocide is at once within history and human comprehension, that its most distinctive testimonial voices have nonetheless to be understood and assessed in relation to other voices, and even that the wounds or trauma resulting from the Holocaust are also subject to the common capacity or, just as likely, *in*capacity of expression. It would then seem to follow that in these respects (and presumably others that follow from them), the Holocaust becomes only another historical moment—one among the many atrocities that the twentieth century so inventively contrived; that there is nothing distinctive about it, in either historical or moral terms.

This conclusion, however, moves in just the opposite direction to that in which I have meant to turn. For I would indeed wish to claim that the Holocaust is distinctive—so much, in fact, that one need not step outside history or the standard patterns of historical, reflective, and social analysis to show this to be the case. The argument seems to me much weightier that through *standard* patterns and categories, one sees more of the individual character of the Holocaust, the deliberate effort at genocide which distinguishes it, and, behind that, the underlying will to violate all moral norms, than one does by projecting the features of that event on an extra-historical space—the tendency encouraged by claims for it as unique or incomprehensible, as requiring privileged statements of witnessing or a distinctive character for Holocaust trauma. This practical justification seems to me only to reaffirm the more basic historical ground that argues to the same effect. In support of such a mingling of skepticism and affirmation, I would repeat a stricture that Primo Levi introduces in his last and, as often noted, his most pessimistic book, *The Drowned and the Saved*. The warning that Levi bequeaths to his readers is this: that whatever testimony we hear and credit, we do not and never will have the most decisive testimony—by which all accounts and understanding of the Holocaust must be measured and in the absence of which other accounts remain provisional, problematic, and open to question. This is the testimony of the witnesses who died. If it is to words in the first person that we defer, the absence of *their* words qualifies whatever significance we attach to the words we do hear; where it is experience that speaks, their experience, after all, would speak last and conclusively.

The idioms or views of Holocaust representation about which questions have been raised here seem to me to converge on the common claim made for the uniqueness of the Holocaust—its incomparability—which are in effect, again, synonyms for its incomprehensibility. Like the Uniqueness thesis itself, however, such claims seem to me to have precisely the opposite effect from what they intend. For the distinctiveness of the Holocaust becomes most visible not through the lenses of extra-historical categories but in the material and moral history of everyday causality and judgment—which is where, after all, difficult as it is to comprehend and still more to believe, the Holocaust originated, grew, and numbered its victims.

SEVEN

Undoing Certain Mischievous Questions about the Holocaust

Certain questions frequently asked about the Holocaust have been, are—quite simply—mischievous. I mean by this that at the same time these questions ask or inquire, they also mislead, distort, cause trouble—and this in a setting that is already so very deeply troubled. The mischief caused in this way will not be undone only by emphasizing the fact or by gaining an understanding of how it was caused—but I hope by such means to advance that undoing. I propose, then, to identify the most notable of these mischievous questions, to show how they are harmful—and then also to suggest how this harm can be avoided, since the questions themselves, almost despite themselves, are capable of re-habilitation, and that, too, I attempt. In this way, the same questions may be preserved, asked and even answered—but without their mischief. It is not their fault, at least not *entirely,* that they have been misused.

The account given here is less concerned with the motives or intentions be-hind the questions than with their consequences—specifically with the way they coerce or slant the responses to them. For against the background of the Holocaust, where even slight missteps in understanding loom large, the effects of mischievous questions about that event—not outright falsifications, but subtler, more angular shifts—take on larger proportions. The "manifest" con-tent of these questions *appears* innocent—so much so that the mischief "latent" in them often passes unnoticed; at times it has even been praised as honest or courageous. Much of the trouble that these questions cause, in other words, is hidden behind a mask of the commonplace. And the problem is not that the questions are simply "rhetorical" or assertions in disguise. They do pose au-thentic queries and so also warrant answers—but what is authentic in them will remain concealed or distorted until what is *not* authentic in them is diagnosed.

I probably should by this point have named the guilty questions, but my delay in doing this reflects their own indirection—the covert way in which they attempt to shape responses to them. For the "mischievous" questions in effect tie the hands of the audience whom they address; more basically, they tie their *own* hands, prejudicing the line of inquiry so that the responses to them mirror the questions themselves. Thus, the questions falsify the representations of the Holocaust for which they claim accuracy and fairness. Admittedly, it might be objected that no questions are entirely innocent: all questions, after all, originate in limited contexts, are driven by partial concerns—and always they lean toward answers from one direction or other. But the mischievous questions criticized here are so slanted in their usual appearances that it is their prejudice, not the substantive issues they raise, that warrant our first attention.

But how, it might be asked, can *questions* be mischievous? After all, they inquire rather than assert, always allowing at least some freedom of response—at times, the freedom not to respond at all. But we know, too, that questions can also be "loaded"—and this quite precisely describes the questions criticized here; their air of innocence only adds to the harm they cause, which follows from a three-step progression. First, the questions draw on an accepted basis in fact which then provides a cover once the questions leave that starting point behind—which they quickly do. Second, the questions are posed apart from any comparative historical context—falsely implying that such a context would make no difference. In this way, what is made at first to appear to be a historical question remains in fact *a*-historical. Third, the "implied author" of the question, the voice asking the question, assumes a privileged position in respect to the people referred to by the questions, at the same time offering the same privilege (something like a bribe) to the question's reader or audience. In this last respect, then, the questions reach beyond the Holocaust as a past event into our own present: now. For not only do the questions I am challenging pronounce a moral judgment on actions taken (or avoided) during the Holocaust, but the person asking the questions also implies that he himself would have acted more commendably than did the people in the Holocaust about whom he speaks. And unintentional as this projection backward may be, its conclusions add self-righteousness (and further mischief) to an already severe moral judgment.

What, then, *are* these mysterious questions? Not mysterious at all, I should claim, but all too familiar. So familiar, in fact, that their usual appearances rely entirely on pronouns, with no need, evidently, to name specific names or referents. Thus, the best known and also, in my view, the most mischievous of these questions:

Question 1: "Why didn't they resist?"[1] There will be immediate recognition that the *they* in this question designates the Holocaust victims. The question thus sets out from the generally accepted contention that they, the victims—principally, the Jews of Europe—went from life to death largely, mainly, without open or physical resistance. And so, the question seems to follow of "Why? Why, with the cruel and certain fate awaiting them, *didn't* they resist?"—with all of that question's harsh but unstated implications. For what the question itself clearly suggests—in effect, asserts—is that the victims could have resisted when they did not; that had they resisted, they might not have become victims—or if they did, they might at least have helped others. At the very least, even if these other possibilities were not realized, they would have won respect for themselves by the act of resistance. But none of this, or very little of it, happened.

Now the basis in fact underlying this first question could not be more concrete or specific—or accurate. The numbers driving it are the most basic numbers of the Holocaust—since it is the number of Jews murdered that is central here—and so the figure generally accepted among historians of between 5,200,000 and 6,000,000. (Such numbers, it is obvious, must be approximate; it is quite improbable that history itself would round off its totals as neatly as historians do; in the context of *writing* history on this scale, hundreds or thousands or tens of thousands and even hundreds of thousands do not substantially alter its overall shape). Juxtaposed to that number, furthermore, is the statistical record of Jewish resistance—at least as defined in terms of instances when members of the Jewish populace fought openly against the fate of deportation, or subsequently against the concentration and death that awaited them in the ghettoes and camps. And this number, although over time it has been recognized to be larger than had at first been acknowledged, yet remains small compared to the mass number of dead. Partisan groups, yes: in the Baltic States, Poland, Russia and Slovakia—but, in terms of numbers, this only in the thousands, hardly more. The Underground in the ghettoes of Poland and Lithuania, yes—but always with the burden of the Nazi threat to obliterate the ghettoes if that opposition came into the open; thus effectual if at all mainly at the end of the ghettoes' existence (as in Warsaw), by which time fewer able-bodied fighters remained in the ghettoes who *could* resist—thus, at a point when hope was virtually lost. And in the camps themselves—yes, too, but minimally and almost harmlessly (that is, for the Nazis and their collaborators).[2]

None of these efforts, then, however one honors the courage represented in them, makes much of a dent in the impression of the millions who were killed; the proportion of resisters to victims remains small. And so, on the face of it, it seems reasonable to call attention to the power that the millions *might* have had if they had joined together in resistance—or even if, singly, they had struck at individual executioners. Why not, after all? In this way, too, the question (and the questioner) link the small proportion of resisters to still another assertion: that if *other* groups of people had stood in the place of the Jews, they might have reacted differently: more courageously, more strongly, more honorably, not at all like "sheep going to the slaughter," as that memorable phrase has been applied to a world which its Psalmist-author could not possibly have imagined.

Well, why not resistance? The implied answer to this question, set in the question itself, is that there must have been some fault in the people who became victims in this unusual, and discreditable, way, one that made them react as they did—which was, the question supposes, hardly to react at all. Seen from this perspective, the victims were to some extent—harsh as the verdict sounds—responsible for their own fates: a short step from blameworthy. And the reasons or causes behind that are also often hinted at, although they are usually left deliberately vague. Perhaps as reflecting ideological or cultural infirmity: the "ghetto" mentality, bred of centuries lived in the shadow of the political power of others; perhaps from religious passivity, faith in a God whose intervention was, at least in this instance, vainly awaited. Perhaps, more prosaically, because of a failure in overcoming economic or class liabilities, the social dependencies of the victims having become ingrained or inbred, and in any event leaving them unfit for practical or instrumental action. Each of these possibilities, and various combinations of them, have figured in histories and theories of the Holocaust. Indeed, the specific explanation hardly matters to the person who asks this first question, since it is the prima facie evidence (the *supposed* evidence) that speaks here: approximately six million dead without much cost to their attackers or much honor to themselves. To be sure, the victims paid dearly for this supposed incapacity—and so the implied charge of failure is usually left muted, concealed in the question. Everybody more or less knows "why" they didn't resist—and at any rate, the question and its basis in fact are more important than any possible explanation: "they" didn't resist when they might have and when, for a multitude of reasons ranging from justice to self-respect to revenge and even to the natural instinct for survival, they should have.

On the surface, then, the question of "Why didn't they resist?" seems not unreasonable—harsh, but not unfair. Where, in any event, is the mischief in it? And the answer to *that* question comes quickly on the heels of a well-hidden premise assumed in the question; namely, the assumption that the Jewish passivity alleged was at once exceptional and remiss—an atypical failing in the reaction of people to threats against their lives. But is the truth of this hidden premise so obvious? Is what it asserts true at all? Does it rest on evidence of how *other* groups or individuals reacted in similar circumstances? The answer to all these "counter"-questions is, I believe, *No*—with the last of them the most important of all. Because far from supporting the criticism implied in this first question, the comparative evidence argues for a contradictory conclusion. I mean by this, quite simply, that in the context of the systematic brutality of the Nazi regime, resistance on all fronts, in all circumstances—including circumstances much more favorable to resistance than those in which the Jews found themselves—was far from common; it was and would be out of the ordinary, notable just because it was exceptional.

In the considerable body of evidence that supports this claim, one item among many stands out. During the Nazi war against the USSR, which began in June 1941, approximately 3,000,000 Russian prisoners of war (out of about 5,000,000 who were taken) are generally recognized to have died in captivity. These 3,000,000 were members of the Russian armed forces who had surrendered or been overpowered by the Germans. Some of these prisoners were killed immediately, others were placed in "camps"—some of the latter improvised and temporary encirclements, some of them (as the War went on) the concentration and death camps that have since become well known.[3] A significant feature of this number of 3,000,000 is the fact that these Russian prisoners had been fit enough to serve in the armed forces; they also—again unlike most of the murdered Jews—had had military training; approximately two of the three million, moreover, were taken prisoner in the first year of the Nazi attack—which meant that when captured they would have been relatively fit. Yet the record of resistance among these prisoners, although there is some, is sparse—not notably stronger, in any event, than that of the Jewish ghettoes or camps. Should we then infer a collective disability also in this second, quite different group? Or should we rather begin to consider more intently the force and design of the Nazi system—and what the requirements are, humanly, psychologically, for conceiving and initiating acts of resistance. The necessity for this comparative perspective is further underscored by other Nazi atrocities carried out against non-Jewish groups, including both civilian and military victims (albeit on a smaller scale). Recall, for example, the razing of the Czech village, Lidice, and the execution of its male inhabitants, the executions at Oradour in France, the murder of the Italian prisoners-of-war on the Greek island of Kefalonia—all instances of massacre and also without evidence of significant resistance. Most often the victims were killed in cold blood, sometimes with torture, frequently with great humiliation, almost always with the victims conscious beforehand of what was being done to them. And again, with little or no resistance.[4]

On the basis of such evidence, then, if we are to ask fairly, "Why didn't they resist?"—that is, if we are to avoid its mischief—we must expand its reference beyond the Jews alone. For a more responsible phrasing would ask why didn't more of the captive populations under Nazi control who were victims of persecution and punishment—more or all of these groups—resist more quickly or fully or actively? And even *this* question is pertinent only as it also considers what is required to conceive and initiate acts of resistance—avoiding the assumption that lack of resistance by these groups necessarily reflects a common social or cultural defect.[5] To be sure, the reasons for failing to resist more than they did may have varied among different groups. It might also be objected that because no other group faced genocidal extermination, their awareness of that fate should have evoked a stronger response from the Jews than from other groups. This objection might be debated—but well before we come to that we encounter the evidence of the widespread common reaction and its most obvious explanation. The nations occupied and the groups held captive by the Nazis indeed shared something in common: each was confronted with an organized system of command through the Wehrmacht and the SS—a system which, even given the practical "difficulties" it faced, was quite precise and competent in its planning and organization, and which, most importantly, admitted few if any limits on the brutality it was prepared to use in implementing those plans.[6]

The degree of control achieved by the Nazis in their campaigns and in their occupation of conquered countries was, for all its occasional gaps, sustained if not total; this was accomplished by a combination of force and various economic and ideological pressures, abetted in these by local collaborators acting for their own motives. In this sense, the answer to the question of "Why didn't they resist?" seems obvious—so obvious that the question becomes mischievous insofar as it implies that the answer is *not* obvious, that there are reasons, putatively in the victims themselves, for their lack of resistance. It is true that as a group singled out for destruction, the number (and still more, the percentage) of Jews killed by the Nazis was high; it is also probably true that Jewish communal responses to this threat reflected collective dispositions and the tendencies of historical institutions that had evolved among the Jewish communities of Europe (how could it be otherwise?); in this sense, there may indeed have been something typical and symptomatic in the "Jewish" reaction to the menace of the "Final Solution." But even allowing for such features, the more basic response to the question of "Why didn't they resist?" ought to look not at the Jews but at the Nazis—and how any, and then all, the other groups they conquered and then ruled and then often also persecuted, reacted. Only then, it seems, would the question, "Why didn't they resist?" be fairly put—and then too, would the answer begin to emerge, but from the opposite direction than the one usually cited. For just as we have to consider the extremity of the measures that the Nazis were prepared to take, we must also consider, also comparatively, the "normal" human response to extreme situations; that is, the common reaction to them of avoidance or denial—at a farther extreme, a sense of fatalism and acceptance. Could the Jews, even in the midst of the Holocaust, have done more than they did to save themselves or others? No doubt. But this by itself hardly distinguishes them from other groups confronted by the Nazi onslaught (Jehovah's Witnesses are perhaps, as a group—a small one—the sole exception to this; they, it seems, could not have done more than they did, refusing to compromise even when, unlike the persecuted Jews, they were given an option that would have ensured their survival. But it is also true that they were not automatically condemned to death—and it is also true that they are exceptional.) The reason why there were not more heroes among Nazi victims is undoubtedly the same reason there are so few heroes ever or anyplace.

Question 2: "How could they have done what they did?" The *they* inquired about here differs radically from the "they" of the first question, but its reference seems just as clear and transparent. For when we attempt to understand how the country of Bach and Goethe, of Dürer and Kant, of many of the great universities and great libraries and great cities of the world, how this same people would go on to imagine and operate the death factories—gas chambers and crematoria working in concert—the disparity commands attention: Is it the same country or culture? Could those responsible for the death factories have possessed human conscience or emotions at all? How could they (or anyone) do what they did? But the mischief in this question is nearly as evident as that in the first one. For behind the large gap it finds between Nazi actions and "normal" evildoing is the implication that the people responsible for this disparity—for its terrible violations of Germany's cultural heritage and of international moral norms—must also have been extraordinary. In other words, the criminality of the Nazis and their collaborators was so excessive that explanations in terms of "normal" wrongdoing fail. A quite different order of explanation is required—one that speaks of more than human, of demonic evil.[7]

But once again: Instances of extraordinary evildoing initiated by individuals or by specific groups surely have occurred historically, and it seems clear that certain individual figures within the Nazi hierarchy ought deservedly to be judged in these terms. But the question of "How could *they* have done what they did?" as it encompasses the "Final Solution," that is, the entire process of genocide, must include not only the echelons of the Nazi hierarchy responsible for making policy, but also the larger group of Germans, numbering in the millions, who did not make policy or give orders but who nonetheless contributed to the advance of Nazi plans, who—finally—made the "Final Solution" possible. (We are speaking, after all, of a population of about 70,000,000, with little more than 10 percent of that populace members of the Nazi party at its peak).[8] So there were workers in the industrial factories producing shoes as well as crematoria, railroad workers maintaining the transportation system and schedule, postal and telegraph workers, farmers who earned their livings by provisioning the armed forces, and then too, as we work our way upward, the middle-aged and often apolitical "ordinary men" (as described, for instance, by Christopher Browning in his account of Police Battalion 101) who took part in extraordinary atrocities but whose most notable feature, nonetheless, seems to have been their "ordinariness."[9] All of them taxpayers, most with families, few differing in any apparent way from their counterparts elsewhere in Germany or, one might surmise, in other countries. Whatever is and probably will remain unclear about their motives or characters, these millions of contributors to the "Final Solution" seem indeed "all-too-human," providing no reason to believe—and much reason to doubt—that the roles they played which were indisputably crucial to the Nazi project as a whole differed significantly from what many (not all, but many) people of other nations, classes, religions, or ideologies, had *they* been suddenly transported into that same set of circumstances, would have done.

This contention does not in the slightest measure exonerate the Germans who did make policy or those who, however "ordinary," directly committed atrocities or those others who did neither but simply "went along" with these other actions. Nor does it elide the difference between any of these groups and other people, elsewhere, who (as I have proposed) might in the same circumstances have acted in the same way—but who were not present and did not. It does mean, however, that the question, "How could *they* have done what they did?" implying that what the Germans did individually or as a nation sets them apart from other groups or people by a more than human-sized chasm, is misleading—and more than that, because of the moral stakes at issue, mischievous. It pushes responses to that question in a direction that would let both questioner and respondent off the hooks of history and moral responsibility—on both of which hooks they (and we) *should be* stuck.

Again, it is the Nazis and their collaborators—corporately, Germany—who did what they did, and who remain responsible. But the reasons and causes for what they did are neither outside history nor outside human nature. Others could have and might have done what they did, including, we might surmise, the person asking the question of "How could *they* have done what they did?" It is, in other words, mistaken—groundless—to assume that a unique disposition or character is required to understand why the Germans, as a group or individually, acted as they did in the context of the Third Reich. Prima facie, a much less inflationary, more banal explanation is indicated—one that locates the Germans of the Third Reich in the domain of conventional human nature, impelled by such "normal" human features as (perceived) self-interest, social pressures that readily turn into cruelty, frustration as it turns into anger, economic uncertainty and need, even simple greed or self-indulgence. To find such commonplace motives leading to acts of extraordinary brutality is no doubt unsettling—and it should be. But those ordinary human motives ought to be faced in their own terms, not by evasions that explain the Nazi Genocide by a distinctive social (let alone, genetic) trait that sets the Germans essentially apart from other people or groups. This second mischievous question seems finally to suggest that what the Germans did in the Holocaust was due to the fact that they were German. And although it is surely pertinent to inquire in respect to the Germans, as for any group or individual, what accounts for their specific decisions or actions, to explain these by positing some mysterious (and ad hoc) characteristic is as mystifying—and mischievous—as it would be to deny the possibility of any explanation at all. Which is in effect what this question does.

Question 3: "Why didn't more people do what they did?" Once again, there can be little doubt about the reference of the third person pronoun in this question. For among the large group of "bystanders" in the Holocaust, we know that a small number tried to help victims of Nazi persecution—extending themselves to Jewish strangers, many of them alien in language and manner, all of them in peril of death. And the question—again, superficially plausible—asks why, with the plight of these victims often in full view, more bystanders, who were themselves under no immediate threat, did not offer help: food or money or—on a larger scale—shelter and hiding places. Here again, the person asking the question privileges himself: not only should more people have offered such help, but the questioner (we are to suppose) would have been among them. This insinuation adds weight to the question—since if the questioner is so confident that *he* would have been among the rescuers, why should there not also have been many others?

This implication is assumed in the phrase "Righteous Gentiles" that has been applied to the rescuers—and again, with some warrant. It is the non-Jews as a group who were in a position to extend aid, but who, in much their largest numbers, did not. Why—the question implies—if some of them could be righteous, were not more of them, if not all, also righteous? It is indeed a matter of fact that almost sixty years later, fewer than 20,000 names appear on the list vetted by Yad Vashem's special committee—20,000 out of 300,000,000, to give an approximate figure for the non-Jewish population of countries under Nazi control at the peak of their power. And such disproportion appears in this third question as evidence not so much of the heroism of the "Righteous among the Nations" but as proof of the moral failure of the hundreds of millions of others who were not "righteous"—but who could and should have been.

But is it so obvious that there *should* have been more "Righteous Gentiles" than there were? The requirements set for this group in the Yad Vashem register (putting aside for the moment the phrase's invidious distinction between Gentiles and non-Gentiles) are explicit and, superficially, simple: they must have risked their lives in order to help Jews threatened by the Nazis, and they must have done this without expectation of compensation or reward. But these requirements are, of course, not simple at all. We know that under Nazi rule, punishment for aiding or concealing Jews often included the threat of death and always of incarceration in the camps; often the threat of such punishment did not stop with the "offenders" but extended to their families—and so, one must add that those who risked their own lives to save Jews would also have been risking the lives of close relations: spouses, children. And now, turning inward, if we ask *ourselves* who among our relatives or friends—not strangers, which the Jews often *were* in the misfortunes of war, but people close to us—if we ask who in this circle of ours we could rely on for such help if the penalty was probable or even just possible death for the person and possibly also for his or her family: how large would this number be? To what extent could we honestly include *ourselves* in that number?

We hardly have to take this thought-experiment any further to see the hollowness of the third question, with its implication that there *should* have been more such rescuers; that what they did was to have been expected of them, and thus also of others. By widely accepted moral standards, the rescuers were not simply righteous but heroes; for they acted beyond the call of duty—doing more than they or anyone was obligated to. In none of the principal religious or secular moral codes is there a *duty* of self-sacrifice, of acting heroically. And the reason for this is clear: heroes, by definition, do more than is obligatory— where most people, most often, are hard put to do even as much as they ought to. Certainly we honor acts of self-sacrifice—but that is because such acts are not required. (Remember that the acts involved are entirely voluntary; they are not, for example, rejections of a command to kill someone else or to be killed oneself. To die rather than to do that would, in many moral codes, be a moral obligation—but the issue for the "Righteous Gentiles" was quite different, with the decision whether to risk their lives and the lives of others in their families entirely in their hands.) Again, the issue here is not whether to risk one's life in order to save someone else's is praiseworthy, but whether it is obligatory—with the answer to that, by the moral standards generally accepted, being "Surely not." Indeed, a more responsible version of the mischievous question, "Why weren't there more of them?" could well ask instead, "Why were there as many of them as there were?" The paucity in numbers of the heroic rescuers, furthermore, reflects the broader difficulty of ever finding an adequate explanation for their extraordinary acts of conscience or courage. This difficulty might recall the failure of explanations elsewhere of artistic or scientific genius: their occurrence is too exceptional to fit ordinary or perhaps any categories. And why, after all, should there not be a place for moral genius as well?

This third mischievous question, furthermore, has the added consequence of drawing attention away from another, and more basic, issue than the one referred to. This is the issue of what could reasonably have been required of Holocaust bystanders, given that they were *not* obligated to act heroically. For the focus on extraordinary requirements and responses has the effect of pushing aside more reasonable ones. It seems obvious, for example, that, in the context of the Holocaust, many more bystanders than did so could have acted in ways impeding its process without putting themselves or others in danger— and that such acts, in contrast to more dangerous ones, might indeed be termed obligatory. No German citizens were required to volunteer for the SS or to join the Nazi party; none was required to smash Jewish shop windows or to take over vacated apartments or to appropriate other abandoned property; nobody was required to replace Jewish professionals or businessmen who had been forced to leave their positions or practices; even soldiers under military command were typically not *compelled* to participate in atrocities. Had rudimentary moral dictates entailing no dangerous consequences been followed here, the "Final Solution" might not have been avoided, but it would almost certainly have been impeded. And that means that this third question of why there weren't more rescuers in the Holocaust willing to risk their lives to save others has two harmful consequences: it undervalues the actions of the people who did so by suggesting that they were only doing what they (and everyone else) ought to have done. And at the same time, it ignores obligations reasonably assigned to bystanders who, like most of humankind, were not heroic (and could hardly be blamed for this) but who still had an ordinary and common ideal of humanity to live up to, but who often did not.[10] A mischievous question, indeed.

* * *

The three questions cited are the most egregious of those that in their familiar form speak misleadingly about the Holocaust. It is worth noting, and probably not accidental, that the three correspond (respectively) to the three Holocaust "principals" commonly distinguished in analyses of the Holocaust: victims, perpetrators, and bystanders. Clearly nobody is exempt. To be sure, additional such questions are readily evident. So, for example, in the question *"Why didn't they just leave?"*—the *they* here again obviously referring to the Jews who, because they didn't leave their homes in Europe when they were able to, would soon after that turn into victims. This question usually points at the German Jews who had immediate experience between 1933 and 1939 of what a Nazi regime would hold for them. In point of fact, there *was* a substantial exodus of Jews from Germany, and ultimately, the percentage of German Jewish survivors was higher than that of most European countries. Accordingly, this question should be understood as asking, "Why didn't *all* of them leave? Why would anyone stay?"—and in these terms, once again the mischief in the question shows itself, specifically in two assumptions: First, that it should have been obvious to German Jews that the future would be much worse than the past, that it would indeed put their lives at risk. And second, that they should have been readier than they were to give up their homes and possessions, to leave family, professional positions, and community—all this in order to depart for alien lands and an uncertain future. (The question has no point for German Jews after 1941 when emigration was forbidden—but the "Final Solution," it needs to be recalled, was decided upon and implemented only after that.)

In retrospect, of course, the Jews of Germany, and of Eastern Europe too, would indeed have been better off had they left when they were able to (carrying this frivolous argument to its extreme, they would have been still better off if their ancestors had not settled in Europe in the first place). That it was possible up to a certain date for more of them to leave than did leave is also true. But the implication of the question as it is usually put is that the decision to leave should have been obvious and easy—and easy *because* obvious. But the fact is that it was not obvious—and even when obvious, certainly not easy. To be sure, we know that people faced with adversity often resort to avoidance and self-deception—and when they do this against convincing evidence, they may indeed be held accountable. But at least until 1938, the belief that there were limits to the extent of Nazi designs was arguable—and so, too, was a ground for expecting something less than the catastrophe that ensued. The mischief here is not especially in the easy wisdom of hindsight but in the distance asserted between the person asking the question and those about whom it is asked—as if to say, once again, that what held the Jews in their places, blocking the obvious step they should have taken, was a group defect of sorts, a collective illusion of their own making. And that claim seems to rest on nothing more in the way of evidence than—circularly—the very fact it purports to explain. To say that people were mistaken on human and understandable grounds is quite different from explaining it by a common collective defect.

Not only the Holocaust itself, moreover, has occasioned mischievous questions of the sort mentioned. The sixty *post*-Holocaust years have nourished their own varieties. A number of recent books with such titles like *Selling the Holocaust* or *The Holocaust Industry* purport on the surface to call attention to the exploitation of the Holocaust, objecting to the use made of that event for political or ideological or commercial purposes.[11] Now it might be supposed that charges of such exploitation (and who, after all, would deny its occurrence?) would also acknowledge that notwithstanding such abuse, the core of Holocaust history remains an important matter of historical record and moral conscience, one that warrants continued study as well as commemoration and other forms of representation. In other words, there should be, there could hardly not be, it would be wrong to do without, talk about the Holocaust. But the thrust of this recent "genre" of Post-Holocaust literature suggests that not only have there been excesses in specific representations of the Holocaust, but that the attention given the Holocaust has been excessive as such. In other words, the mischievous question asks: "Why do they talk *so much* about the Holocaust?"—the implication here being that there is *too much* talk: too many books, too many memorials, too many museums; that other events are no less deserving, that the undue attention paid to the Holocaust diminishes or trivializes other comparable events. Some of these critics then conclude that the Holocaust should not be talked about by itself at all; for some of them, in order to right the balance, the Holocaust should be talked about less and less; for all of them, the question they ask of why there is "so much" (that is, *too* much) talk about the Holocaust assumes for the speaker a privileged role as judge of how much talk about the Holocaust is proper or not. But here, too, the question posed undoes itself. No doubt there are various reasons for "so much" talk about the Holocaust—and some of these, no doubt, are bad reasons. But even to consider regulating such talk suggests the waywardness of the question itself: who is in a position to do this, by what standards, and to what purpose? The refrain from a familiar children's story seems to stand in the background here: there should not be too much such talk, not too little—but just right. But where does that leave us that we have not already been? And why should we accept the question's premise that there is "too much" talk at all?

A related Post-Holocaust question concerns the truth status of Holocaust historiography. Once again, the question begins with a basis in fact: historical analyses of the Holocaust do disagree on certain important matters of interpretation, including so fundamental an issue as the nature of its causes. Given disagreements of that magnitude, then, it might seem plausible to hear a question that asks, "*Don't they realize that history is all interpretation, all the way down—from start to finish; that there isn't any way, at any point, of getting it (that is, history) right?*"[12] This question moves quickly from the fact of differences in interpretation (which nobody would deny) to skepticism about the possibility of true or false historical statements at any level—which is, however, a very different matter. The mischief in this question, although subtler than in the others, in the end requires less elaboration than they do—since it implies that even about the most basic elements of Holocaust history, there is no way of "getting them right." And to carry this skeptical claim to its logical conclusion would also be to claim that there is no basis for choosing between the assertion that the Holocaust occurred and the assertion that it did not—since, again, if they are equal as hypotheses, neither (by its own terms) would be entitled to claim that it had gotten the history right. Indeed, the two views could hardly claim that they disagreed—since they would have previously agreed that there is no "thing" or matter of fact to disagree about. The harm in this conclusion may seem more prospective than actual, since it is the possible future of Holocaust-denial rather than its past or present that is most troubling. But the issue of objectivity in historical judgment is very much a present one. Difficult as it is for us who live in the tradition of liberal political discourse to admit, it is simply not true that there are two sides to every story.

I have written here of these various questions as mischievous, meaning by this that the answers they invite misrepresent important facets of the Holocaust. It is not only that the questions cited are "leading" questions, but that the directions in which they "lead" are specious, both from the standpoint of the person asking the question and in the representation conveyed. The questioners, moreover, repeatedly privilege themselves: the failings noted in the questions do not apply to them (they claim). Still more to the point of mischief-making is what the questions do to their subject, with each of them misrepresenting the Holocaust by moving it outside the categories of "normal" history and moral analysis. The effect of this, I hope to have shown, is not only mistaken in fact, but mischievous beyond that, insofar as it locates the Holocaust in an ahistorical vacuum, and then blames and praises in the wrong order or on the wrong grounds (or both).

More positively, what I have been arguing *for* is that reflection about the Holocaust, whatever direction it takes, requires as a premise recognition that the distance between us now, looking back at that event, and those who sixty years ago were caught up in it, is a human-sized distance, not at all beyond the reach of human possibility in our own world and—more to the immediate point—in us. If any single lesson can be drawn from the Holocaust, surely it is that if such an event happened once, it can happen twice. But to say this, and to mean it, is also to understand that questions we ask about the Holocaust will be falsified if we treat them impersonally, as though the enormity of that event, insulated by the sixty years since, places its motives and causes as well as its consequences beyond our own capacity and surroundings. The evidence—historical, moral—argues strongly against that belief. Are there then any questions about the Holocaust that are not, or *cannot* be mischievous? At this point, the only answer I can think of to that question is "Probably not—except, of course, for that one. . . . "

EIGHT

From the Particular to the Universal, and Forward
Representations and Lessons

When we hear the phrase *"representations of the Holocaust,"* we think first of artistic representations: novels or films or paintings or even, as Art Spiegelman has demonstrated, comic strips, all of them incorporating events or themes linked to the occurrence of the Holocaust, now almost sixty years in the past. We may also in this connection think of Holocaust memorials—which, like other memorials or monuments, recall particular events or figures in that past, re-presenting them for the present. These indeed yield forms or genres of Holocaust representation that deserve attention as well as respect, as they provide access to the past from the present. But it is also important to recognize that representations of the Holocaust originate at a more basic level than those of art alone; indeed, that as soon as we find ourselves outside the event of the Holocaust—which is where everyone now stands in respect to that event, including those who were once most directly inside it—we immediately find ourselves in a field of representation on which also artistic expression depends: first in historical representation, as historical writing and discourse deploys its own characteristic genres and tropes, but then also, prior to that, in linguistic representation. That is, in the currency of language itself, as its images and icons and connectives at once express and shape the "prose of the world" in the articulation of commonplace events, but also and more notably, of extraordinary ones. Like the Holocaust.[1]

The most pointed appearance of linguistic representation in relation to the Holocaust occurs in the phrase, *the Holocaust* itself, which has come now to designate (that is, to represent) broadly if not universally the Nazi Genocide against the Jews—the attempt, to repeat again Himmler's memorable words, to make that group of people "disappear." In what way is *the Holocaust* a representation? First, of course, in the term *holocaust* itself—a word not commonly used either before or after "the Holocaust" and which in its origins in the

Greek Septuagint refers to the type of sacrifice at the Temple in Jerusalem that was "consumed entirely" (in Hebrew, *Olah*) in contrast to other sacrifices that were not burnt in their entirety. The term's English meaning since the seventeenth century has shifted to suggest large or intense destruction—early on, natural destruction, but increasingly including man-made occurrences as well. (In *The Great Gatsby*, Fitzgerald concludes the scene in which Gatsby's body is found floating in his swimming pool: "The holocaust was complete.") But the original layer of religious connotation and to some extent of sacrifice still clings to the usage in a way that critics of that representation (I include myself here) find problematic.[2] The process by which the term *holocaust* came to be *the Holocaust*—the shift to upper case and the application of the definite article—is also, of course, part of this history of representation. (Prior to 1960, fifteen years after the Holocaust ended, the New York Times Index still did not include an entry for *Holocaust*.)

The use of the definite article in association with *Holocaust* adds to its representation the implication either that there was only one *holocaust* or that even if there were others, the one designated by the phrase stands out among them in a way that requires no further explanation. When Americans speak about *the Civil War*, there's no doubt in their minds about the specific war they refer to, although many other countries have also had civil wars; *"the" Crucifixion* refers to one crucifixion in particular, although crucifixion itself was a common means of execution among the Greeks and Romans. So, too, *"the" Holocaust*— as the phrase implies that the event referred to differs from other past and even possible holocausts: not only a representation, but an unmistakable one.

Much more might be said about this one example, but the point at issue is a broader one, claiming that the study of language used and created during or after the Holocaust provides an important and still unfolding means of analyzing that event. And if thinking about the Holocaust, as indeed thinking about any historical event, is locked into the world of representation in this way, shaping and then interpreting tokens or figures that serve as the necessary medium for thinking, remembering, feeling—then the importance of examining the representations we use, often unconsciously and as a matter of habit, should be clear: the more so, as what they are representations of carries unusual moral weight. Only by such scrutiny of public representations ("public" here redundant but not irrelevant) is it possible to measure or test our own private selves, since they are, after all, the outside of our own insides.

I propose to consider here two common representations of the Holocaust that warrant attention in their conjunction for an odd reason: the fact that at one level, they appear to be—they *are*—contradictory, but that viewed from another perspective, they require or entail each other, with each of the two claims plausible in its own separate terms. The two representations, then, turn out to be at once contradictory and necessary. How can this be?

The answer to that question appears in the two claims advanced through the representations themselves. The Holocaust—one of them asserts—can be understood only as a particular historical event that involved individual perpetrators and individual victims. This is what happened, and this is the way it happened—and representations that stray from this particularist ground, that attempt to place the event in a more general or abstract context, falsify it, necessarily blunting the edge that made it what it was. But—on the other hand—the Holocaust can only be understood in universal terms, since it *could* have occurred at other times and places than it did, with other victims and with other perpetrators. To regard any aspect of the Holocaust as distinctive or particular, let alone as unique—aside from the general truth (virtually a tautology) that every historical event is particular and unique—is in this respect to falsify history and, for the case at hand, also the Holocaust itself.

I do not attempt here to reconcile these two conflicting views—each apparently valid in its own terms—mainly because I do not think it can be done. But there is a way, I believe, of placing them within a single and broader framework that establishes an informative relation between them. The direction in which the attempt to do this might go is suggested in the first part of this chapter's title: "From the Particular to the Universal, and Forward." For indeed, it seems that in order to understand the Holocaust (at least to come as close to understanding as possible), those three steps, in that order, are required: to consider the Holocaust first as "particular," then as "universal," and finally (as understanding and, I should argue, history itself require), to advance past the joint grounds of the particular and the universal.

First, then, to the first "particular"—and the central question it raises concerning the Holocaust, the one question on which all other questions about that event (together with their answers) depend. This is, it might seem, a straightforward, even obvious question that, transparently, *would* come first in any address or consideration of the events now gathered together under the heading of "the Holocaust." Like so many other such questions, however, this one turns out on reflection to be much less obvious or transparent than it first seems: What *is* particular or specific or distinctive in the Holocaust, as its very title implies?

Claims for the uniqueness of the Holocaust as the source of its particularity have fastened on the event as a whole as their basis, and in doing this, they miss the more fundamental particularity within it on which any claims for uniqueness (questionable on other grounds as they are) would depend. That more fundamental feature is the character of the Holocaust as a series of acts committed by one group of people against another—a campaign of extermination launched by one people and government (Germany and the Germans, during the twelve years of Nazi rule (1933–45)—against another people, the Jews. Both these groups were specifically (that is, particularly) defined in the context of the Holocaust: the perpetrators on one side, the victims on the other, each distinctively marked. Admittedly, the process of this demarcation was imposed not jointly but by one of the groups on the other; it was the Nazis who in the Nuremberg Laws of 1935 introduced their own definition of who was a Jew (namely, anyone with three Jewish grandparents and/or who identified with the Jewish community)[3]—as it was also the Nazis who would decide, on the basis of a determination of their German bloodline, who was eligible or not to become a member of the SS, forcing would-be volunteers to trace their lineage back not just to their grandparents, but to the eighteenth century—in some cases, it seems, to 1648. (Genealogy, we know, became a thriving business in Nazi Germany.)

To be sure, the Nazis had collaborators in carrying on their campaign of the so-called "Final Solution of the Jewish Question." Italy, Germany's principal European ally, also implemented laws of racial distinction and discrimination against Jews—even if tardily (in 1938, sixteen years after Mussolini himself came to power) and reluctantly. So too, similar laws would be applied in virtually all the countries that the Nazis occupied (including France, Belgium, the Netherlands, Norway, Greece, Yugoslavia, as well as Poland, Lithuania, Hungary, and Russia: the list is itself imposing). In all these countries, furthermore, local collaborators appeared among the local populace who then took active roles in the roundups and deportations and often in the executions required for the "Final Solution." It also needs to be remembered that, as has been described in Chapter 1, Jews were not the only victims of the Nazi regime; the Nazis were also responsible for non-Jewish civilian deaths in the millions, from all the countries they occupied and including non-Jewish German citizens (as in the so-called "Euthanasia" or T-4 campaign).

Even after recognizing such other murderous elements of the Nazi project, however, the "Final Solution" directed against the Jews remains unmistakably a more central purpose within that project than others; that is, in terms of the deliberate persecution of a specified group. The estimate of between fifty and sixty million "innocent" deaths caused in World War II staggers the moral imagination—but the number of victims *by design*, through the process of genocide, is considerably smaller, if no less difficult to grasp or explain. The roots of the "Final Solution" were present in Nazi plans before they came to power in 1933—and the "Solution" itself became a significant factor in their planning (at first, vaguely and tacitly; later, more explicitly) once they obtained that power. Europe was to be made "*Judenrein*"—"cleansed" of Jews (thus, the euphemism of *cleansing*, as in *ethnic cleansing*, is also indebted to the historical design of the Holocaust). And if that goal of cleansing could not be achieved by forced emigration or expulsion which was Nazi Germany's original proposal, well, then it would have to be accomplished by annihilation—the systematic effort at genocide that was historically distinctive in the deliberate and cohesive effort and organization that the Nazis brought to it. This essential part of the Nazi "ideal," then, was notably specific—that is, particular. It pitted the power and people of Germany (and its allies) against the Jews—first, against the Jews of Germany, but then, ultimately, against the Jews of all Europe and part of Asia—and then too, as Hitler himself affirmed, against all Jews wherever they lived. "Just as the Jews had been 'smashed down' in Germany, so they would be in the entire world. The Jews of England and America . . . could expect what had already happened to the Jews of Germany."[4]

The twofold particularity of this effort—in the victims, on the one hand, and in the perpetrators, on the other—also opened the way to certain basic, and also particularist, questions that remain, and may always be, unresolved: *Why,* after all, was it the Jews whom the Nazis would single out?—an obvious question, and one for which there have been both too many and too few answers. And a parallel question—raised before in Chapter 7—appears on the other side: "Why, after all, was it the Germans, inheritors of a great and enlightened culture, who would launch and support the barbarous campaign of extermination that settled on the Jews as its victim?" Many historians have noted that had they been asked beforehand in which country an event on the order of the Holocaust was likely to occur, they would have predicted its appearance not in Germany, but elsewhere: in France, for example, or Poland or Russia—in each of which antisemitism had more deeply rooted and openly expressed histories than in Germany—and in which, unlike Germany, outbreaks of lawlessness driven by that view had previously, and not very long before, occurred. For much the same reasons, it could be further argued that the Holocaust, as it originated and unfolded in Germany, *might* have taken place in those other countries; in this sense, Germany's role in the Holocaust seems underdetermined, and certainly few historians would claim, against a background of historical determinism, that it *had* to happen when and as and where it did. In these terms, as the Holocaust did not have to occur at all, it did not have to occur in Germany with the Jews as victims—and from this perspective of logical or historical possibility, the claim being addressed of historical particularity seems challenged by history itself.

Even viewed together, however, these reservations do not override the claim for that particularity. For however broad the background of possibility against which the Holocaust emerged, the fact remains that the Holocaust as it occurred was not only possible but actual—an actuality, we know, that essentially involved two principals: the Germans and their collaborators, on the one hand—and the Jews, on the other. This is the most immediate and conclusive reason for recognizing the Holocaust's particularity, and it remains—will always remain—as the first step in understanding that event, however far the latter's consequences extend beyond Germans and Jews in the contemporary world. For both those groups, the Holocaust remains a weighty and distinctive part of their respective collective memories—on both sides, a significant wound or trauma (to be sure, in different ways), and one that distinguishes their "particular" histories from other group histories, whatever other trauma may figure in the latter. The only means by which Jews or Germans could forget or blot out that event would be by an extraordinary act of repression, the deliberate rewriting of history on a very large scale.

To be sure, the particularity of the Holocaust is important also for non-Jews and non-Germans—most notably as proof that ethical choices and decisions are inherent in the process of history (and then, of course also in the writing of that history as that becomes itself part of history). There is, in other words, no way of divorcing the living or the writing of history from the role of ethical judgment that is, as hard experience teaches, individual and particular. In *all* ethical decisions the agents decide for, and by, themselves—that is, individually and particularly. The value of holding this feature of contingency and choice steadily in mind is not primarily to soften or to justify making judgments on the past, but to emphasize that choices, and often *moral* choices, are as much an element or factor in the historical past as any of the "hard" data that historians more often dwell on. To retell human history without holding a place in it for ethical value and assessment is, quite simply, to distort that history. Natural histories—of a species or a volcano—can be written without introducing moral judgment; but these are quite different from human history, where human agents are responsible for much if not everything that happens, as well as, of course, for much that does not.

But is there a reason, beyond the description itself, for *emphasizing* the particularity of the Holocaust? Two justifications emerge for doing this. The first is quite simply the importance of getting and keeping the historical record straight. *"This is what did happen."* There are and will continue to be disagreements about why and how "it" (the Holocaust) occurred—but there is no debate, except at the unimportant margins, that it did occur and that its occurrence can be represented in terms and numbers and dates that are well known and in many of their details agreed upon. Contemporary analysis is not very much interested in or devoted to history; much of what figures in cultural studies and still more in public discourse bridles at the restraints that history imposes, and it is a predictable consequence of this tendency that some writers (and readers) should view history as only another type of narrative, of a likeness to the discourses of fiction: both, after all, have to be imagined and constructed.

That there is *some* basis for this view, however, should not override the importance of keeping in mind that wherever else the reach of history extends, it begins and ends with particular fact: who did what to whom, and when. This remains the case no matter how partial or oblique even conscientious representation of such facts must be. To reject, or to claim to do without such a foundation for historical understanding would be also to imply that there is no reason why history should not be written simply to fit the (particular) historian's taste, as though one were cooking a favorite dish. And to proceed in that direction is in effect to equate all historical interpretations—in both practice and principle. In these terms, furthermore, the denial that the Holocaust happened would become just another way of telling the story of the Holocaust—to be registered and left in the same hypothetical status that any other account is, with none of the alternate narratives conclusively accepted or excluded. But it seems important—urgent—that we recognize, and say, that although there are two sides to many stories, for some stories there are not two sides but one. At times, in other words, the facts *do* speak for themselves—and when they do this, their contradictories would be, *are*, silent. Not because of censorship or prohibitions, but more simply because they have nothing to say, or to have said, for themselves. The historical occurrence of the Nazi Genocide against the Jews, its particularity, is not the only example of a fact (or collection of facts) that speaks for itself in this way—but it is a notable one. The consequences of crediting its denial—that is, the denial of the occurrence of the Holocaust—demonstrates as clearly as any proof could the connection between history and ontology: what is said to have happened and what did happen. In this sense, the strong case can be made that particularity is all.

But then, on the other—the second—hand: we often think and speak in general or universal terms, and there are good reasons for this. It is impossible to imagine what ethics or politics, let alone science, would be if their founders were compelled to think or act without general principles or general findings. The law of gravity gains its force just because it applies to everybody and everything on earth; so too, when the Declaration of Independence speaks of the three "unalienable" rights of "life, liberty, and the pursuit of happiness," it attributes those rights to all mankind—not to a particular person or group. And when the sixth of the Ten Commandments proclaims "Thou shalt not murder," it addresses that prohibition not only to one, but to every "Thou." Even if we recognize these implications, however, there is no avoiding the starting point observed above—that people live their individual lives as particulars, not as general rules or doctrines. The decisions they make, the work and relationships they give themselves to—these are necessarily individual, their own particular choices, often irretrievable and always contingent. Even if at times individuals succeed in redoing or changing them, they cannot hope to *undo* them; that is, to turn history backwards. And always they make such decisions historically, in time—where the past, they quickly learn, is indeed past, not something anyone can reach back into and reverse.

In other words, general principles are even at best applicable or useful only up to a point—the point at which they have decided, often perforce, *between* two (or more) such principles. If ethical decisions were always or even often one-sided, with all the weighted principles at one extreme and none at the other, life would indeed be beautiful. And easy: practiced and lived in general. But in fact, particular and conflicted decisions are constantly with us, by invitation or not. To be sure, the world has rarely confronted events on the scale of the Holocaust—but this makes it all the more important to understand events on that scale as well as lesser ones not primarily through abstract principles—not even by such compelling explanatory concepts as antisemitism or fascism, but as acts or series of acts that particular people have done to other people, that they *chose* to do, for reasons also of their own choosing. *And* that the decisions enacted in this way were, as much as any decisions ever are, freely made. The agents and contributors to the Holocaust could have acted differently; what occurred could have happened differently; indeed, the Holocaust need not have occurred at all. Each survivor bears witness, particular and concrete, to this possibility—as does also each agent who imposed himself on them. This sense of contingency—that what happened might have been avoided—is the single most important implication of the particularity of the Holocaust. It points in the direction of the future as well as toward the past—and still more dramatically, it points at us, at our own contingency in the present as we look back at the past, asking us, too, what we are prepared or willing to do, now, in the present, about it.

Stage 2: "To the Universal": Even in the specific features of the Holocaust emphasized up to this point, however, the shape of certain universal or general implications emerges. As intently as we focus on the particularity of the Holocaust and the two individual groups at its center, we recognize that nothing intrinsic in them brought either the perpetrators or the victims to those roles. Each of the two sides could have been and acted other than they were or did; they could have been other than what they were. Obviously, there was a great difference in the power relation between the two and thus also in their freedom of action—but, again, the point here is directed against the notion of an *inherent* identity. To deny this view, with its implication that the identities and actions of the Holocaust principals were "hardwired" presupposes what would itself be a racial theory of history. If such things as national traits exist at all, it goes beyond any evidence yet found to claim that particular acts or sets of acts are determined by such traits. Antisemitism, viciously and systematically as it expressed itself in the Holocaust, depends finally on a belief or dispositional system, not the human genome. It is precisely *because* the Germans and Germany were free to do or not to do what they did that they could and can be held responsible for what they did.

An implication of this premise, however, is that the actions of the Germans and their collaborators during the Holocaust were indeed human and thus universal possibilities, not essentially linked to Germans or Nazis—acts that might in principle as well as in fact have been initiated by other people in other countries at that or at other times. There is little basis and certainly no means of proving that "It [the Holocaust] could not happen [or could not have happened] here"—wherever "here" happens to be. The evidence argues strongly in precisely the opposite direction: that if the Holocaust happened once, it can happen twice; if it happened in one place, it could have happened, and could yet also happen elsewhere; if it was done by one particular group to another particular group, it can also be done to and by still other (particular) groups. Thus important as it is to keep in mind that when the Holocaust did occur, it was the act of one specific group against another in a particular place at a particular time, the nature of the act compels recognition that nothing intrinsic in those groups or in the place or the time would prevent its happening elsewhere, at another time and place. Thus, there *are* general principles impelled by the occurrence of the Holocaust: evidence of what human beings are capable of and willing to do to each other, person *to* person, person *as* person—a universal that exempts no one and no group.

An alternate way of underscoring this universal implication of the Holocaust —what amounts also to its ground—appears in the concept of genocide. That term itself has become part of our everyday vocabulary, sometimes used precisely, sometimes as an all-purpose epithet for brutal acts of mass killing. In the latter sense, the term has in effect come to designate metaphorically the worst crime humanly imaginable—a socially acceptable curse word. What is often less fully appreciated is that the term itself is of relatively recent origin— having been coined in 1944, by the Polish-Jewish lawyer, Raphael Lemkin. To be sure, the fact that the word for genocide came into existence as recently as that does not mean that acts of genocide had not preceded the Holocaust. (A fuller account of this historical issue appears in Chapter 12.) But words also have a power of their own—and we recognize now, as would not have been generally acknowledged before the Holocaust, that genocide is indeed a human, and thus universal, possibility—a "live" and constant option: it has a name, it comes in a variety of forms, it is the subject of a United National Convention declaring it a crime—and most importantly, it has occurred and has been recognized *as having* occurred.

In these respects, the phenomenon of genocide is comparable to the discovery —or should it be the invention?—of the act of individual murder. The biblical story of Cain and Abel is familiar in its account of Cain's murder of Abel out of anger and jealousy at the rejection of his (Cain's) sacrifice. And we understand that, in biblical terms, this is a report of what is "historically" the first murder. What is often obscured in thinking about that story is its suggestion that not only was Cain the first murderer, but that with his act he invented the *idea* of murder—which would thereafter be an option for all other human beings and thus also a continuing feature of human history. One does not have to accept the account of Cain and Abel as literally true in order to recognize this point: at *some* historical moment, the possibility of individual murder entered history—to which we now find added the additional larger possibility of genocide and its effect of a double murder: murder of individuals and also, apart from that, of the group of which they are members.

In this sequence, then, we follow a thread from the particularity of the

Holocaust—what happened at one time to one group as the result of the actions of another, single group—to the feature of universality: what the Holocaust portends about human nature and history as such, wherever we find evidence of them. This may suggest a certain symmetry of historical analysis, perhaps also the temptation to leave the account of moral history leading up to it at that: to reflect on, to try to understand, and beyond that, to teach. Indeed, there seems no more formidable task than to enable (or more strongly, to convince) people to think of themselves *both* in particular and universal terms. It is apparently more tempting for people to identify themselves as only one or the other of these: either by membership in a particular group (a family or gang or nation or race or religion), with those not in the group consequently viewed as aliens or "Others"—or, on the other hand, by the self-image of a universal being, as a member first, and perhaps only, of the human race, with no allegiance to any particular group or tradition or history (as though created magically, sprung full-grown from the earth). The latter view, I should argue, is as much an illusion about the way human character and culture work as is the first, exclusionary account. Neither one, taken by itself, matches experience—and what seems necessary once the two views are seen as opposed to each other is to find a way of joining them, of living in the one without denying the other, and in the other without denying the one.

Is a conjunction of this sort *possible?* As a goal or ideal, it is much more easily set (or said) then done; but there may indeed be a way of effecting this bridge through the third stage mentioned in this chapter's title: "From the Particular to the Universal," and then forward once again. But "forward" to *what?* it might be asked. Well, forward once again to the particular, but at a different level and in a different sense from its first appearance. An episode described by Primo Levi suggests how this synthesis might be realized; it appears in his memoir *Survival in Auschwitz,* in which Levi describes the eleven months he spent in that camp (from the end of February 1944, to the end of January 1945). His "survival in Auschwitz," Levi recognizes, was due finally to chance; but it was also due at a lesser level to his profession as a chemist, which provided him with a work assignment in the camp that gave him a greater chance of survival than he would have had otherwise. Thus Levi describes the interview that tested him for the "job" with a German chemist named Pannwitz who ran a laboratory in the camp and who, having learned about Levi's training, was deciding whether to accept him as an assistant. It would have been natural for Levi to recall from this encounter the desperate possibility it posed for him of obtaining work in the camp that might have helped him survive. But what Levi relates from the episode is something quite different.

In his account, Levi has been brought to the interview with Pannwitz by Alex, a Kapo; once the interview is over, Alex reappears to escort Levi back to his barracks.

Alex enters the scene again. I am once more under his jurisdiction. . . . Here we are again on the steps. Alex flies down the stairs; he has leather shoes because he is not a Jew, he is as light on his feet as the devils. . . . At the bottom he turns and looks at me sourly as I walk down hesitantly and noisily in my two enormous unpaired wooden shoes, clinging on to a rail like an old man . . . to re-enter Bude, one has to cross a space cluttered with piles of cross-beams and metal frames the steel cable of a crane cuts across the road, and Alex catches hold of it to climb over: *Donnerwetter,* he looks at his hand black with thick grease. In the meanwhile I have joined him. Without hatred and without sneering, Alex wipes his hand on my shoulder, both the palm and the back of the hand, to clean it; he would be amazed, the poor brute Alex, if someone told him that today, on the basis of this action, I judge him and Pannwitz and the innumerable others like him, big and small, in Auschwitz and else.[5]

Now, let us ask, What has happened here? Levi is in Auschwitz, the largest death camp among the six organized by the Nazis and in which upward of a million and a half people, mainly Jews, would be killed, mainly by gassing. Levi himself was fully aware of the camp's purpose, as he was aware also of how slight his own chances of survival were even if he did get the job for which he had just been examined. And yet at that moment, he focuses his attention on what by comparison seems a trivial matter: not torture, not beating, no special threat of death—only the thoughtless act of someone wiping his soiled hands on Levi's ragged clothing which was, we may assume, already soiled.

But is it really so difficult to understand the importance Levi attaches to this moment, what it represents for him? Precisely *because* the act was limited, so partial and slight in comparison with others that he had seen and might see around him at any moment (probably at that *very* moment), it symbolized for Levi something very large indeed, and—it is not too strong to say—universal. It may be possible, the Nazi regime proved repeatedly, to commit murder impersonally and bureaucratically and on a large scale—with the orders for those acts delivered from afar. But here, in the moment to which Levi calls our attention, there were no orders; nobody could claim that Alex's act was not freely chosen, made up on the spot. The Kapo, Alex, quite on his own, *chose* to treat Levi as a rag on which to wipe his hands. To be sure, murder on the spot would have had more flagrant consequences. But here the intention was no less murderous—in one sense, perhaps more so, because there could be no question, as there may at times be even about murder, that the act was indeed voluntary, willful, and that Alex could have found other means of wiping his hands with little effort or loss. But he chose not to.

Now, why recount this episode? The title of this chapter promised to describe not only how what was particular in Holocaust led also to a grasp of its universality—but, beyond this, how such universality would in turn move on to still another, concluding mode of particularity. And this is, it seems, what the incident with Alex recounted in Levi's memoir does. For we see there clearly on one side that general ethical principles are at stake: how it is possible to treat human beings not as persons but as things, and to do this as a principle or *rule*. But we also see, from the other side, that the way we come to know and recognize that first point, and also to teach about and against it, comes in very specific, and as it turns out even trivial, day-to-day circumstances. Furthermore, we see here how the test of general or universal principles might grow out of the particularity of the Holocaust itself, represented in the person of Primo Levi as he was caught in the grasp of Auschwitz. Only consider the dimensions of that particularity: a member of the small Italian Jewish community (fewer than fifty thousand in all), captured by the Fascist Militia in a chance raid on Italian partisans, transported seven hundred miles in a freight car to a camp in an otherwise invisible town in Poland by Germans who had conquered it—a camp set up, after a search for the "best" means, for the sole purpose of turning people into corpses. No fiction writer would attempt to bring the pieces of such a narrative together; they are by themselves too improbable. But now Primo Levi leads us forward, following a first jump from the particular to the universal as the Camp Auschwitz takes on the dimensions of a world—forward again but also back to the particular: the story through his own life of what happens when general principles, on the one hand, and history in its specificity, on the other, collide. One would expect an explosion of sorts under these conditions, and that indeed is what happens. The "Big Bang," we learn, occurs not only on the scale of the universe; it happens first and just as explosively in everyday life, as the particularity encountered there extends far beyond itself.

* * *

Undoubtedly, there are lessons to be found in the sequence so far described, as in the Holocaust more generally—lessons to be learned and so also to be taught, in classrooms or outside them. I have said little explicitly about what such lessons might be or how they can be conveyed, and this is in part because so little is known about how lessons can be drawn in general, even about subjects set to a much smaller scale than the Holocaust. And then, too, we recall from common experience how little people seem to learn from history, whether individually or collectively. (Hegel's words echo here, as he wrote, "The one thing we learn from history is that we do not learn from history.") We also recognize the danger of trivializing the Holocaust by looking at it as a school from which we are entitled to derive lessons: whatever else Nazi Germany was, it was not a classroom—and whatever else is taught about the Holocaust, surely it ought first to convey, as accurately and concretely as possible, the harsh reality, the immediacy, the unexpectedness, and the severity with which that event struck: not quite what classrooms are understood to include under the heading of the "disinterested search for knowledge."

One way of quickening the sense of this immediacy, however, is through an aspect of the experience of the Holocaust that although often remarked in passing, has not been discussed systematically and indeed, has hardly been discussed at all. This is the response of incredulity or surprise or disbelief frequently noted in accounts of individual reactions to events of the Holocaust as they unfolded—sometimes on the part even of its perpetrators, most commonly among its victims. Innumerable reports speak of people destined for the death camps who heard stories about them but refused to believe them, arguing against what they heard as possible, let alone actual. This was a common reaction, furthermore, not only in places yet untouched by Nazi roundups and deportations, but in the ghettoes themselves where death was a daily presence and which were themselves often in close proximity to the death camps. Indeed, and still more ominously, the same reaction commonly appeared in the camps themselves and at other scenes of executions, as we read of people facing imminent death who did not believe what was happening before their eyes, indeed what was happening *to* those eyes.

Now it might be claimed that such reactions of disbelief, of surprise, were—are—entirely understandable, that they were understandable just because what was happening was so *un*natural, so improbable. (Levi and other writers describe the people who adapted most successfully to the requirements for survival in the camps as those who were and would be social misfits in "normal" circumstances.) Again, there is the familiar phenomenon of not believing something because of our wish that it should not be true, the state of denial. And if anyone ever had cause for such denial, surely the inhabitants of the ghettoes of Vilna or Warsaw, of Lodz or Lublin did—as enclosed there, they anticipated, knowing without quite knowing, what the future had in store for them. But also people who were in no immediate danger, who were able to look at Germany and Europe from distant shores, were incredulous; recall, for example, the famous exchange in 1942 between Justice Frankfurter of the U.S. Supreme Court who was also a confidant of President Roosevelt, and the Polish emissary, Jan Karski, an extraordinarily brave and dedicated man, who had voluntarily entered certain ghettoes in Poland to observe for himself what was happening there and then traveled to the United States to spread the word. On hearing Karski's report of what he had seen in the ghettoes, Frankfurter responded that he did not believe him. The Polish ambassador who had accompanied Karski to the meeting protested: "Do you think he is lying?" "No," Frankfurter answered, "I don't say that he is lying, but I cannot believe him."[6]

Is there a lesson in *this*? Surely the lesson cannot be that we ought to believe whatever we hear. Nor would the lesson be that we ought to believe all the bad news that comes our way. A likelier if more sobering lesson, it seems, would be that we should not be surprised to find that improbable or unexpected events do in fact occur, and that we may indeed find ourselves in unlikely, in improbable—*first-time*—situations. The problem in this, of course, is that it is so obviously difficult for people to prepare themselves for what has not happened or for what does not typically happen: the truly novel, what is beyond human expectations or imagination will—arguably *should*—surprise them.[7] Yet perhaps we may learn from reading, hearing, talking about such occasions when they have occurred (and so also, about the Holocaust), how to bring a sense of them also into the present as a possibility—to bring their particularity into our own, and so also to learn to foresee, perhaps (as we extend ourselves) to guard against, the unexpected—at least not to disbelieve the appearance of the unexpected when it shows up even when we could not ourselves have imagined what in particular is unexpected. That is, to learn how to be surprised without becoming its victim.

Here, in this connection, another episode recounted by Primo Levi shows at once the difficulty of such an accomplishment and yet how necessary it is. This occurred soon after the transport that had brought him from Italy reached Auschwitz. The newly arrived prisoners had been forced through showers, they had been tattooed with numbers, and were then shut up in a barracks; the journey had lasted days with little food or water, and none was provided now either. Levi picks up the narrative at that point:

> Driven by thirst, I eyed a fine icicle outside the window [of the barracks], within hand's reach. I opened the window and broke off the icicle but at once a large, heavy guard prowling outside brutally snatched it away from me. "Warum? [Why?]" I asked him in my poor German. "Hier ist kein warum" ("Here there is no why"), he replied, pushing me inside with a shove.[8]

Can we prepare ourselves for a situation in which all *whys* are forbidden? Probably not. But we can tell ourselves, and others, that there have been situations like that—and that if those situations occurred in the past, they may occur again. And that even as we ought then to value the importance of being able to ask that question, we ought also, telling ourselves and others, to recognize the possibility of situations in which the question itself would be denied— where, if it were asked, the answer would come not in words but in the silence of brute force. Perhaps in this we might find an unexpected and improbable lesson: that we know now, looking backward through the lens of the Holocaust as we did not before it, that we should not be quite so surprised, in the interruption of the orderly world of our expectations, to find ourselves surprised.

Part Three

For and Against Interpretation

NINE

Oskar Rosenfeld and Historiographic Realism
(in Sex, Shit, and Status)

There is nothing startling by now in the claim of a role for style in writing (or reading) history, but most working historians would probably still vote against it, the more so if the claim included Hayden White's conception of historical discourse as based on "emplotments" shaped by literary figuration or tropes. Votes, however, are not arguments, and the case that White presented in *Metahistory* for historiography as a form of writing causally intertwined with the traditional projects of historical explanation and/or a search for the "eigentlich" ["actual"] has survived the many attacks directed against it.[1] This conclusion holds, I believe, even if one adds to the mix the qualifications that White subsequently made (more correctly, that he made *explicit*, since he had always assumed them) for the relevance of certain non- or extra-stylistic criteria of truth in the process of emplotment itself.[2]

White's later references to such non- or extra-stylistic criteria appear largely in response to the demands made on historical writing in its representations of the Holocaust, most urgently as those representations confront a "ground zero" in the non- or extra-stylistic claim of Holocaust denial: the assertion that there was no Holocaust (since no "Hitler-order" for genocide has been recovered, or since, in any event, the Nazis used no gas chambers, and/or if they did, the gas chambers had some other purpose and, anyway, could not have "accommodated" the numbers of victims claimed). In terms of Holocaust history, Holocaust denial is a marginal phenomenon, but for historical methodology, it poses a radical "either/or": between the acceptance or rejection of its claim, there is no third way.[3] The implications of recognizing the non- or extra-stylistic referentiality in the challenge of Holocaust denial, furthermore, extend to historical discourse more generally, and it should be clear by now that readings of White's "meta-history," which infer from it the writing of history as one among other varieties of fiction, are mistaken in that interpretation (as well, I should argue, as in their own endorsement of that view).

Yet there *is* an issue here that "will not go away" for any writer or reader of history who hopes to give each of the (now) two facets of historical discourse its conceptual due: on the one side, admission of the literary or discursive character of history as a substantive element in its writing (that is, style as a contributor to "making" the historian's subject); on the other hand, recognition that events of history do not wait for such accounts or explanations, let alone for the historians' confirmation, in order to happen. And although the Holocaust is one among an indefinitely large number of events that provide evidence for the latter claim, it makes the point with unusual force. For obvious reasons.

I do not attempt here a stylistic analysis of Holocaust historiography as such or even of the volume of Oskar Rosenfeld's writing from the Lodz Ghetto that serves as the primary text for these comments.[4] More restrictively, I shall be considering Rosenfeld's "ghetto writing" in a framework of Holocaust historiography that reaches, however, beyond that single volume—specifically, as his advocacy and practice of "Realism" bear representationally on the writing of Holocaust history as such. On this conception of Realism (using the term alternately—I hope distinctly—for both its stylistic and extra-stylistic applications), it designates representation that aspires by way of verisimilitude to a referential or intentional object; that is, as it asserts a relation between a representation and the Real—the latter understood, indifferently, as the "really" real or (only) the real.

Even this relatively limited project is formidable in relation to Rosenfeld's "ghetto writing" because of two aspects of that work that are unusual in the domain of historical discourse. One of these is the fact that Rosenfeld was writing about contemporary, not past, events—events, furthermore, that were happening to him. He thus set out to do the work of an historian but in the manner of a diarist—in this, differing from the usual character of both historians and diarists. Typically, the diary as a genre emphasizes—it is *about*—an author's mind and heart, with the events that set those organs in motion of secondary importance to the diarist's reactions to them. The most memorable diarists are recalled for what they wrote rather than for the independent importance of what they wrote about. As external, furthermore, the events about which the diarist writes are ordinary and equal—no matter how "extraordinary" any individual moments among them are. Even at their most unusual, they remain less noteworthy as events than in the writer's response to them—since, like the writer as person, his responses are uniquely his in a way that the events occasioning them are not.[5]

In Rosenfeld's ghetto writing, however, this "normal" rhetorical order of the diary is reversed—implying for his readers that if Rosenfeld as author could have made himself disappear entirely from his text, he would have. Much of his effort rhetorically is turned toward this effect—a disposition summarized by Rosenfeld in a statement that might serve as his credo for historical writing more generally. His ideal, he proposes, is to have his writing "entirely factual [*sachlich*], short sentences, everything sentimental set aside . . . without thought of the context, alone in space, not intended for others, as a remembrance [reminder] for future days." Historical discourse on this view would occlude the presence of the writer or any hint of his *rendering* what is represented in it; it would avoid all accommodation by the writer of readers' interests or expectations. Whatever is recorded, in other words, is to be non-perspectival and impersonal—camera-like in its detachment and disinterest.

Admittedly, this atypical ideal of Rosenfeld's for his diary/journal will be familiar to readers of the sub-genre of Holocaust diaries. The latter—still in the process of discovery and numbering in the thousands, most of them yet unpublished—were typically written with an awareness of the contingent present as that consciousness figures in all diaries, but also with a sense of the writer's *own* contingency as exerting a constant—often imminent—pressure. The tersest and most dispassionate Holocaust diaries (e.g., Adam Czerniakow's) and the most elaborately associative ones (e.g., Etty Hillesum's) are alike in making a place for this random and arbitrary and thus crushing presence.[6] That presence is, of course, further intensified by the Holocaust diarist's feeling of urgency at making and bequeathing his or her account—responding to the likelihood that the writing in hand might be the only record to survive the writer's and/or the diary's destruction. Rosenfeld's writing thus aims for a convergence between (on one hand) the genre of the diary—speaking in a particular voice from a radically contingent setting and attempting to suppress both its particularity and its contingency—and, on the other hand, the genre of the historical chronicle: evoking the neutrality and indisputability of dates and events that, however, are continuously qualified by the single-minded and directive thread of genocide. The representation intended is to be history lived as documentary.

A second aspect of Rosenfeld's writing, more speculative than the first, is no less relevant for the reader. This originates in Rosenfeld's own history and his early efforts as a student (as in his doctoral thesis) and then as a journalist and novelist that disclose the strong influence, the "hangover," of nineteenth-century Romanticism.[7] If it is too much to claim that Rosenfeld's ghetto writing thirty years later was impelled by the "anxiety of his own influence," there is at least a hint of this in his shift from the characteristic hyperbole and inwardness of Romanticism to the spare minimalism and impersonality of Realism. To be sure, the nineteenth-century elaboration of Romanticism had demonstrated that also Realism can be a figurative means or literary trope—a "style." And indeed, a compelling formulation of that style appears in Rosenfeld's own historiographic ideal (as cited above)—an ideal realized in much of his writing from the Ghetto, as it merges the genres of diary and chronicle in his staccato, ostensibly unfiltered, non-sequential observations of the pitiless everyday life of Lodz Ghetto inhabitants. So, for example [from Notebook H, 12 June 1943]: "Three Tliah's [Hebrew for "hangings"] at the central prison. Execution ten o-clock in the morning carried out by the Jewish police. Two candidates went from a work camp to a village, begging Polish peasants for bread. Caught. The third one tried to escape from the ghetto. Silence. The delinquents were screaming. No use. Orders from the Gestapo. The hearse was waiting in front of the prison."

Nothing in this brief, fragmented sequence appears as opinion or "point of view"; each of its pieces is meant to be understood as true or false—and presumptively *true* because the individual claims are unlikely to have been made in error or even open to question. (Could an observer be mistaken in that four men were hanged, not three? That the hanging was carried out at nine rather than ten o'clock? Etc. In principle, of course, yes—but not in the practice of the discourse.) To think of the brief passage cited in literary terms is to see the writer limning the external world not on a personal screen but as an objective replica, designed to approximate the "thing itself." The staccato fragments are so deliberately set apart from each other that they might be interpreted as a series of author's notes meant to be reserved for use in a later project—in effect as a *list* or other mnemonic device—rather than as a piece of discourse or "statement." But this would be at once an unduly literal and insufficiently literary reaction. Spareness or ellipsis (parataxis, in rhetorical terms) is in itself no more incomplete or prefatory than a contrasting fullness need be redundant. The crucial question for either case is whether, and how effectively, the form of discourse functions representationally—and about this Rosenfeld's portrayal is both clear and compelling. (Even lists, after all, constitute a literary genre—historically, a very early one.)

Walter Pater wrote in a comparative statement about the arts, that "all art aspires to the condition of music," thus suggesting that music exemplifies most completely what makes all of the arts art. I have elsewhere related a version of this statement to Holocaust imaginative or fictional writing—inferring from the latter's repeated appeal to verisimilitude and truth as preeminent values, that "all Holocaust writing aspires to the condition of history."[8] To extend this thesis about imaginative literature to include *historical* writing would be also to claim that Holocaust historiography (including now Rosenfeld's journal/diary) yields still another variation on Pater's statement—thus, that "Holocaust *history* (that is, its written history) aspires to the condition of history (history in the sense of the events themselves)." Not, to be sure, in order to revive their actual contingency or presence, and not even to represent their contingency in linear or chronological order—but by assuring a place for contingency as one (an important one) among the other features of the events or actions or even objects represented.

Admittedly, even an emphasis on verisimilitude by way of the representation of contingency would not account for all of the most ardent Realist's work, and

Rosenfeld himself, in any event, often moves outside this line in his forays as commentator and ironist. So, for example, he also provides glimpses of Holocaust humor, e.g. [24 February 1943]), "We see ourselves as three Jewish holidays: We eat as on Yom Kippur [that is, as fasting], live as during Succoth [as in huts or shanties], and look like we do on Purim" [in costume or caricature]. This particular report, it should be noted, is immediately followed by a stark reversal in which irony has no part at all: "Rumor that in a discussion outside [the Ghetto], the butchering of all Jews was asserted. Cannot be verified." It is not that the two parts of this sequence do not exhibit continuity—but that the continuity is established by principles of Realism rather than by an internal or "writerly" relation between the parts. The reporting of a joke may not entirely quash its humor, but reporting it is clearly different from "telling" the same joke—and if there were any doubt of this in relation to the quotation cited, it would be dispelled by the statement immediately following the joke as the diarist recorded it.

The ground attributed above to Rosenfeld's conception of Realism points to a crux in Realist discourse—as that discourse leads toward *either* factual or imaginative (fictional) representation. I speak of this crux as the "Historian's Antinomy"—with Rosenfeld standing in here for "Historians" more generally. Antinomies typically involve a conjunction of two principles or claims, each of them supported by sufficient evidence, yet which, viewed together, result in apparent contradiction. That the Historian's Antinomy is especially pressing in relation to Holocaust history is a reminder that many critical categories are pushed to their limits by that event's extremity, not that it applies *only* there. It can be shown, in any event, that the "Historians' Antinomy" applies more generally to historical discourse as such.

The terms of the Antinomy come from two opposing sources: On the one hand, Realism has served the literary imagination as a figurative or stylistic "choice" with no place for truth or falsity among its criteria. Proof of this is evident in analyses of artistic style whatever its medium or context; even period or group styles that often override individual styles do not "disprove" them, any more than the work of an individual artist "disproves" the work of lesser predecessors from whom he has nonetheless learned. The assessment of style, in other words, involves many but always other factors than the standard of truth or falsity. And yet, on the other hand: the foundation of historical writing—of *all* historical writing—consists precisely in descriptive claims the truth of which (in some sense of "truth") is assumed not as a rhetorical function but as non-rhetorically factual ("*sachlich*," in Rosenfeld's term). That is, historical discourse, whether stylistically Realist or not, presupposes a foundational understanding that something—some particular "thing"— happened, this "happening" then occasioning the further elaboration that becomes history. Realism is thus a style—but also not a style. And how can this be? Thus, the Antinomy emerges.

There seem to me only two possible resolutions for this "Historians' Antinomy." The first would be to conceive of historical discourse (the genre of historical writing) as a meta-trope; that is, as a more inclusive version of realist style that applies to all historical discourse, with its specific expressions branching out to sub-genres (like the monograph or the autobiography)—also, as White suggested, to sub-tropes like tragedy or the romance. On this solution, the meta-trope of Realist historical discourse would have no more cogent claim on representing or expressing truth or fact than any other stylistic choice (than, for example, those stylistic decisions which "figure" the genre of fiction). Stylistic choice within the bounds of historical writing would thus remain only another manner of speaking or writing, with its assessment dependent not on a standard of truth but on aesthetic or moral or perhaps still other criteria.

The second alternative would be to think of Realism as double-edged: stylistic on one side, but non- or trans-stylistic, on the other, with the first of these dependent on the second. It seems to me that Holocaust history—and within that, Rosenfeld's writing—provides both evidence and argument for this second alternative, and thus also evidence and argument against the first. It does this in part by an implicit reductio argument that shows what consequences follow for Holocaust history on the assumption that the limits of that history *are* set by the limits of rhetoric, but also (on the other hand) by the evidence of practice; that is, from the actual writings of Holocaust history and what thus emerges as its own, by now substantial history.

To be sure, historians are as liable to illusions about the character of their own work as anyone else. But since a necessary feature of all style is that it should be recognizable as *a* style (that is, no one style except in contrast to at least one other), then also on this ground, the Realist base of historical discourse would necessarily be more than only a stylistic decision. This is another way of saying that for Realism in its non-stylistic historiographic occurrence, there is no second, non-realist option—since the alternative, with "non-Realism" here amounting at best to indifference to claims or denials of referentiality, is not an alternative, but a rejection of the project itself.

Is it excessive to claim this as the only means of explicating Rosenfeld's ghetto writing—and still more, as exemplary of Holocaust historical writing in general? Statements by two other writers of Holocaust history seem to me to underscore, and to support, just such a view. The first is from Victor Klemperer's *The Language of the Third Reich*, which builds a theory of language on a ground that joins autobiography and diary (another example of the mixed genres that characterize so much Holocaust writing). Klemperer, describing the act of writing both for that book and for his diary, tells the reader about the criticism he had received from friends who learned about his project: "'Stop doing all that writing and have an extra hour's sleep. . . . Your writing is merely putting you in danger. And do you really think that you are experiencing anything special? Don't you realize that thousands of others are suffering thousands of times more than you are? And don't you think that in time there will be more than enough historians to write about all this? People with better material and a better overview than you? . . . ' [But] I didn't let myself be led astray at the time. I got up each morning at half-past three and noted down what had happened during the previous day. . . . I told myself: you hear with your own ears, and what matters is that you listen in specifically to the everyday, ordinary and average things, all that is devoid of glamour and heroism. . . . I kept hold of my balancing pole, and it kept hold of me."[9]

The second passage is from Raul Hilberg's book, *The Politics of Memory*—an unusual memoir insofar as it has less to do with his recollection of his own life and doings than with the "memory" (and so in effect the autobiography) of his major work (*The Destruction of the European Jews*) which, forty years after its publication, remains a central text in Holocaust historiography. So, the voice of the book describes itself:

> The printed pages at least would be devoted to the subject, not the person who wrote them. To this end I banished accusatory terms like "murder," as well as such exculpatory words as "executions," which made the victims into delinquents, or "extermination," which likened them to vermin. . . . Above all, I was committed to compression. I had to avoid elaborations, detours, and repetitions. [My father] tried valiantly to have me memorize in the original as much of Genesis as possible. The brevity of Hebrew, he assured me, was one of the marvels of the world; the power of its sentences could not be duplicated in any other language. The literary impact [of Genesis] on me was unmistakable. "You write short sentences," an editor once complained to me. I still do, though sometimes I hide this quirk with . . . connectives and, on rare occasions, semi-colons. . . . Beethoven sketched the finale of his Eroica symphony by pairing what he placed first with what he put down last, and so on. I [did] . . . something very similar with my twelve-chapter work. . . . The longest of my chapters was the one on deportations. It was the andante of my composition with a theme and multiple variations that mirrored the special conditions under which deportations were carried out in each country.[10]

Again, Hilberg's self-analysis represents his historical style as not only subordinate to the event, but as a mirror of it—and so, again, the more general claim of style itself as referential, with historical style, then, referring to history not only (although first) as written but then also and still more basically as it had occurred. Historical styles have varied historically at least as markedly as have the historiographic or methodological assumptions of working historians. But however diverse those styles, the element of referentiality remains a constant and common aspect, the axis around which stylistic variations move when the project is the project of history. The alternative, if it avoided an open denial of referentiality, would be indifferent to the latter's presence or absence—and it is difficult to imagine, let alone to name, historical narratives that advocate, or more to the point, that practice such abstention.

To be sure, it might be objected that in reporting their aspirations for a realist historical discourse, Klemperer and Hilberg—and Rosenfeld—were dreaming an impossible dream: the myth of an immaculate perception in which the author-historian—very much a person, indubitably a "subject"—aspires to escape that subjectivity, in effect, to jump out of his skin. But if the possibility of fully realizing that ideal is remote, there are certainly, and visibly, degrees of proximity and distance to and from it. And the crucial differences among those degrees are comprehensible only insofar as the ideal itself is viewed as real (that is, as it functions). What is factual on this account goes beyond—or below, or at least, apart from—rhetoric; it is in this sense that the claim is made here for Rosenfeld's writing as approximating the vanishing point of those apparent degrees of difference.

* * *

Lest this assertion for the inevitability of historiographic realism seem blind or overstated, I would call attention to certain limitations of realism even in its own terms—limitations that although sometimes regarded as only practical, turn out to verge also on principle. These are especially notable in Rosenfeld's diary/chronicle because although he often explicitly challenges those limitations and attempts to overcome them more consciously and deliberately than most other Holocaust diarists, he nonetheless falls victim to them—most suggestively, if silently, in the phenomenon of self-censorship or repression. For also in Rosenfeld, and still more in other Holocaust diarists (and Holocaust historians more generally), all of whom claim for their accounts authenticity and if not completeness, at least fullness, certain standard and repeated omissions are evident. That these are not accidental seems clear both from the amount of other historical detail provided, and from the independent evidence of a variety of discursive taboos on certain aspects of daily life that pass largely unspoken and unwritten even outside of historical discourse. These "habits of the mind," it seems, are sustained or renewed even for writers committed to Realism in all its facticity, and even under conditions as urgent and unmistakable as those constituting the Holocaust as an historical subject.

The sequence of "S's" in the sub-title of this chapter mentions three notable instances of such repression in Holocaust realism: Sex, Shit, and Status—an absence notable in the relative silence about them even in a writer as fully and consciously committed to Realism as Rosenfeld. So, in respect to the first of these instances: like a number of other ghetto or camp diarists, Rosenfeld notes that over time, under the press of starvation and disease—to say nothing of torture and the threat of death—it was common, and predictable, knowledge that the erotic impulse diminished among ghetto dwellers and "Häftlinge" [captives]. But there are, we also know, numerous brief references in Holocaust writers (sometimes, as in Primo Levi, oblique to the point of obscurity) to sexual relations in the ghettoes, in the deportation trains, and in the camps themselves. Rosenfeld himself notes, although also with restraint, that even late in the history of the Lodz Ghetto, when there was no longer reasonable doubt about the fate of the Ghetto, and when the sight of people dying on its streets of starvation or disease was commonplace, he observed young Jewish girls, dressed up and made up, walking about on the arms of ghetto "Prominenzen." How much more is there to say about this phenomenon, or about the patterns and forms of sexual relations more generally? Numerous brief references have appeared to brothels and prostitution in the ghettoes and camps, to sexual relations within and across the sexually segregated camps (this invariable segregation itself has been largely undiscussed), and to pregnancies and births continuing to occur in the camps and ghettoes notwithstanding the dangers that these brought with them. Even without such reports and even supposing, as one must, that conditions in the ghettoes and still more in the camps would substantially inhibit this elemental feature of everyday life, the characteristic silence about it in personal memoirs speaks loudly. What went on, how much, and how? We don't know—because so little has been said about its many aspects, singly or in their varieties. Yet enough has been alluded to or implied to warrant the conclusion that what is absent here is a function not of the facts but of the not-telling; that is, of its repression. Would the knowledge of sexual conduct be important or especially relevant to an understanding of the Holocaust in its "concentrationary" world and the effects on life in that world? But there can be no answer to this question in the absence of the information itself—and a prima facie implication from the principles of historical realism would be that the lack of such information—its absence—is not random or accidental, but specifically an exclusion.[11]

Again: Rosenfeld refers a number of times to the "excrement cart" in the Lodz ghetto, at other times to the overflowing toilets, also to the penchant of SS men for taking photographs of the communal earth latrines in use: men and women, young and old, sitting side-by-side in the open, poised there as subjects of amusement for the cameras of the captors. The known facts are plain: that there was terrible overcrowding in the ghettoes (as also in the deportation trains and the camps) with virtually no working plumbing. Toilets were primitive—from buckets to holes in the ground—and invariably (and deliberately) inadequate; dysentery was common, the norm. Does it require more than an awareness of these rudimentary facts to imagine their effect on everyday life? The consequences extend farther than to the smell or stink—but let it for the moment be limited to that: the shit together with the waste and dirt of other kinds—garbage, dead and sick bodies, the refuse of everyday life after anything with the slightest possibility of use had been appropriated and removed. What *would* be left? And how would its presence be marked?

The most realistic pictorial representations (films, documentaries) of the Holocaust do not have the means for conveying smell; and literary representation has always, for evident reasons, had difficulty in finding a place for that sense (together with taste) in its structures. But aesthetic tradition in itself is insufficient to account for the absence of such reference in Holocaust diaries—the records of present impression, since we know more certainly and more emphatically than for other settings that the stench would have been constant and unavoidable. (However one credits the claim that constancy dulls the sense of smell, it does not imply the oblivion of consciousness.) Certain writers (e.g., Jorge Semprun) have noted the absence of birds in the vicinity of the death camps in Poland, although the surrounding countryside had many. What kept them away? It is true that the vocabulary of smells and odors is relatively limited, but the absence of reference here does not seem due to that limitation, since even the available vocabulary goes unused.[12]

The third and last of the repressed *S's* is a moral issue related not to the Nazi perpetrators but to the Jewish victims. This concerns the influence that social and/or economic status exerted in the ghettoes (and even, with variations, in the camps), most crucially of course in the process of selections: selections for permits or particular jobs or, in extremis, for deportation in the ghettoes; for killing, openly known and anticipated, in the camps. That a person's status, according to some hierarchy or other, would play a role even in the commonly shared captivity and dangers of the ghettoes or camps is in its own way not surprising. As that practice figures at so many junctures of "normal" or everyday life, one could hardly expect it to disappear when what was at stake was the difference between life and death; indeed, the pressure there would be still greater. The topic itself, to be sure, is difficult and dangerous—ample reason for the taboos that have surrounded it. To be sure, scattered accounts are available of the methods of the *Judenräte* [the Jewish Councils] in the ghettoes and of the Jewish police carrying out the "roundups" ordered by the Nazi occupiers; of selections in the camps themselves for labor, for other tasks, finally also for execution as those selections were at times carried out by the "Kapos" or even lesser functionaries.

Although the Nazis themselves or their collaborators sometimes took charge of the process of selection (most often, in the camps), they were also willing, even eager, to leave the process in the hands of the Jewish captives themselves—partly, one supposes, to spare themselves the trouble but also, almost certainly, as an addition to the process of dehumanization. The question here is not what justification there was for the fact that economic or social status would affect this process even when Jewish "rule" had the authority of choice; it is the fact itself that has gone largely unspoken—at least in part, one supposes, not only because of the painful decisions that such selections would necessarily involve, but also, almost certainly, because of the forms that the process took. There are occasions on record where certain individuals eased the process of selection by "volunteering" themselves; I do not know of an instance where the notion of a lottery—with members of the group allotted an equal chance at whatever danger or advantage was in the offing—was adopted on a communal basis. To be sure, silence is not proof, and the invidious comparison between this impersonal method and the alternatives to it might have contributed to this silence. But there are also reasons why, had it been practiced, we *would* have heard about it—and we haven't. Rosenfeld himself, again, only refers to this contrast, tacitly condemning the more usual practice, but without elaborating on that or the practice "normally" followed. Most Holocaust diarists, however committed to writing and sustaining the record, however committed to realism in principle, say nothing about it at all.

Could there be Realism—or history—that entirely avoided or repaired such omissions or acts of repression? Surely not—unless, for some reason, we decided that that it was the responsibility of realism to provide for the literal reproduction of historical events; that is, as they had been actually lived (and died). But whether or not formal provision is made for omissions (and the more deliberate, surely the more covert such practice would be), omissions are as constitutive of any representation—in some cases, more so—than what is openly presented. What is omitted thus becomes as substantial and revealing an element of Realism (and historical discourse, realist in style or not) as any elements more explicitly cited and named, no less present or historically significant than what appears in the flesh. Even to judge such significance, furthermore, presupposes a view of the two aspects—what is present and what is absent—side-by-side: a view, that is, of what is present as present but also of what is absent as present. Oskar Rosenfeld demonstrates the apparatus, the possibility, and finally the necessity of these features of Realism more clearly and fully than most, arguably any other, Holocaust diarists/chroniclers. First, as he includes in his observations aspects of the ordinariness—including the perversity and brutality—of everyday life in the Holocaust as these reach farther than are usually shown or noticed. But then, also, by what Rosenfeld— against himself—omits: responsibly if not consciously, perhaps incidentally, and yet also, in the end, as still fuller confirmation of the claims of realism.

TEN

Lachrymose without Tears

Misreading the Holocaust in American Life

In 1988, Peter Novick published *That Noble Dream: The "Objectivity Question" and the American Historical Profession*,[1] in which he criticized the sometime ideal among American historians of writing neutral or objective historical accounts—epitomized in Ranke's conception of history written *"wie es eigentlich gewesen"* ("as it actually was"). That ideal, Novick argued, was—*is*—illusory: a "noble dream," in Carl Becker's phrase (and not always, according to Novick, all that noble). In *The Holocaust in American Life*, Novick provides a vivid illustration of his own thesis, although not, one supposes, by design.[2] The tendentiousness and ideological tilt he found in the work of other historians is here on prominent display; also *his* conclusions go beyond the evidence from which his accusations of the artifice of Holocaust "centrality" and its harmful effects on the American Jewish community and the larger American public allegedly follow. "Allegedly," because the three conclusions to which Novick lays claim do not in fact follow from his premises:

1. Question: What is the place of the Holocaust in American life?
   Novick's answer: Large. Too large. For American Jewish life, *much* too large.
2. Question: What caused this?
   Answer: Interests and calculations unrelated to the Holocaust: An uncertain American Jewish identity that looked to a "new antisemitism" (or a new version of the old) for sustenance; the fading Cold War that opened the door to repressed recriminations against Germany; threats to Israel in the Six Day and Yom Kippur Wars inviting the use of the Holocaust as a metaphor (or more). And—nourished by all of these—a self-serving cadre

of Holocaust-memory professionals (Novick's version of "Shoah Business").

3. Question: What are the consequences of Holocaust-centrism?
   Answer: Bad. Competition for the title of victim among religious and ethnic groups. Disdain and insensitivity (in Jews) to the suffering of others. Self-definition by American Jews in terms of suffering and the Holocaust—thus as victims, thus also warranting compensation and privilege. A swing to the political right among American Jews. Advocacy of a hard-line Mid-east policy against Arabs. "Un-Jewish" (i.e., "Christian") ritualization of the Holocaust in Jewish practice. A search for lessons in the Holocaust despite the fact that no morals can be drawn from cases.

None of these parts of Novick's thesis is beyond the reach of evidence. Each might in principle be demonstrated—but as they appear in his account, none of them is. The evidence he does provide is partial in both that term's meanings, undermining his conclusions at every juncture that goes beyond the commonplace assertion that the Holocaust has at times been exploited by different groups for their own interests. (And who would deny this? Novick's indignation comes twenty years after Robert Alter tellingly wrote about the "deformations of the Holocaust," with Alter himself not the first even then to express such misgivings.) He raises this objection, furthermore, as if it had nothing to do with the by-now wholesale exploitation of *every* notable event that the media get their arms around. (In this respect, Novick's objection to claims of uniqueness for the Holocaust is surely warranted.) Novick's conclusions, then, emerge as caricatures: near-tautologies, on one side, and on the other, in their specific historical reach, disfiguring. They are no more warranted by his evidence than are their contradictories—although the latter indeed have been defended by other writers and with stronger arguments. He is, to be sure, not alone even in his politically tendentious *explanations* of the exploitation of the Holocaust in American Jewish life that he criticizes; but if his writing and thinking are qualitatively at a different level from knockoffs of his work like Norman Finkelstein's *The Holocaust Industry*,[3] a common thread of mean-spirited moralism nonetheless connects them and skews their conclusions.

The "few cheap tears" with which Novick characterizes the exaggerated view of the Holocaust in post-Holocaust eyes is thus not an accidental metaphor: it fills the vacuum between his evidence and his conclusions. To be sure, Novick does not contend that the Holocaust as it is now addressed is *only* a "retrospective construct" (p. 20). But he does view that event largely *as* a construct and has almost nothing to say in developing his account about the significance of the Holocaust *un*-constructed; that is, in fact. His readers are meant to understand that the Holocaust was substantially less than it has been touted to be, certainly less consequential than its afterlife has represented it as being. But exactly or even approximately how much less it is or was in fact than the touting would have it—an important question, after all—he leaves to the readers to manage on their own. And this stands in contrast to the *present appearance* of the Holocaust that, whether or not it is more important in itself, more urgently requires the help of his de-construction.

* * *

Thus, to the evidence of my own claims that begin with a challenge to Novick's assertion of the harm caused by Holocaust-centrism—the claim at the center of all the other parts of his account. And indeed, it is in enumerating those (allegedly) harmful consequences that Novick begins to leave historical analysis behind in favor of a combination of moralizing and special pleading. Perhaps the most important effect that Novick attributes to the undue attention given the Holocaust is its minimizing of public moral sensitivity (among both Jews and non-Jews, but especially among the former) to *other* horrific acts. As a consequence of this diminution, he claims, those other events have come to be taken less seriously, with the further consequence that less or little is done (and even more than that, felt) about them. Hence, he criticizes what he regards as the feeble U.S. response to a more recent atrocity than the Holocaust: "American debate on the bloody Bosnian conflict focused on whether what was going on was 'truly holocaustal or merely genocidal' . . . a truly disgusting mode of speaking and decision-making."[4] This supposed effect of the exaggerated Holocaust, however, raises a question about Novick's own method and assumptions. For his assertion here presupposes an instrument capable of measuring not only degrees of moral sensitivity but also the causal origins of variations among them. Novick's claim to possess such an instrument is a bold one that he might reasonably be expected to support with an account of the evidence (pro- and contra-) picked up on his moral seismograph. The published statements that Novick cites would obviously be part of the record here (assuming they *are* part of the record), but there are equally relevant—and conflicting—forms of action or practice that he ignores, virtually as a group. That he is himself aware of this omission becomes apparent as he mentions but then moves quickly past the contrary view to his own: the contention that emphasis on the Holocaust has *increased* sensitivity to oppression and atrocity. "In principle . . . [such emphasis] might [have this effect], and I don't doubt that sometimes it does. But making it [the Holocaust] the benchmark of oppression and tragedy works in precisely the opposite direction" (p. 14). Readers who find their way through the subjunctive mood and the double negative in the first sentence of this sequence find themselves buffeted by his categorical assertion in the second—with no indication of method or evidence for either.

The evidence he might have turned to for judging whether Holocaust-centrism has been responsible for increased rather than decreased moral sensitivity to other atrocities is by and large absent; and the moral seismograph Novick invokes in support of his own view draws mainly on anecdote and stray quotation (some of them, as indicated, without attribution)—but not, in any event, on anything approaching a systematic search for evidence.

Is such evidence available? One obvious way to gauge public sensitivity or opinion in a society is to examine its laws. Since the end of World War II, a network of international covenants, law, and courts has evolved which focuses on human rights—individual and group—and on the crime of genocide. The contrast between this many-faceted development and the pre-World War II status of international jurisprudence concerning group and individual rights is notable, and there can be little doubt that a large part of the impetus for this development came not only from the Holocaust itself but also from "the Holocaust"—that is, the period since the event itself against which Novick directs his fire. It might be objected that the legal formulations that have evolved during this time still lack teeth; it might be argued (it would not be surprising if Novick went in this direction) that compared to the harm caused by Holocaust-centrism, these other developments do not amount to much. But neither of these counter-arguments is self-evident, which is the way he apparently regards them, or that the evidence is in their favor, since he does not consider the issues involved in them at all. Thus, Novick makes an ostensibly historical assertion but at the same time ignores its historical context. Even if the evidence on balance supported his claim of the harm caused by Holocaust-centrism, furthermore, reference to the possible contrary evidence would be required for verifying his claim. As it stands, however, Novick's thesis considers no counterevidence, hypothetically or in fact, and in this way taints both the slight evidence that there is, or other evidence that might have been presented in favor of his own thesis as well.

What, then, of the related and no less fundamental claim in his account of Holocaust-centrism, that the Holocaust, through its exaggerated role (and the related, more general threat of antisemitism), has become the basis of Jewish identity in the American Jewish community? Also here, Novick relies in good measure on an Argument from Ignorance: "So far as self-understanding is concerned, there's no way of knowing just how many American Jews and which American Jews ground their Jewish identity in the Holocaust, but the number appears to be large" (p. 201). We hear first the concession that "there's no way of knowing," followed by the similarly concessionary phrase "the number *appears* to be large." But readers who expect to find proportionately qualified conclusions following from these moderate premises must look elsewhere—since the qualifications simply disappear when the connection between Holocaust-centrism and its alleged effects is asserted: that connection is then held to be not only actual but decisive.

This dogmatism becomes most noticeable in Novick's analysis of the causes of the supposedly exaggerated attention to the Holocaust: Why, after all, should what in his view is so obviously exaggerated and skewed a phenomenon have occurred—presumably influencing a large (naive) part of the American Jewish community and much of the non-Jewish American community as well? Here his response cites principally the threat to American Jewish identity in a liberal and open society. Given the fading appeal within the Jewish community of Zionism, on the one hand, and traditional religious practice, on the other, Novick regards it as natural, even inevitable that American Jews should turn for nourishment to the Holocaust: what else would they have to draw on? That this reaction also coincides with an increasingly widespread "culture of victimization" and the growth of identity politics among other ethnic groups proved serendipitous, according to Novick, since the Jewish community has then been able to build on these in drawing from the Holocaust a spirit of Jewish solidarity and identity—even if this is the solidarity and identity of victimhood.

To be sure, this supposed role of Holocaust-centrism in the construction of American Jewish identity derives from a still more fundamental but never more than tacit premise of Novick's argument. That the issue of American Jewish identity has been a widespread communal concern is evident and would be generally admitted on all sides of the "identity" spectrum. That antisemitism has been a factor in shaping Jewish identity in the United States and elsewhere in modern history is also widely accepted, even if the claim is also difficult to demonstrate because of the lack of control groups on which to base it (i.e., societies in which Jews lived as Jews but with no external civil or cultural liabilities). Novick takes these commonplaces for granted, but goes much further than they do in their assertion of antisemitism as one among other influences in the construction of Jewish identity. For him, antisemitism is not one among *other* influences, but, as his analysis turns out, one alone. Thus: "Two factors had been the guarantors of a substantial Jewish presence in the United States over the centuries . . . renewal through immigration [and] . . . anti-Semitism" (pp. 185–86). In logical terms here, the "two factors" cited amount in effect only to one. Since immigration would depend on the existence of a Jewish presence elsewhere, and since immigration must (presumably) begin someplace that is not itself dependent on immigration, the Jewish "presence" in that place would evidently have been sustained by the one, and only one, source of antisemitism. That a Jewish presence or identity might, in the United States or anyplace else, have been impelled by a positive sense of self, by a group of people creating or finding value in that tradition and identity, seems not to be considered by Novick as a possibility.

In this sense, the more general framework of Jewish history in which Novick sets his account fits squarely what Salo Baron famously titled the "lachrymose conception of Jewish history": Jewish history as essentially a history of victimization and suffering, thus of Jewish identity as essentially imposed from without, sustained in response to persecution. Baron, however, in labeling and calling attention to this conception of Jewish history, emphasized its status as *one* view—to his mind, a faulty one—among others. No such self-consciousness, however, affects Novick's account that assumes not only a direct but an exclusive causal connection between Holocaust-centrism and the search for Jewish identity in the contemporary United States (and ultimately, as he implies, wherever Jews are or have been): what other (non-persecutory) explanation could there be? Novick does not claim that this "lachrymose" basis for Jewish identity originated with the Holocaust, but the latter event clearly gave that basis significant support, both because of the dimensions of the Holocaust, but even more importantly, because of the serious contemporary challenge of modernity to sustaining Jewish identity.

Again: few commentators—Baron least of all—have denied, or would deny, that antisemitic persecution has been one factor among others in shaping Jewish history and identity. It would also be generally granted that historical representations of this persecution have at times been exaggerated, even mythologized within the Jewish community. Novick's reduction of the sources of American Jewish continuity to this one source alone, however, goes beyond the reach of such evidence—or of logic. It amounts to the claim that without the prominence of the Holocaust as an emblem of victimization and hostility (along with other factors in the "new antisemitism"), Jewish identity in the United States would have foundered—as it also may yet and as it would have done even before the Holocaust if not for the sustenance provided by earlier, if milder varieties of antisemitism. This persecutory genealogy of Jewish identity recalls Sartre's *Reflections on the Jewish Question*, according to which the antisemite *creates* the Jew (and presumably Judaism)—a thesis that mischievously begs the question of how the process it describes in putatively historical terms ever originated. Unless, that is, antisemites preceded Judaism, which they then created in order to have something to be antisemitic about. The lachrymose view of Jewish history in this sense simply avoids (or begs) the central historical question of origins; indeed it *has* to avoid it, since it can give no account of it that is consistent with its theory of Jewish continuity. In this sense, the Holocaust might seem to provide substantial evidence for that theory (and Novick builds on this)—but only for a truncated view of the history that it allegedly is a theory *of*.

To be sure, the further question remains here of exactly who, in order to further its dubious means (together with its dubious ends), orchestrated this campaign for Holocaust-centrism—and how did they manage it so effectively? Also at this crux in his argument, Novick protects himself by evasion; the categorical insinuation contrasts with the evidence required for it which is either equivocal or, more often, simply missing. On the one hand, in Novick's reasoning, there must have been such a campaign in order for the Holocaust to have reached its present proportions: accidents like that don't happen. But then, there must also have been (and be) active conspirators, bent on Holocaust-centrism for the reasons Novick identifies. On the other hand, to "have" intentions only unconsciously or covertly, buried in a collective will of sorts, is not quite to have them at all, and there is nothing more than this to go on. Thus, Novick threads his way through the thin opening between, or more precisely, around these two alternatives:

> It is not that Jewish leaders deliberately . . . latched on to a fashionable victim-hood as the basis for an identity that could mobilize Jews. . . . The "culture of victimization" didn't *cause* Jews to embrace a victim identity based on the Holo-caust; it *allowed* this sort of identity to become dominant, because it was, after all, virtually ["virtually" is meant here to serve as the author's life preserver; but what exactly does it save?] the only one that could encompass those Jews whose falter-ing Jewish identity produced so much anxiety about Jewish survival. (p. 190)

In other words, the "hyping" of the Holocaust did not result from a conscious decision by the Jewish leadership—but then no such *conscious* decision was re-quired. Since no other solution to the problem of Jewish identity was avail-able, the decision somehow made itself—a magical turn of events that at once gets Novick off the hook and the American Jewish leadership and community onto it.

And so also in returning to the fundamental claim of Novick's thesis: that the Holocaust occupies a large—too large—place in American Jewish life and in American life more generally. In its own terms, viewed methodologically, any such claim would be impossible to assess- or before that, to make—except comparatively. "Large" in comparison to what: Yom Kippur? the American Civil War? MTV? And of course, beyond this and once again, the contention that the Holocaust occupies a too large place brings us back to the question of evidence. In addition to the doubtfulness of the grounds already cited, another source of doubt occurs in respect to Novick's critique of the history of the manipulative campaign that, in his view, created "the Holocaust": the fact that this campaign took effect so late in the day—beginning in the 1960s and reach-ing a full head of steam only in the 1970s. For "generally speaking," he argues, "historical events are most talked about shortly after their occurrence" (p. 1). That the Holocaust did not appear as "The Holocaust" until two decades after "it" occurred thus also becomes for Novick a reason for questioning its authen-ticity. If the Holocaust actually mattered as much as we are now given to be-lieve, it would, he alleges, have been more quickly noticed and asserted.

To be sure, Novick himself supplies a number of reasons why talk about the Holocaust might not have appeared more immediately or prominently in the post-war years: the Cold War, in which Germany as an American ally was not to be embarrassed by reminders of its Nazi past; the fight against Na-zism in the World War had Russia as an ally, and Cold War reminders of this would evoke the specter of the Jewish association with Communism; resistance among survivors to speaking about the horror they had escaped; fears in the American Jewish community that to call attention to Jewish affairs, including even the Holocaust, would inflame antisemitism (in citing this reason, Novick conveniently finds antisemitism responsible for silence—as he elsewhere, more prominently, finds it responsible for utterance: it thus serves as an all-purpose historical cause).

Each of these factors surely did figure in the immediate post-Holocaust period; arguably they could serve as a sufficient explanation for the "delay" in Holocaust discourse. But also another, perhaps still larger consideration than any Novick mentions pertains to the character of that response, one which suggests that it might not have been delayed at all in the usual sense of that term. This is the fact that the process of gathering evidence to show that the events that had occurred and constituted a, or even "The" Holocaust would necessarily take time—emotionally, conceptually, probatively. Historians commonly acknowledge the difficulty of writing contemporary or even near-contemporary history. Raul Hilberg's monumental *The Destruction of the European Jews,* which he began writing as a doctoral student (in the face of scholarly opposition; there was no professional future in it, he heard), was published in the same year as the Eichmann trial (1961)—those two events coinciding with the beginning of the period in which Novick locates the origin of Holocaust-centrism. Hilberg's book remains a marker at the beginning of a now forty-year period of intense research, with scholars in virtually every Western country still turning up new data and records *and* contributing substantially to "The Holocaust" as phenomenon.

Except for brief reference to Hilberg himself, however, Novick has nothing to say about this scholarly aspect of Holocaust-centrism in which historians and other academic writers—his professional colleagues—have figured prominently. (Nor does he consider that without the Holocaust "centrality" that he objects to, whatever the source, such historical and moral issues as the role in World War II of the supposedly neutral countries or the question of reparations for Nazi slave laborers or the conduct of the various professions in Germany in support of the Nazi "project" would almost certainly have never seen the light of day. All these, too, however, as part of the alleged excess?) Admittedly, the academy is often marginal to significant social trends and discourse—but this does not apply to the emerging area of Holocaust Studies whose influence on the "phenomenon" of the Holocaust has been substantial. Even allowing for changes in academic fashion, moreover, it seems impossible—and would in any event require more evidence than Novick provides—to attribute that scholarly work, coming from many disciplines and many countries, to a conspiracy of Holocaust-centrism. Novick hardly mentions this source, however—even as a possible factor in the phenomenon at the center of his criticism.

Finally: Novick's fundamental claim remains his contention that the role ac-corded the Holocaust in American and American Jewish life is *de trops:* too. prominent, too oppressive, too *much*—for himself and, still more importantly, for the many other people (Jews and non-Jews) who, unlike him, have not man-aged to see through it. Such judgment implies not only superior moral self-knowledge on the part of the person making it but also the authority of that person in deciding what the *proper* dimensions of the role of the Holocaust should be, again not only for himself and his own conscience but for the lives and practices of other people as well. This moralizing undercurrent runs throughout Novick's book. Constantly the author presents himself as a monitor not only of deformations of the Holocaust but also of other, conceivably *justi-fied* responses to that event: expressions of mourning, of commemoration, of re-identification, of a call for moral conscience, even of the search for revenge. Admittedly, since Novick never mentions possibly authentic responses as fac-tors in the growth of Holocaust-centrism, perhaps he should not be blamed for ignoring those possibilities in the context of detailing its faults. But one hardly knows which is the more serious liability: the failure to acknowledge authentic impulses as factors in shaping "The Holocaust," or the moraliz-ing that criticizes the supposed excess of that phenomenon quite apart from the recognition of its historical origins. Novick's paternalistic subtext here ech-oes a familiar children's story: he warns his readers against paying too much attention—deference, concern—to the Holocaust. They would, if they listened to him, manage all these responses in their proper dosages: mourning, memory, conscience. Not too much, not (presumably) too little, but just right.

The Holocaust in American Life is meant as a provocation, and in this it cer-tainly succeeds. Readers who, like myself, disagree with the book's design and with its principal claims may nonetheless find parts of it illuminating and some of the information it provides useful. It is Novick's conclusions that mischie-vously exaggerate the evidence from which they supposedly follow and that thus echo hollowly as well as loudly. It is difficult to avoid the suspicion that if those conclusions did not fully precede the evidence presented for them, they at least had a role in shaping it; in any event, the dissonance between evidence (stated or ignored) and conclusion is sufficient by itself to attach to the whole the mark of special pleading—much as Novick himself had claimed in his ear-lier indictment of American historians. Along the way, his defenders and critics alike may notice the irony that in contesting the prominent place of the Holo-caust in American life, Novick has himself added to that prominence. He has clearly also accorded the Holocaust a substantial role in his own American Jew-ish identity. Too large a role? Perhaps. But probably not.

ELEVEN

"Not Enough" vs. *"Plenty"*
Which Did Pius XII?

That Susan Zuccotti and Ronald Rychlak—joining many others—find themselves quarreling about the actions or inactions of Pius XII during the Holocaust does not necessarily mean that they disagree.[1] More precisely, it does not
mean that they disagree on what they think they are disagreeing about—or
that they disagree as much as they believe they do. Zuccotti claims that whatever Pius XII did in confronting the threat and events of the Holocaust, especially as these occurred in Italy, it was not enough; Rychlak claims that whatever Pius XII might not have done during the Holocaust, he still did plenty. It
is important to recognize that these two claims, so often repeated by themselves as if they refuted the other, are by no means contradictory: it could be
the case that Pius XII did not do enough and yet that he did a good deal. So
these two authors, and the many other disputants on both sides of the divide,
might all be correct and even in agreement when they believe that they're disagreeing and that the "other side" is flatly mistaken—although they might also
disagree with *this* attempt at reconciling them.

Even if they accepted it, moreover, that would not resolve the controversy
in which they have taken part with their assessments of the initiatives and
responses (or lack of them) by Pius XII during the Nazis' "Final Solution of
the Jewish Question." For the crucial measure in conducting a moral inventory of Pius XII's conduct and policies—indeed, what is required for a moral
inventory of *anyone's* actions or inactions—is not a verdict based on abstract
principle brought to bear on whether Pius XII, during that fraught time, did
as much as he could have (which few people ever do) or whether he did plenty
(which more people do, and even in that context, did), but the assessment of
specific actions that he took when he need not have or that he failed to take when
he could (and should) have. In the end, moral decisions are singular and concrete, irrespective of how general or broadly applicable the ideals that guide or

ground them are. Moral assessment of those decisions, furthermore, must be similarly individual, concrete, and unequivocal—however abstract or general the principles under which they retrospectively are held to fall.

To be sure, in the judgment of any act, other parts of the larger whole of which that act is part may, or arguably must, be set aside (every context, after all, will itself be part of a larger one); and it could be objected that this process of deliberate exclusion necessarily undermines any assessment arrived at (since the "larger" context might well have altered it). But the counterargument to this objection is that if we were obliged to take into account for every practical judgment we make the larger and still larger contexts within which our present one lodges (and to do this until reaching the largest one possible), no decisions or judgments would be possible at all. And yet, of course, decisions *are* made, judgments *are* passed (and needed)—all the time and if only because they must be. In other words, moral acts and judgments are singular, individual, and re-alized on the single occasions in which their contingency is also set—because that is what they are and do (and cannot be or do otherwise). And if this means, for the "case" at hand, that other or even contrary instances of Pius XII's actions and inactions vis-à-vis the "Jewish Question" than the three I consider here might be cited, that possibility does not dull the moral edge that the three examples in themselves have. That edge concerns Pius XII's refusal to act in defense or in aid of Jews during the Holocaust: "refusal" rather than "failure"—since the inaction alleged, on the occasions cited here, could only have resulted from conscious decision. This is to say that, quite apart from any judgment on them, in the instances to be cited, the decisions made at the time were made in sufficient, if not full, knowledge of the Nazi persecution of the Jews. There is ample evidence for this claim, and the question that remains, then, is about the justification for the decision, not whether the decision was indeed a decision.

Both Zuccotti and Rychlak mention the three examples that are the focus of discussion here, but each finds a somewhat different turn or moral in them, different from each other and from what is suggested here. All the examples in-volve acts of omission; all of them, even in a world where moral ambiguity is a familiar, arguably unavoidable, presence, seem nonetheless straightforwardly wrong; that is, morally wrong. I would argue for this judgment even when the acts are defended, as they often have been, on prudential or instrumental grounds. Not because moral reasons can never be outweighed by prudential reasons (although the burden of proof is heavier then), and not because pru-dential reasons themselves cannot sometimes take on moral weight, but be-cause the prudential factors cited in these particular cases do not, in my view, balance, let alone outweigh the moral ones.

The first of the moral "omissions" is the fact that not once in the twelve years of Nazi rule or in the six years of World War II did Pius XII use the instrument or even the threat of excommunication against the leaders of the

Nazi regime or their accomplices inside or outside Germany. This failure occurred despite the public knowledge that many of those perpetrators and much of the populace at large who took their cues from them—again, inside and outside Germany—grew up as and (albeit to a lesser extent) maintained their identities as Catholics at the same time that they were participating in or abetting the Nazi "project." To take one prominent example among many that might be given: Ernst von Weizsäcker, the Nazi ambassador to the Holy See at the crucial moment in the history of Rome's Jews about which Zuccotti writes—their imminent deportation—found, and was made to feel, no incongruity between his religious commitment to the Church and his political and professional commitment to the Nazi government. Indeed, it was his mission at that crucial moment to disarm potential objections by the Holy See to the deportation of Rome's Jews—a mission that he carried out effectively. There is nothing in the record reported to suggest that the Vatican gave him (and millions of others in less prominent but still active positions) any reason to think there was an incongruity, let alone incompatibility, between what thus figured in his thinking and conscience as two quite basic commitments of principle.

The possibility of excommunication was an instrument directly in the Pope's control. Pius XII did not require an army to issue or enforce it, he did not have to conquer or imprison the people affected by the decision, and he did not even have to name them individually (although of course, he could have). He would have been able to act by will and by words alone. And indeed, only a few years after World War II ended (on 1 July 1949), Pius XII acted in exactly this way—in a blanket condemnation of Communism and those of its adherents thoughtless enough to believe that *that* political allegiance was compatible with Catholicism: those adherents, he warned, must make a choice: Either/Or—one or the other, but not both.

Yet during the years leading up to and then of the "Final Solution," Pius XII refused to take such action with respect to the Nazis or their accomplices. And he refused to do this although he was aware (and after a relatively early point, certain) of the Nazi policy of extermination of the Jews, and although the Nazis, imposing their rule on heavily Catholic countries like Poland, France, Hungary, and the Pope's own Italy, were in the end responsible for the deaths of millions of Catholics as well. The latter total, furthermore, included Catholic priests numbering in the thousands (mainly from Poland, but including some in Germany itself). If the threat or act of excommunication was not warranted against that "ecumenical" background, it is difficult to imagine what conditions could (then or ever) provoke such a reaction. That the excommunication of Communist Catholics was mandated only after there was no need (or possibility) to do so against Nazi Catholics seems at least as much part of the explanation as it is something *to be* explained. Pius XII, during, and certainly after, his Munich years as papal nuncio beginning in 1917, became an early and fierce critic of "Bolshevism"—and insofar as the Nazis represented an aggressive threat against the USSR, the view often ascribed to him of regarding the Nazis as a "lesser evil" than the Bolsheviks becomes more than only plausible. Only on that basis, it seems, would it be likely that the ban on Communists could wait until it did not have to be joined to a ban on fascism even in its German version, let alone in its Italian appearance (more about this point below).

Against this charge of failure to use a means of protest immediately available to him, an argument on the grounds of prudence often appears as a counter; namely, that if the Pope *had* asserted his opposition so publicly by the act or even the threat of excommunication, placing himself more directly and explicitly at odds with the Nazi regime than did the hints or covert instructions for sheltering the persecuted he allegedly issued, he would have made conditions worse, not better for the victims—the Nazis using the occasion as a pretext for intensifying their campaign of persecution. The instance of the fate of Dutch Jews is the item of evidence most often cited to support this view—the timetable of deportations and the number of those liable for deportation having been increased after Dutch bishops registered a collective protest against that process. The force of this objection, however, is substantially weakened by the fact that the bishops' protest itself was made in defense of Jewish converts to Catholicism, as it were leaving those who remained (unconverted) Jews to whatever fate awaited them. Still more than this, of course, and even if the timetable of deportations was at that stage accelerated, it is difficult to imagine what Pius or anyone else surveying the scene with the information at his disposal could have imagined as making conditions "worse" for Jews in Nazi-occupied territory than those conditions were or would become.

A second reason given as part of the prudential justification for the Pope's refusal to use the instrument of excommunication has been that the Pope and the Church were themselves at risk in the face of the Nazi onslaught—and that any more explicit statement or action than those which they made would provoke a violent response against *them* (that is, against the Pope and/or the Church). And indeed, evidence indicates that plans had been drawn (and were known to have been drawn) by the Nazis for the possible takeover of the Vatican, and even for the murder of the Pope.

There is significant doubt about how serious the intent behind such contingency plans was, but even aside from this, two objections apply, respectively, to the parts of this counterargument. The first is that, on the evidence, the first prudential consideration—that more public or dramatic efforts by Pius XII would have produced an intensification of Nazi persecution of the Jews—seems at least as likely to be mistaken as to be correct. The second is that even if the argument from prudence were not mistaken (something that could not in any event be known with certitude), it was—and remains—to a large extent irrelevant. It could well be mistaken, because however the Nazi hierarchy might have intensified its racist campaign as a consequence of the act or threat of excommunication (again, aside from the question of how much worse any possible reaction by the Nazis could have made things than they were in fact to become); or however the Nazis might have turned more openly against the Vatican itself, the *contrary* effect on the attitudes toward Nazi policies of hundreds of millions of European Catholics would almost certainly also have been significant. How much of a difference would that potential effect have made? Nobody can estimate this with assurance, but such uncertainty cuts in both directions: it would have been at least as likely to have positive effects as negative ones. Furthermore, since even without explicit papal statements there was already *some* resistance to the "Final Solution" in the occupied countries (and to the Nazi occupiers more generally), it is reasonable to infer that the Pope's voice would have added to the several levels of resistance which occurred without it—as these ranged from armed partisan attacks to the passive refusal to collaborate or inform or, even more simply, to a refusal to take advantage of opportunities for material gain based on the losses of victims. To be sure, it is unlikely that excommunication would have deterred Hitler himself, even taking into account his birth in a Catholic household. But it does not follow from this that his *being* excommunicated would have made no difference to those still professing Catholics among his followers; indeed, the fact that many of them could consider themselves "professing" Catholics and at the same time Nazis or Nazi supporters suggests the contrary.

Furthermore: the same argument from prudence against any explicit and more public intervention by Pius XII—even if it were compelling in its own terms—seems also, in the end, irrelevant. This is only in part because, where moral issues are at stake, prudential arguments may always, arguably, be beside the point. With the exception of the philosophical position of Utilitarianism—with its own serious problems of internal consistency—the conceptual frameworks in which ethical judgments are set invariably go beyond prudential or instrumental considerations. But also and more substantively: the question can surely be raised of whether in this *particular* case, judged as it presumably was by the Church also on religious and spiritual grounds, prudential or instrumental reasons should have been summoned to oppose reasons or ideals of moral principle and then been allowed to carry the day. If individuals can be called on to sacrifice practical interests—at times life itself—in the name of principles or ideals, as they often have by the Church, is it too much to apply the same expectation to the Church itself? The chief executive of a business corporation might arguably defend executive decisions on the basis of corporate and economic—in short, institutional—interests alone, and national authorities often typically find refuge in "reasons of state" for actions that on moral grounds alone would be condemned. But whatever institutional concerns the Church may at times reasonably take into account, there is hardly a basis in its own terms for giving those concerns the priority they would understandably have if the Church were simply a national or an economic—

"interest-bearing"—institution. For surely, it does not profess to be primarily either of these.

The second instance of moral failure I adduce is related to the first, but counts nonetheless as a separate finding. On 24 December 1943, Pius XII, in his annual Christmas broadcast, pronounced what he regarded as the strongest condemnation he had made or could offer of the unfolding "Holocaust." He did this by referring in that broadcast to "those hundreds of thousands who, without any fault of their own, sometimes only by reason of their nationality or race, are marked down for death or gradual extinction." Some listeners to that Christmas message noted that even on this portentous occasion and at that relatively late date, with knowledge of the Holocaust widespread and clear, the Pope refrained from mentioning both the Jews and the Nazis by name. This itself is (and was) worthy of notice, but the "failure" I call attention to here is less concerned with that omission than with the justification that the Pope afterwards gave for it. Certain foreign dignitaries appointed to the Vatican met with the Pope soon after the Christmas broadcast and asked him, directly and pointedly, about the omission: Why *not* mention the Nazis by name, as primarily responsible for the "death or gradual extinction" to which he had referred? Harold Tittman, the American emissary to the Vatican (equivalent to, although not with the formal rank of, ambassador), reported the Pope's response to this question in a telegram to the American Secretary of State, Cordell Hull (5 January 1943): "He [Pius XII] explained that when talking of atrocities he could not name the Nazis without at the same time mentioning the Bolsheviks."

Pius XII himself, reportedly, had been taken aback by the question to which he gave this response; he clearly believed that the reference in his broadcast had gone very far indeed toward putting himself on record. Even if we accept this judgment for the sake of argument, however, his response to the question *about* his statement emerges in itself as an instance of omission or failure: *Why* could the Pope not have mentioned Nazi atrocities without also mentioning those of the "Bolsheviks"? It is obvious that at the basis of this response is Pius XII's conviction that those two sources of wrongdoing were at the very least equivalent ("at the very least" since he might have judged the "Bolsheviks" even more severely than the Nazis). In other words, on his view, the two regimes were responsible for committing the same kinds or qualities of act, as measured by whatever general standard of wrongdoing national regimes could reasonably be judged. But was this indeed the case? And was the impact of a papal condemnation likely also to have identical consequences for the two?

The answers to both the latter questions seem clearly to be "No"—but there is even a still more basic matter at stake here. In terms of what principle is it necessary to condemn all (similar) wrongs in order to condemn any one of them—especially when the condemnation of one of them by itself might produce more results than condemning the other by itself or even by condemning the two together? It is evident, in fact, that some other factor than only the question of equity—a sense of impartiality toward wrongdoing—influenced Pius XII's response to the question he had been asked. The conjecture that the Nazis, no matter what wrongs they committed, were also a bastion against the Bolsheviks (hence useful in a way that the Bolsheviks were not) may remain unproven as a decisive motive—but the assumption of something close to it appears required to explain Pius XII's refusal to condemn Nazism without condemning Bolshevism. There is no intrinsic reason why the two should have been linked together—and so the explanation must be sought elsewhere. That he was subsequently able to condemn Communism with no reference, even looking backward, to Nazism is another item of supporting evidence for this interpretation.

The third example of moral failure adduced here provides the title for Susan Zuccotti's book: what Pius XII refused to do at the time of the roundup of Jews in Rome on 16 October 1943. One point in relation to this event remains inexplicable, even apart from any question of direct opposition: the failure of the Vatican, which almost certainly knew beforehand of the impending roundup, to convey a warning to the Jewish community of Rome—a warning that would have allowed the Jewish populace to go into hiding. It is difficult to imagine a plausible explanation for this omission: the hypothesis that fear of being held accountable for any such warning was responsible would condemn the silence as much as explain it. The more notable breach in moral terms, however, is the fact that after the roundup took place—"under the very windows of the Pope," as von Weizsäcker himself put it—and with the trains standing by to deport more than a thousand Roman Jews (the "Pope's Jews") to Auschwitz, not a single public word of protest was uttered by the Pope even in private, let alone publicly. Soon after the deportation, Weizsäcker could accurately (and apparently with no intent of irony) report to Berlin that the Pope "has not allowed himself to be carried away making any demonstrative statements against deportation of the Jews. . . . He has done all he could . . . not to prejudice relationships with the German government."[2]

To be sure, and once again: the argument from prudence often surfaces here in defense of the Pope's position—prudence dictated here by the Nazi threat to occupy Vatican City and to take the Pope prisoner: Would not *this* have been sufficient reason for a muted response, for resorting to "silent diplomacy" rather than open opposition? But aside from the question of how active the alleged "silent diplomacy" was, a more substantial question arises in this context: is there no time and no occasion when the Vatican, or the Pope himself, should be willing to place themselves at risk? Admittedly, it is difficult (or it should be difficult; at times it is made to seem far too easy) to impose on someone else an obligation for martyrdom. But there was slight reason to believe that the Nazis had in mind literal martyrdom for Pius XII. And it is a fair question to ask whether anything less than that (and perhaps, for the spiritual leader of the Church, even *that*) should be a sufficient reason for silence where large and fundamental moral principles were at stake. One might have thought that the question of what the order of importance was between the sacred and the profane would not be in doubt for the Church.

In conclusion I offer an analogy—a thought-experiment in something like the form of a parable, concerning the disagreement between "not enough" and "plenty" as those conflicting assessments have persisted of Pius XII's role in the Holocaust. Imagine that a person who is morally conscientious arrives after much grappling and reflection at a policy about giving charity. He or she makes substantial monetary contributions, *more* than a tithe; he or she also spends much time in working for good causes. And then, having considered the various levels and means of giving, this person decides that on balance a certain combination of such contributions is as much as he or she can reasonably offer, given the resources of income and time available, and given the other responsibilities and obligations to family and self that the person has. In other words, a limit is decided on—a generous one by any standards, but still a limit: this much and no more. But then one morning not long after having made the decision, the same person opens the front door to pick up the daily paper—and finds a stray young child sitting on the steps: emaciated, weak with hunger, alien, obviously without resources. The person who finds the child has at that point a choice between two courses of action: to apply the reasoned conclusion that had been conscientiously arrived at about the limits of charity and time— and so to pick up the paper and shut the door. Or to bring the child inside, overturning a policy thoughtfully decided on and the violation of which might entail harmful consequences to both others and the person himself. What then, reader—you decide—would be the right course of action?

TWELVE

The Evil in Genocide

A different title that I decided *not* to use for this chapter would have been more explicit—but also offensive: "*What's so bad about genocide, anyway?*" That wording sounds flippant, and the topic of genocide warrants something more than that. But the flippancy has a serious side to it, since although what is bad or wrong in genocide is often regarded as self-evident, it is in fact far from that; the assumption that it *is* obvious has led to both overuse and misuse of the term and to distortions in understanding its reference. The question of the evil in genocide—what *is* so bad about it—is, at any rate, my subject here, with my premise the claim that genocide is indeed "so bad": evil, if any human act is or can be. Nobody is likely to find this assessment surprising or contentious. On any ranking of crimes or atrocities, it would be difficult to name an act or event regarded as more heinous; genocide arguably appears now as the most serious offense in humanity's lengthy—and, we recognize, still growing—list of moral or legal violations.

This view of genocide's public standing is supported by two pieces of evidence in particular. The first is that the charge of genocide has become a metaphor for atrocities as such, some of them clearly not genocide even when we make allowance for a certain vagueness in that phenomenon's formal definition. Poverty, disease, and slavery (for examples) have at times been labeled genocide or genocidal, and although these *have* sometimes been associated with genocide, it is doubtful that there is any intrinsic connection between the two. Human history includes many terrible acts and events—but not all of them, indeed relatively few, are or were genocidal. Nonetheless, *genocide* has become a virtual synonym for atrocity, the equivalent of a curse more damning than any other. And this figurative expansion has been possible, I suggest, only because the term's *literal* meaning made it so; figurative expression, after all, is anchored in the world as it is.

The second piece of evidence for the extreme character of genocide stems from the history of the word itself: the fact that a new term had to be coined (recently, in historical terms: 1944) in order to name the crime it denoted—implying also that a new concept had to be *thought*, one reflecting new circumstances or old circumstances newly pushed to an extreme or to an expanded moral consciousness. To be sure, this relatively brief history does not mean that genocide had not *occurred* previously (events often take place that at the time have no name), and there is continuing disagreement on genocide's historical status—with claims on one side, for example, that the Holocaust, the Nazi Genocide against the Jews, was the first of its kind or (more strongly) unique; on the other side (here, with majority opinion), that earlier occurrences of genocide, from biblical and classical times forward, had all its requisite features, however distinctive the *scale* of the Holocaust as genocide was.

There is no disagreement, however, about the novelty of the term "genocide" or (by implication) of the concept at its basis. These were shaped largely by the efforts of a single person, the Polish Jewish jurist—and then émigré to the United States—Raphael Lemkin who, after a number of other starts at the concept in the 1930s, in his book *Axis Rule in Occupied Europe* (1944), applied the term as we now know and use it.[1] During this period, Lemkin was working his way toward a definition of his new term as a needed development, since, in his view, no other term or phrase available in the legal or moral vocabulary adequately expressed its meaning: not murder, not mass murder, not even the catch-all but also vague phrase of "crime against humanity." Genocide, the phenomenon of *group murder* (joining the Greek and Latin roots: *genos* and *cide*), was, in his view, distinct from all of these, distinct as an act and distinct also in its moral weight. And for its evil—the latter, both for the wrong *specific* to its occurrences but also (as I shall attempt to show) for its enlargement on evil as such.

First, then, to the evil specifically in genocide. To represent this adequately requires retracing certain steps in the concept's history, with a focus on the *gap* that it was meant to fill. Legal and moral thinking—like nature in its classical formula—at once abhors a vacuum and seems to do nothing in vain. When a new concept appears, then, it is reasonable to assume that it does so because something had been found missing in the extant array of legal and moral categories. Just such a lack stands behind the formulation of the concept of genocide as a distinctive crime that Lemkin set out to identify, beginning with his initial effort at an international congress in Madrid in 1933, and moving then to a fuller articulation in the book from 1944 just mentioned, which he wrote with the Nazi atrocities in full view (which included the murder of forty-nine members of his own family). The concept of genocide that emerged from this process was subsequently put to use in the articulation of the Nuremberg trials (the International Military Tribunal) of 1945 and the many war trials following them, in both Germany and the countries it had occupied or attacked (although genocide as a formal prosecutorial charge figured only rarely in the immediate post-war trials).[2] And this phase of the new concept's history culminated in actions taken by the newborn United Nations, first in a General Assembly resolution in 1946 and then in the 1948 Convention on the Punishment and Prevention of the Crime of Genocide. The most recent development in this continuing history has been the formation of the permanent International Criminal Court established for prosecuting the crime of genocide, active since July 2002. Other tribunals initiated earlier under the auspices of the United Nations (for the former Yugoslavia and for Rwanda) are also still conducting hearings on charges of genocide in those locations—the best known of which is the case of Slobodan Milosevic; findings of genocidal guilt have already been determined—as in the judgment in August 2001 against the Serbian General Radislav Kristic.

The extraordinary figure of Raphael Lemkin affected *all* these stages of thinking and legislation about genocide. The "crime" he labored to bring to the world's attention seems now so obvious that we might well conclude that there were reasons (not necessarily good ones) why it had not been identified earlier —with one such reason especially relevant to understanding the concept itself. International law in its modern history has viewed the nation-state as its basic structural unit; international crimes—which nations always had regarded warily because of the possibility that any legislation they agreed to might later be turned against them—were, on the standard model, crimes committed by one nation against another. The implications of this taboo were straightforward: within the boundaries of a given nation, no other country had a recognizable "interest" in the first country's treatment of its citizens or minorities; so far as concerned individual inhabitants of *another* country, the obligations even of nations at war were primarily to other nations, with little thought to spare for the other's non-citizens and none at all for groups not defined *by* their citizenship. To be sure, international conventions had been adopted for protecting prisoners of war and "civilian populations" in conquered and occupied territories. Omitted from that protection, however—as came out more graphically in World War II than ever before—was protection for groups who either had never been citizens of a host country, or had been citizens of that or another country but were then persecuted because of some group feature either after having been disenfranchised or after having an alleged (negative) group feature judged sufficient to override whatever rights they had. These groups, Lemkin saw, were quite without internal protection— since a reigning government could believe itself entitled to do as it wished to its own populace (as the Turks made clear in persecuting the Armenian minority in Turkey in 1915–17, and as also the Nazis did to German Jews, beginning in 1933—both of these under a fig leaf cover of internal legality). On the other hand, such groups were also unprotected externally, from an *occupying* power, since the legal apparatus imposed by such a power might override whatever protections the occupied country itself had set up—the more readily, of course, if no such legislation existed.

The concept of genocide verged in this way on a distinctive, if not novel domain of law—breaching the traditional boundaries of national and international law by rejecting the "hands-off" doctrine that gave nations free rein in respect to members of their own populace, and disputing the premise of international law that granted full standing only to nations. The UN Convention on Genocide thus moved toward a conception of "*meta*-national" law that would protect groups *aside* from (and sometimes, of course, against) the political authority that had formal jurisdiction over them. Admittedly, a lengthy theological and philosophical tradition of natural law and natural rights antedated this development[3]—as had earlier been demonstrated, for example, in prominent political texts of the Enlightenment like the U.S. Declaration of Independence (1776) and the French Declaration of the Rights of Man and Citizen (1789). But also these texts turned quickly to the more readily applied dualism between intra- and international law, leaving groups that were other or less than nations to fend for themselves. The texts referred to did indeed speak of "natural" or "unalienable"—that is, *inherent*—rights as more fundamental than any granted by national affiliation or citizenship, asserting that every person, quite apart from the question of national citizenship, possessed such rights that *could* then have been extended to associations or groups of citizens within the body politic. In practice, however, such rights, important as they were as a rationale for the American or French revolutions, gave way in practice to a less generous model that associated them with the national citizenship of individuals—in effect abandoning groups of citizens as groups to the space between individual and nation, a space that subsequently remained almost empty.

It was these unprotected groups, outside the law as groups even in supposedly enlightened societies, that Lemkin saw as requiring protection against the threat of genocide—the murder or destruction of a group qua group. The act of genocide thus rests equally on the two parts of the term itself: on *genos* (groups), and on *cide* (murder). The first of these parts raises more complex conceptual issues than the second (what, after all, *is* a group?), but much might be said about the latter as well. Lemkin himself, and then the UN Convention, found, for example, that the destruction of a group did not require the physical killing of its members. A group *could* be destroyed by killing, of course, and this remains the term's most definitive application—the reason why the Nazi Genocide against the Jews is a paradigm, if one can use that term, of genocide. (There could be no clearer expression of genocidal intent than Heinrich Himmler's words to the SS in 1943 (cited in earlier chapters), that "that people [the Jews]" must be made "to disappear from the earth."). But there are also other ways of destroying groups of people, and if these are less certain or their results less easily determined, their consequences are equally destructive. Thus, the UN Convention includes four means of genocide in addition to physical killing: the forcible transfer of children, imposing measures to prevent births within the group, inflicting conditions of life on the group calculated to bring about its destruction,[4] and causing "serious bodily or mental harm" to the members of the group. These means differ in the range of their immediate cruelty, but any of them, it is evident, could lead to the destruction of the group over a period of time—and it is clearly *this*, the demise of the group, the death of potential future members, against which the formulation of the crime speaks.

In addition to the differences among these means, there is also some lack of clarity in their terms (as there is even more obviously in the Convention's stipulation that genocide may be directed against a group "in whole or in part"). The need for greater precision in the Convention's wording has been widely acknowledged, and undoubtedly the Convention will be progressively modified, if only through the weight of precedents as these emerge from actual genocide trials. Its essential principle, however, is clear and unambiguous: genocide entails the intended destruction of a group—and it differs in this not only from the destruction of individuals, but also from destruction or murder on a large scale where that act is directed at individuals as individuals and not as members of a group. (Genocide is thus not a function of numbers; mass murder that is not genocide may account for larger numbers of victims than particular instances of genocide.) What is distinctive about the murder in genocide is not killing, then, but its object; namely, the group. For it is the intent of genocide, as Himmler's statement notes so decisively, to destroy the group, with the group identity itself, apart from its individual bearers, "made to disappear." Of course, the surest and quickest way to destroy a group is by the physical destruction of its members—but the latter is the means to the end represented by the former, with a recognizable distinction between the two.

We find here, then, the first aspect of the evil in genocide: that, as in genocide's most explicit example, it involves a twofold murder, killing at two levels: the murder of individuals, but that as a means to the second "murder" of the group of which the individuals are members. This twofold murder is the basis, again, for distinguishing genocide from individual murder, on the one hand, and from mass murder, on the other. The murder committed is of two kinds of beings: individuals—yes; but also, and distinctively, the group of which the individuals are members. Certain objections to this formulation may appear quickly. Are not groups only the assembly of a number (and an indefinite one at that) of individuals? How can groups be substantively distinguished from the individuals who make them up? Something more will be said about this issue below, but the short response to it is that we do in fact make the distinction referred to *all the time*. For groups—at least, some of them—are not simply individuals added to each other; at times they have an identity larger than and separable from the individuals who make them up. They appear, in effect, as corporate or collective persons capable of actions and achievements, sometimes in ways that individuals by themselves or even randomly joined are not. To be sure, groups do not have the *physical* "vital signs" of individual human beings, but they do constitute lives and histories apart from the lives and histories of their individual members. And they can also, as genocide makes clear, suffer death. (The analogy to the threatened deaths of biological species is only approximate—but the various movements to protect animal species are so confident in the justification for their cause that it typically goes unstated.)[5]

A pressing question recurs here as to *which* groups can be subject to genocide, since the definition of what counts as a group is elastic: they may, for example, have as few as three or four members or as many as millions (Thoreau, we recall, could think of himself as a majority of one.) Membership in a group, furthermore, can be fixed by an indefinitely large number of indicators—from eye color or occupation to the first letter of last names, and so on. Genocide as defined in the UN Convention, however, refers to groups with special significance in social and cultural life. This does not mean, of course, that the murder of other groups would not be criminal or evil—only that it might nonetheless be distinguishable from genocide. And although there has been disagreement about which groups *should* be covered by the Genocide Convention, there has been none about the groups that the Convention *does* name; that is, "national, ethnical, racial, or religious groups."

Why should these groups in particular have been singled out for protection? The UN Convention itself offers no justification or explanation, but the reasoning behind its choices seems clear enough: that these groups contribute more essentially to social structure and life (collective or individual) than others of the indefinitely large number of groups that might be named—from the college class of '04 to the residents on Main Street to Sherlock Holmes's "red-headed" league. (The most contentious exclusion debated in the UN was that of "political" groups; that category was finally excluded—on what were patently political grounds). And indeed, whatever other candidates might be added to the UN's list, it seems indisputable that the groups presently on that list have without a doubt been primary in shaping cultural and individual identity in contemporary societies: West or East, First World or Third. A test of this claim would be the thought-experiment of imagining what societies or individuals would be like without them, and it seems clear that the outcome here would be social and individual life radically different from anything familiar to us—a life difficult even to imagine. The difference made evident in this way would not be due to the absence of this or that feature or individual, but to the absence of a *group* identity as that shapes individuals in a way that no other influence on them—including biology itself—can.

The first aspect of the evil in genocide, then, comes to this: that the types of groups against which genocide is directed—those "*eligible*" for genocide—are types in the absence of which the lives of individual (and collective) humanity would be inconceivable or at least, radically diminished. And this, it seems, is a principal justification for thinking of genocide as the murder referred to by the term: not only that genocide may involve individual murder as a means to its corporate end, but that the corporate goal is murder, the destruction of the group identity without which the individuals would not have been, and could not be, the individuals they were or would be. Genocide in this sense represents the group as in effect a "person"—arguably, as Aristotle proposes for the polis in the *Politics,* an entity *prior* to the individual person: life-*giving*—and understood in this way, reflecting the difference between death and life as well for the individual. This claim might seem exaggerated if we think of ethnic or religious or national groups and identity as made up of many small and discrete parts, a large number of which might be altered or excluded with no *essential* loss. But it is important to keep in mind that the destruction intended in genocide is not piecemeal but total. (Individuals may also "lose" parts of themselves without ceasing to be the same individuals.) Murder here, in the first evil of genocide, involves the destruction of the means of existence or personhood.

A second and different facet of the evil in genocide is only obliquely related to the first. This is the intent of genocide to destroy members of a group not because of anything they have *done*, but solely because of their identification *as* members of the group. In other words, genocide kills individuals not after finding them responsible for doing or failing to do some specific thing, but just because of their identity—with the determination of that to a large extent externally imposed. What I mean by the latter point is that identification of the group and its members is typically determined for the purposes of genocide by the agent of genocide, not by its victims—since here as elsewhere, the power structure also controls the categories or labels of identity. What results is typically a process of imposed identification that is also, to that extent, arbitrary. So, for one example, the Nazi definition in the 1935 "Nuremberg Laws" of who was a Jew drew the lines around anyone with three Jewish grandparents. This, however, represented a substantial reduction in the ruling issued two years earlier according to which *one* Jewish grandparent sufficed. But there is ample evidence that the basis for this change, which by the stroke of a pen sharply reduced the total number of "German Jews," was not biological, but practical, and so, in racial terms, arbitrary: the earlier, more inclusive definition would also have been much more difficult to enforce—however odd it may seem that the Nazis would under any circumstances object to having "too many" Jews to persecute. Or again, to show how the process of group identification can come even closer to absurdity, we recall the alleged (disputed, but alleged) policy of the Khmer Rouge of identifying for genocide those of their Cambodian countrymen who wore eye glasses—as marking the dangerous group of intellectuals. What happens in these cases is that within the vague initial boundaries of a group marked for genocide, further specification is made—but this identifies group members neither by their own assent nor for reasons related to the group identity itself. Yet a death sentence nonetheless emerges.

This grounding of genocide on involuntary identity or character—the denial of individual autonomy—appears also in relation to the question of how individual membership in the four groups named by the UN Convention is determined. For although membership in those groups is voluntary in principle (race, to be sure, the least so, but also there, insofar as the actual definitions of race are social constructs), to a great extent the reality of those identities is involuntary, certainly initially (ethnicity, for example, is transmitted first and strongly through language and the home)—but then also, with continuing external pressure. Religion and nationality, to be sure, are more clearly voluntary features of individual identity than the other categories, but for them, too, the pressures against "opting out" are often intense and at times overwhelming: many people manage to do it, but many more do not—and even for those who do, it is often a difficult process. Also in this respect, then, for those subjected to genocide, the group identification that is the necessary first step in that process (and a universal mark of it), is if not entirely, largely imposed. Even at their freest, these elements of identity are distinguishable from other, fuller decisions or choices made by members of the group—which means that genocide acts against its victims, once again, on grounds for which they have at best only limited responsibility.

To be sure, the justification for genocide by its agents often cites the responsibility of the group attacked for decisions or actions of its members, claiming that these have caused harm or represent a danger to others. But even the semblance of evidence for these claims is usually lacking, and a stronger objection still is that on this justification, the group attacked is held responsible for dispositions or conduct for which they are in fact not responsible—in the sense that they were not able *not* to engage in the acts or conduct they are charged with. This is one reason, it seems clear, why the language of genocide so frequently turns to medical or biological metaphors: the Jews, in Hitler's own language, were "germ carriers," "a virus," "a racial tuberculosis"; this representation of the Jews' conduct as symptomatic of a dangerous disease would then justify genocide as surely as would the menace of any other deadly pestilence. One does not *blame* a virus or bacillus for the harm it causes; the moral issue simply does not arise.

Admittedly, societies do act against even involuntary conduct when that seems a menace. But such measures are based on individual *conduct,* not on a presumption of group identity—which is at once larger than anything the individual does but also smaller, in the sense that there is no necessary connection, where genocide emerges, between the group and the action initiated against it. Genocide, in these terms, adds to the destruction of the group identity murder which rejects the humanity of its victims in denying their autonomy or freedom of decision. Members are killed *not* for choices they have made or acts they have committed, but either for alleged dispositions beyond their control or for others that they might have acted upon but have not been shown to. The verdict against them, then—the genocide—is first (whatever else ensues) a denial of them as persons, as responsible moral agents—a denial otherwise intimated in genocide's twofold murder, but distinctive enough in this second aspect to stand for itself. In the first facet of the evil in genocide, the denial of the victims' humanity appears as a prior condition or preventative, declaring that there shall be no such group or individual members of it *in the future*—where the second aspect of evil in genocide comes to the denial or reduction of humanity in the group *at present*, as and when it exists. Whatever else can be said against the Nazi denial that the Jews were human at all, the internal logic leading to its consequences was rigorous: given their essentialist—biological—conception of Jewish group identity, genocide was not simply the "Final" Solution; it was also the only solution.

If one asks how these two facets of the evil in genocide fit into or reshape any more general conception or understanding of evil, it seems to me that in one way they conform to a standard view—and in another way, they challenge it. Both facets conform to what seems a minimal standard view of evil as value destroyed with no commensurate recovery—the destruction affecting not only the potential that exists in any human being, but also the *means* (through group identity) by which, and only by which, that potential can be realized. But genocide also goes beyond this, it seems, in arguing against a common view of evil that holds that evil has an intrinsic relation to ignorance, to an absence of deliberation or intention; that in the end, when people do evil or wrong, it is not because they have chosen these goals fully cognizant of the evil or wrong in them, but because they mistakenly believe that what they are doing is good—or at least, that it is better than the alternative. Thus, this position argues—standing on the shoulders of Plato and the Platonic tradition, of the seventeenth-century rationalism of Spinoza and Leibniz, and of at least a part of the Judeo-Christian heritage—if people who do evil only knew better, if they *really* understood what they were doing, they would not do it; they would choose differently.

There is much to be said—and much that has been said—about this view of evil (some of it in Chapter 3). What is at issue here was dramatically brought face to face with the occurrence of genocide in Hannah Arendt's analysis of Adolf Eichmann's character and role in the "Final Solution" which has become familiar through her phrase, the "banality of evil": the claim that Eichmann managed to do great evil although neither his intention nor he himself was at all great.[6] He was no Iago, Arendt claims, nor a Richard III; he did not think enough about what he was doing to qualify as authentically or radically evil— indeed, he hardly thought at all. He was—in her words—"thoughtless," a "clown"—unfortunately finding himself (he spoke of his own "bad luck") in a position that placed fateful decisions in his hands. That thoughtlessness, Eichmann's reliance on clichés not only in speaking but in *thinking*, was his, and his evil's, banality—with the clear implication, according to Arendt, that if he *had* been capable of thought, he would not have done what he did. Iago and Richard III, after all, in the forms that we know them best, are products of Shakespeare's imagination: there and there only, we infer from Arendt's account, is where radical evil, evil deliberately chosen, is to be found—in fictional worlds, not in the course of ordinary human agency and responsibility. She had come to realize, Arendt concluded not long afterward in a letter to Gershom Scholem (just before he cut off all communication with her), that "*all* evil is banal."

Insofar as this alleged impossibility of voluntary or willed evil is open to verification at all, however, the phenomenon of genocide seems to me to provide certain counterevidence, or at least to raise doubts about it. For it is a feature of genocide as conceived in the UN Convention, that it is always intentional; and although in this respect genocide may seem no different from other premeditated acts, an implication of what I have been saying here *also* suggests that genocidal intention is not only directed at the destruction of the group, but that it aims at that destruction while *knowing* the act's wrongfulness. In other words, that those who commit genocide both recognize the wrong and do what they do at least in part for that reason—in effect making that knowledge itself an element of the intention. This is obviously a large claim to make good on, both about genocide in general and about its specific instances. I have elsewhere attempted to show how an awareness of their wrongdoing figures in the Nazi's "Final Solution"—arguing that the moral *quality* of that process appears in the conscious *style* of Nazi expression and actions where, in addition to their specific wrongdoing, the will to transgression itself is also evident.

I can here rehearse that argument only in an abbreviated form, relating it as well to the still more difficult challenge of proving that genocide as such—as an institution of war—involves conscious wrongdoing. On that point, I would claim that the rationale for killing on the basis of an imposed group-identity always betrays itself—can never be undertaken in good faith—because of the evident disproportion between the object and the act: it is the group traits that are condemned, but it is individuals who are killed, and the disparity between those two, no matter how much effort is made to align them, do not match up, in fact or theory. This contention is supported by certain apparently accidental, albeit typical features of genocide—which are, in my view, not accidental at all: the invariable practice of secrecy and denial on the part of those carrying it out, the elaborate—and one has to say, imaginative—efforts at dehumanization that typically accompany it (not simply direct physical or brute torture but measures directed against the person as a member of the *genos*); the subsequent psychopathologies suffered by its agents. All these features of genocide require explanation—and *one* such explanation points to an awareness of the evil being committed on the part of those doing it. Some of the features mentioned, to be sure, may appear in atrocity as such—but the requirement in genocide of both imposing and then annihilating group identity increases both the opportunity and the need for the consciousness of transgression. I realize that the broad thesis of intentional and knowing wrongdoing (inside or outside genocide) requires more evidence and argument than I provide here, but even its possibility seems to me important as one basis for disputing the view that wrongdoing can never be fully voluntary—a basis to which genocide may contribute as distinctively as genocide itself is an historical occurrence.

At the beginning of this chapter, I offered a possible offensive alternate title to the one given—and I would balance that now, in concluding, by another possible offense, proposing that beside what I have described as the evil in genocide, we do well also to look for the good in it. The immediate response to any such proposal will undoubtedly be, "No! No good *could* come out of genocide, no redeeming features, no, none!" But a slower response that begins with the same condemnation might yet also turn its attention sideways to one historical aspect of the conceptualization of genocide that indeed promises—I can think of no other way of describing them—positive or even good consequences. In this age of social self-consciousness, the relationship between immoral practice and moral prohibition hardly needs retelling. Even the gentle skepticism of a writer like Montaigne would remind us that one thing we know when we read about various religious or cultural prohibitions or taboos is that practices that are prohibited have in fact occurred—and with sufficient frequency to be regarded as a danger. There *would be* no prohibitions against murder, robbery, adultery, incest—unless they had first been part of the moral (or immoral) landscape, unless they had occurred. Furthermore, for all these prohibitions and their attendant punishments, something more seems to be going on than only the delineation of individual offenses. Set in motion here is also a stirring—and further construction—of the moral imagination that in some way anticipates specific violations and prohibition but comes into full view only as the pair—act and prohibition together—appear. Together, they then shape further the extent of the moral domain that, it should by now be clear, has a history and is even a "progressive" history. This is not to say that wrongs as they are singled out and identified *become* good or right in this process, or even that, if we had the choice, it would be right or good (whatever that might mean in the context) to choose a world with evil and moral imagination in it over the world without them—but only that in *this*, that is, *our* world, wrong or evil can be, and sometimes are, met by right and good.

Something like this sequence has appeared, I would argue, in relation to genocide as it has been conceptualized, identified, and then expressed in legal, moral, and common discourse. For a concurrent event has been the emergence, also in legal, moral, and common discourse, of "group rights": the concept of the rights of groups (first and foremost) to exist, to *be* groups, that is, of self-determination—but extending from that to other rights implied by or built on that first one. The contemporaneous recognition of genocide as a crime and of group rights as a condition of moral and political justice—both emerging in the aftermath of World War II—is not, *could not* be accidental: they are too closely related conceptually and chronologically, and too much history had passed with neither of them identified, for their simultaneous emergence to be coincidental. Even if one sees the historical progression as moving first from genocide the crime to recognition of the new group's right to exist—first violation, then virtue or justice—there is nothing startling in this; much, perhaps all, moral history follows a similar pattern. Admittedly, all talk of *group* rights faces substantial objections—but so, after all, does, talk of *individual* rights (which, we remember, Bentham unkindly characterized as "nonsense upon stilts"). A common presumption has always been, furthermore, that if group rights are acknowledged at all, they are only individual rights bundled together: since I as an individual have the right to free speech, so, too, any group of which I am a member (together with other individuals) has the same right, but only because of the individual rights of its individual members. But an alternate view of the concept of group rights raises the possibility that group rights may on certain issues precede rather than follow individual rights, or that the two may be co-temporal or co-logical; the concept also proposes a "deep structure" for society quite different from the individualist conception of human nature and social structure deeply embedded in contemporary Western political ideology. In certain respects, the practice of group rights has advanced more quickly than its theory, since many aspects of contemporary political life—from issues of affirmative action to Church–State relations to issues of property rights and taxation—assume not only the possibility but the actuality of group rights. This connection, however, is a topic for another time, and I mention it not to divert attention from the central subject here of genocide but to show that even in relation to that extreme act, moral history and analysis do not escape the reach of dialectic. Certainly the appearance of group rights as underwriting the identification and criminalizing of genocide is not at all meant to provide a concluding "uplift" to the terrible story of genocide that remains, it seems clear, the dominant motif of twentieth century history as a whole. But the two sides do indeed arrive close together, if not quite simultaneously; and so, in the end, they also have to be viewed together, or at least close by. Group rights, yes—because first, group wrongs. And at the very beginning of *that* beginning, genocide.

THIRTEEN

Misinterpretation as the Author's Responsibility (Nietzsche's Fascism, for Instance)

I am terrified by the thought of the sort of people who may one day invoke my authority.

Nietzsche, Letter to Elisabeth Nietzsche, 1884

If . . . the only politics calling itself Nietzschean turned out to be a Nazi one, then this is necessarily significant. . . . One can't falsify just anything.

Derrida, *The Ear of the Other*

The title of this chapter may seem perverse in imposing the two concepts of misinterpretation and responsibility on an author who spent much of his life and work battling against both of them. It seems to me necessary, however, to consider these concepts in order to assess the charges that link—or more point-edly, inculpate—Nietzsche with fascism, if only because Nietzsche's distinctiveness as a writer and his views *on* writing and interpretation directly affect the way we read (or *mis*read) him and his politics (that is, if he has any).[1] Nietzsche himself, after all, created the genealogy as a genre of philosophical discourse, and it is fitting, then, to read genealogically what he himself wrote; that is, through the lineage—not the history, but the begetting—especially of those systematic concepts that he believed he had understood so radically that he could without qualms also will their destruction.

I shall, then, be moving back and forth here between certain general questions in the theory and practice of interpretation and the more specific—for this chapter, the more central—matter of Nietzsche's fascism. *If*, again, that's what it is. A framework for the inquiry emerges from a number of questions that I at first answer briefly and unequivocally (well, almost unequivocally)— those answers that are then to be elaborated, although also, I admit, to some extent hedged and hemmed.

Post-Holocaust

Question:	Was Nietzsche a fascist or an advocate for fascism?
Answer:	No.
Question:	Has he been interpreted *as* a fascist?
Answer:	Yes—by both fascists and anti-fascists (but not by all of either; some of those others—again on both sides—think of him as anti-fascist, some as either so politically retrograde or so advanced as to be neither pro- nor anti-).
Question:	Did Nietzsche anticipate being misinterpreted?
Answer:	Yes—often. Misinterpreted as a *fascist?* Also yes (that is, once we allow for the anachronism: If the doctrines of Mussolini's "fascismo" became actual in his march on Rome, that was in 1922, twenty-two years after, not before Nietzsche died. A second chronological datum makes the same point, although more eccentrically: Nietzsche's madness seized him early in 1889— a useful mnemonic reference for recalling the year of Hitler's birth. Understandably, then, the term *fascism* does not appear in Nietzsche's writing, but this does not mean that the term could not be rightly (and so wrongly) applied to what he wrote—or that he could not, or should not have anticipated those applications.
Question:	Did Nietzsche attempt in his writing to *prevent* the misinterpretations he anticipated?
Answer:	Yes; that is, to some extent.
Question:	Could he have done more than he did in those attempts at prevention?
Answer:	Yes, demonstrably.
Question:	Then is Nietzsche *responsible* for the misinterpretation?
Answer:	Yes, of course. On the standard juridical model that holds people accountable for acting negligently; otherwise, for sins of omission.
Question:	If Nietzsche is responsible for, that is, contributed to—in some sense, chose—to be misinterpreted as a fascist or advocate of fascism, would this suggest that to charge him with fascism is not a *mis*interpretation at all?
Answer:	Maybe. Go back to the first question, and start over.

Thus, now to the sequence of argument underlying these responsa as they revolve around the general issues of whether, when, and how an author may be responsible for his misinterpretation by others. All the words in this phrase of my title, I realize, beg certain well-known questions that I do not plan to "un-beg" here, offering instead only a brief apologia. So: *Mis*interpretation implies that interpretation can go wrong—which in turn implies that it can also go right or at least righter than interpretations that don't. And these together imply that the focus of interpretation (also misinterpretation) is a point or circle, perhaps only a penumbra, that serves the text as a center and its readers as a target. Call this center or target the (or a) *meaning* or *referent* or *signifiee* or even *thing-in-itself*: without *some* one of these, neither interpretation nor misinterpretation would get very far; indeed, they would not move at all.

I know that the links in this chain of inference have been under attacks that dispute the very notion of *good* or *bad* interpretations—still more, of *right* and *wrong* or *true* and *false* ones. On such accounts, *mis*interpretation becomes only a misnomer for an opinion delinquent enough to differ from our own—a conclusion that follows logically if we deny all objective status to the text and/or reject authorial intention as relevant to its understanding. Both of which claims this oppositional view makes.[2] However else one judges this view of interpretation, an immediate advantage it offers for my own conflicting project is that it leaves the argument here free to assume that contradictory—to suppose, that is, that interpretation and misinterpretation do intersect at a common object. At least in this class, then, the answer to Stanley Fish's well-remembered question is "Yes, there is a text"—and the corpse sighted in the "death of the author" was evidently a case of projection, perhaps only of wishful thinking, by certain critics. And then, too, we here have recourse to the concept of responsibility, when the very category of moral categories (thanks in due measure to Nietzsche himself) has come under fire as tendentious, certainly as lacking any foundation worth the name. All in all, then, a reactionary feast—but let us at least see what it amounts to in its own terms

For from this point of view, certain quite plausible conclusions seem to follow—since it asks us to think of writing as if it were an act (that is, deliberate), with an at least one-time agent, that is, author; which at its conclusion produces a characteristic meaning or range of meaning. When to these are added the text's potential consequences for the reader, we find that the process of interpretation meets both the necessary and sufficient conditions of ascribing responsibility to the author, who did, after all, invite the reader in. Consider the transaction here as just that: the author makes an offer, intending to engage the reader; the reader, on the basis of his or her understanding of the offer, then (becoming a reader) accepts. As in any other exchange, the author thus also, sometimes, may be liable for misleading the reader (that is, for the reader's misreading)—an outcome that may itself have been intended or accidental or, in unusual cases, even occur against the author's will; all this, as the text evokes and affects the reader's response. Perhaps authors also bear or share responsibility for consequences *outside* the text—for example, the suicides that (allegedly) followed the publication and first readings of *Young Werther's Sor-*

rows. My interest here, however, is in the more immediate relation between text and reader as the former induces, invites, or even just allows the latter's misinterpretation.

This set of premises, in any event, sets the stage for one large thesis that summarizes the earlier questions and answers as they have been enumerated. Namely:

That Nietzsche is responsible—up to a point, of course—for the interpretation of his work as fascist, even if that reading is (as I also claim) a *mis*interpretation.

Several likely objections to this thesis warrant quick acknowledgment. The first balks at the blatant hedge behind which it seeks shelter: the ascription to Nietzsche of responsibility for his misinterpretation *"up to a point"*—that phrase poised to take away with the other hand what the one hand had given only a moment before. And indeed, how we determine the "point" in "up to a point" without leaving the two theses vacuous, *is* an issue. But conceding this does not threaten the claims themselves, since, at a general level, certain clear cases of misinterpretation and other clear cases of non-misinterpretation can be demonstrated, with some of the former sometimes shown in part to be the author's responsibility. This is in any event what must be shown (and I believe can be) in order to locate the point referred to in the expression "up to a point."

A second likely objection concerns my reference to the "work" of Nietzsche as if it constituted a single whole or system. And one "school" of Nietzsche interpretation has indeed read him this way, sometimes for only particular texts, but at times trans-textually as well—that is, finding unity in the whole of his oeuvre (even where contradictions appear; for philosophers, there's nothing novel in that, after all).[3] But there has also been almost as much opinion directed *against* this unified field theory—as based on Nietzsche's own doctrine of "perspectivism," and his disparagement of "systematic" thinking ("Systematic form attempts to evade the necessity of death in the life of the mind as of the body . . . and so it remains dead. . . . The rigor is rigor mortis"). Or as based on the both literal and literary fragmentation so widespread in his writing that for many readers the aphorism remains his most characteristic or "natural" genre. When these features are added to his subversive views of truth and interpretation (truths: "a mobile army of metaphors, metonyms, and anthropomorphisms . . . which after long use seem firm, canonical";[4] interpretation: "Whatever exists . . . is again and again reinterpreted to new ends, taken over, transformed, and redirected by some power superior to it. . . . All subduing . . . involves a fresh interpretation, an adaptation through which any previous 'meaning' and 'purpose' are necessarily obscured or even obliterated";[5] "There are no facts, there are only interpretations"),[6] the problems facing any would-be *systematic* interpreter of Nietzsche might well appear overwhelming if not, more simply, impossible. Without judging this issue at large,

however, I propose only that on *certain* questions, to read Nietzsche systematically and to read him anti-systematically yield much the same conclusion—or
(in a milder version) that the two modes of reading fit together consistently. At
least on these questions—among them, the ones addressed here—there would
then be only one Nietzsche, not many.

A third problem concerns the definition to be used of "fascism"—since any
charge of fascist allegiance presupposes a definition independent of its particular ascription. But disputes abound about that definition—because of differences alleged between the Italian and Nazi versions of fascism, for instance, or
because of *their* alleged differences from the other totalitarian systems have
multiplied so inventively during the twentieth century. The supposedly neutral
dictionary-definitions of the term are as ideologically complicit as many openly
partisan statements—and indeed I turn for a working definition to the substantial agreement between an advocate and an opponent of fascism on its central
features. So, to one side, Mussolini, writing with Giovanni Gentile, in 1932,

> Against individualism, the Fascist conception is for the State . . . which is the con-
> science and universal will of man in his historical existence . . . [and which] inter-
> prets, develops and gives strength to the whole life of the people [41–42]. . . . It
> affirms the irremediable, fruitful and beneficent inequality of men, who cannot be
> leveled by such a mechanical and extrinsic fact as universal suffrage [49]. . . . It
> thus [also] repudiates the doctrine of Pacifism. . . . War alone brings up to their
> highest tension all human energies. . . . All other trials are substitutes which never
> really put a man in front of himself in the alternative of life and death [47].[7]

And then, less dramatically: the political theorist Walter Z. Laqueur, writing in
1996, with the experience of fascism behind him, and so, as he hopefully expresses it, in the past tense:

> The interest of the state always took precedence over the right of the individual.
> State power was to be based on leadership, and the legitimacy of leadership was
> provided by the fact that the people followed the leader. Seen in this light, the
> leader embodied the will of the people, and fascism was the true democracy. . . .
> One nation is the others' natural enemy . . . and those with the greatest willpower
> will prevail.[8]

Two common themes in these compressed statements seem crucial. The first
is my version of the "Fascist Minimum," which for writers on fascism has been
as constant an issue and as elusive as the Philosophers' Stone. This version
posits the priority of the state over the individual—a priority based not simply
on the superiority of state power to individual power or the imbalance between
state and individual rights (and, conversely, between their respective obligations), but in the metaphysical character of the state as expressive of a common or general will. That collective impulse transcends the will and interests
of individuals within the state, serving them in fact as a rule (inevitably, of
course, in the person of a ruler). The second condition is the premise of natu-

ral (that is, of innate or hardwired) inequality among individuals and nations, an inequality demonstrated for the members of each of those groups by the outcome of conflict among them, with such conflict—less nicely, war—thus becoming itself a constitutive value.

Certain aspects of fascism are quite untouched by these two conditions; for example, the economic structure of the fascist state, as that typically inclines to state-sponsored privatization. But the two principles cited seem to me more rudimentary for fascism in its theory and practice than all others; they will appear here, at any rate, as necessary elements of any doctrine (Nietzsche's or anyone else's) that is termed fascist; taken together, furthermore, in the absence of possibly countervailing assumptions, they constitute a sufficient condition as well. Beyond this definition, I would stipulate rather than attempt to prove two of the steps in the "question–answer" sequence outlined in my opening comments. The issue of Nietzsche's *actual* influence on twentieth-century fascism—through whom and how—is interesting and possibly important, but so far as it can be answered (not, it seems to me, very far), its analysis has led to conflicting results, ranging from the claim that his voice was decisive in the rise of fascism (at least of Nazism) to much more modest estimates.[9] The issue of misinterpretation (and so also of his responsibility for it), however, turns not on Nietzsche's *actual* influence but on his invocation by fascists—that is, in their *professed* debt to him. And about this, the evidence is plentiful. Arguably, Hitler himself never read a word of Nietzsche; certainly, if he did read him, it was not extensively (when he summoned the authority of other "thinkers" than himself, which he does not do often, it is Schopenhauer whom he was likely to mention, or, turning music into idea, Wagner). It is clear, however, that other figures committed to National Socialism did read Nietzsche as a herald of Nazi ideology, bringing Hitler to Nietzsche if not the other way round (this is epitomized in the 1934 photograph of "Hitler contemplating the bust of Nietzsche" at the Weimar archive—a set-up contrived by Nietzsche's sister with whom Nietzsche himself quarreled during his lifetime on almost every philosophical or political matter they discussed). Mussolini, even as a young man, not only read Nietzsche and contemporary commentators on him, but wrote a number of admiring reviews and essays about him,[10] and certainly the intellectual figures whom Mussolini attracted (like Gentile) claimed the affinity of Nietzsche for the tenets of the New Order of Italian fascism.

It might be objected that this stipulation attributes to fascist ideology a blanket acceptance of Nietzsche's doctrines, and that this—if anything could be—is unfair to fascism. Even among the staunchest fascists, after all, Nietzsche did not pass unchallenged. So, for example, Ernst Krieck, one of the most influential of "Hitler's Professors," could hardly have been more explicit in his *bon mot*, that "Apart from the fact that Nietzsche was not a socialist, not a nationalist, and opposed to racial thinking, he could have been a leading National Socialist thinker." But ideologies are typically indifferent to systematic consistency; much the more numerous claims for Nietzsche's fascism by anticipation or affiliation have been quite willing to overlook distinctions in his work between what they find to be consonant with fascist ideology and what is at odds with it. This is indeed part of the problem to which this chapter is a response: considering the misinterpretation of which I claim Nietzsche has been the subject but also, however, for which he is responsible (that is, up to a point).

The second item to be accepted as stipulated among the earlier series of questions and answers concerns Nietzsche's assumption that he *would* be misinterpreted—for here again, the evidence (including the first epigraph cited at the beginning of this chapter) seems unequivocal. To be sure, some of his statements along this line are mainly self-serving. Nietzsche evidently regarded his neglect, as exhibited, for example, in the silence that met his writings, as a form of misinterpretation—an understandable if not quite compelling response by an author who found himself (and the few friends he could impose on) obliged to pay the costs of publishing every one of his books that appeared during his lifetime (that is, when he was still in control of them).[11] But Nietzsche relies on more than only an argument from silence in his anticipation of being misinterpreted; he was aware even in his brief working life (he was only forty-five, after all, when the curtain of madness fell) about the diverse and sometimes (for him) objectionable ideological partisans who claimed his patronage. He claimed to "enjoy a strange and almost mysterious respect among all radical parties (Socialists, Nihilists, anti-Semites, Orthodox Christians, Wagnerians)."[12] This incongruous assortment was for him, however, a "comic fact"—his judgment about a matter that would later turn out not to be comic at all and which then becomes an item of evidence in the record assessed here.

We turn at last, then, to Nietzsche in respect to the two necessary conditions of fascism stated above. About the first of these—the priority of the state to the individual, and the autonomous will of the state in that role—there seems virtually no basis for attributing any such view to Nietzsche and much that argues against it. The evidence for this claim includes both the absence of positive assertions and a bounty of negative ones opposing the view—the latter, in Nietzsche's animadversions not only against nationalism which he repeatedly excoriated, but also, more generally, against the concept of the state as a primary factor in the life of either culture or the individual.

His specific statements against nationalism, principally against German nationalism, are numerous and emphatic. So, for example: "If a people is suffering and *wants* to suffer from nationalistic nervous fever and political ambition, it must be expected that all sorts of clouds and disturbances—in short, little attacks of stupidity—will pass over its spirit into the bargain: among present day Germans, for example, now the anti-French stupidity, now the anti-Jewish, now the anti-Polish, now the Christian-Romantic, now the Wagnerian, now the Teutonic, now the Prussian."[13] "[The Germans] . . . have on their conscience all that is with us today—this most *anti-cultural* sickness and unreason there is, nationalism, this national neurosis with which Europe is sick, this perpetuation of European particularism, of *petty* politics."[14]

To be sure, objections to nationalism are not necessarily objections to a role for the state as such—but also on that more general issue, the sources are ample: "The state is the coldest of all cold monsters. Coldly it lies, too; and this lie creeps from its mouth: 'I, the state, am the people.'"[15] "Only where the state ends, there begins the human being who is not superfluous: there begins the song of significance, the unique and irreplaceable manner."[16] "The state is always only the means of preserving many individuals: How could it be the end! It is our hope that through the preservation of so many inferior types a few individuals in whom humanity culminates will be protected."[17] And then, as if to put a final stop to any temptation: "Madness is something rare in individuals —but in groups, parties, peoples, ages, it is the rule."[18]

When such statements are added to his repeated assertion of the priority of the individual, the single person, in the numerous imperatives of *Werde wer du bist* ["Become who you are"], even in those passages where Nietzsche extols *the* "blond beast" or less pictorially but still, *the Übermensch*, seems clear that it is the individual about and to whom Nietzsche is speaking: always in its grounds the singular, always the particular, never as a social creature, never as part of a collective that might be responsible for what the individual has been or may become. To be sure, the ideal of a culture is never far off, and it is not the isolated individual who will constitute—or enjoy—that form of collectivity. But about the steps which, beginning with the individual, would lead to or shape a culture—that is, where the instrument of politics would be expected to intervene—Nietzsche is largely silent. The "will to power" he affirms is not a collective will—not because a collective cannot have a will (the triumph of slave morality has proved otherwise), but because the will to power acts collectively only when those who comprise the collective are too weak to exert themselves individually. Only the chorus that makes a harmony of individual ressentiment culminates in the travesty (but nonetheless the power) of conventional morality. To this extent, the extreme view sometimes proposed, that Nietzsche does not *have* a politics, seems at least arguable (that is, putting aside the claim that to be a- or non-political is also a form of politics—which is in my view an historical or situational, not a theoretical argument).

What then, of the second part of the "Fascist Minimum": the natural hierarchy in value of individuals and groups—nations, peoples, races—the specific order of which is determined by conflict among them, with such conflict itself then appearing as a value? Indisputably, Nietzsche adheres to *something* in each of the two parts of this claim—but in each of them only with qualifications. So, on the one hand, there can be little question that for Nietzsche, there is indeed a hierarchy of value among individuals: few of either his advocates or critics dispute this. Indeed, on this point, the otherwise conflicting fascist and socialist readings of Nietzsche disclose a notable likeness—affirming the possibility of a superior human being in the future: for the one, however, wearing the new face of fascism, for the other, introducing the many-sided selves of a socialist utopia. Apart from these extreme renderings, Nietzsche's attacks on democratic egalitarianism, epitomized in socialism, are as well known as his more positive claims for the significant differences—culturally and individually and finally in worth—that distinguish individuals. "Every superior human being will instinctively aspire after a secret citadel where he is *set free* from the crowd, the many, the majority, where as its exception, he may forget the rule 'man.'"[19] Or again: "We to whom the democratic movement is not merely a form assumed by political organization in decay but also a form assumed by man in decay . . . in the process of becoming mediocre and losing his value, whither must we direct our hopes? Towards *new philosophers*, we have no other choice; towards spirits strong and original enough to make a start on antithetical evaluations."[20] "One speaks of 'equal rights' . . . as long as one has not gained the superiority one wants."[21] After the Danish critic, Georg Brandes (whose Jewish origin, it might be noted, was known to Nietzsche) gave a series of lectures in Copenhagen endorsing Nietzsche's view as "aristocratic radicalism," he wrote to Nietzsche describing the enthusiastic response of his audience to that view; in his reply to Brandes's letter, Nietzsche cites that descriptive phrase of Brandes's as "the shrewdest remark that I have read about myself till now."[22] To be sure, Nietzsche relished Brandes's attention and regard; it is also true that "aristocracy" has historically been a euphemism for varieties of oligarchy or tyranny. On the other hand, once Nietzsche's claim for differences in individual worth is recognized, the question of exactly how to characterize those differences becomes crucial—and it is clear that whatever "aristocratic" means here (for either Nietzsche or Brandes), it is not simply to be equated with the rule of brute force.

We need recall once again the status of the inequality that Nietzsche finds among humankind—principally the fact that that status is not innate or fixed for either individuals or groups. Not that the natural or biological ground is irrelevant—but that what is decisive in their status is what the individual or the group strives for and achieves, and this as a function of actions, not of "hard-wiring." As individuals create themselves, so also do groups: nations, peoples, or what count for Nietzsche as "races." But at none of those levels is individual character fixed: group features change (as Yirmiyahu Yovel has persuasively argued, this is a key to reconciling Nietzsche's harsh diatribes against "priestly" or rabbinic Judaism and his emphatic praise, by contrast, for both biblical and modern Judaism).[23] In genetic terms, in other words, Nietzsche is a Lamarckian, not a Mendelian—and if the former turns out to be faulty science by comparison with the latter, it makes for more much plausible social theory. (Exactly how *non*-biological—if vague—Nietzsche's conception of race is, becomes apparent in statements like this: "The industrious *races* [my emphasis] find leisure very hard to endure: It was a masterpiece of *English* instinct to make Sunday so extremely holy and boring that the English unconsciously long again for their week- and working-days.")[24]

The second part of the second condition of fascism also has strong grounds in Nietzsche's writings: the contention that given the natural inequality among individuals, the way in which this manifests itself is through its assertion. This means in effect acting at someone else's expense—not simply in order to demonstrate the inequality between the two, but as the expression of inequality in a situation where that achievement makes a difference to the outcome. In this sense, individuals will be constant warriors, and war itself a natural, hence desirable state: "You say that it is the good cause that hallows even war—but I say to you: it is the good war that hallows any cause."[25] And then in still more graphic terms: "Life itself recognizes no solidarity, no 'equal rights,' between the healthy and the degenerate parts of an organism: one must excise the latter—or the whole will perish."[26] Even allowing for the high pitch of Nietzsche's rhetoric, statements such as these cannot be reduced, as some commentators have suggested, to metaphor; here and elsewhere, Nietzsche extols war, combat, and the exercise of power—as *a*, if not the *only*, means for determining the composition of an "aristocracy." To this extent, a distinguishing feature of the rulership of the "best"—and it is *to be* a rule—is indeed linked to, although by no means restricted to, the exercise of force.

This having been said, however, it bears repeating that the "will to power" motivating such action remains a function of the individual, not the group or the state. And once again and still more emphatically, there is no reason for thinking of either the ability or the will to strive in war as a biological given, as hardwired or genetic. Admittedly, Nietzsche offers some harsh words on the "illusion" of free will; he rehearses approvingly the Spinozistic conception of metaphysical determinism. But if the "will to power" or any other basic disposition or capacity were genetically transmissible, all his repeated exhortations (and anger against those who fail) would be foolishly, vacuously, beside the point; nobody would have to *become* what they were because they already *would be* what they were. The struggle or war that determines the hierarchy among individuals thus does not ratify an order already settled but means to create one. That distinction is significant

So far, then, an account of Nietzsche in relation to the "Fascist Minimum"—which amounts to his rejection of the first of the two necessary conditions and his acceptance of the second condition only with substantial qualification in each of its two parts. On these terms, any claim for Nietzsche's "fascism" must then be severely—arguably fatally—limited. And yet it is clear that this association *has* been frequently asserted, by both fascists and anti-fascists (although, again not by all of either)—an association asserted for *him*, not for such contemporaries of his as John Stuart Mill (whom Nietzsche himself called a "flathead") or Marx or Ralph Waldo Emerson whom Nietzsche in fact admired. How does one explain this? And what makes it an instance of misinterpretation rather than a straightforward case of assault and battery combined with an act of theft by someone who, searching for the sanction of authority, simply steals a convenient formula? (As, for example, we might ourselves do with Ernst Krieck's ironic criticism of Nietzsche that was cited above, in order to turn that objection into praise for him as "a leading National Socialist thinker"; all that would be required for such a change would be the omission of the contradictory clauses.)

Misinterpretation as the *author's* responsibility, however, differs from readings of this sort that do not qualify as interpretations at all—and the fascist reading of Nietzsche is, I believe, an instance of the former rather than the latter. Admittedly, it has also been argued that from the variety and extremity of Nietzsche's statements, virtually any philosophical (or political) position can be inferred—indeed, that *this* is the one and only constant in his thinking.[27] Even if we were to accept this exaggerated claim, however, it would not explain why in particular fascist commentators who, after all, do have commitments in principle, have found in Nietzsche a special affinity. Is his partial support of the one of the two conditions cited sufficient to explain this? Clearly, there ought to be more of a basis than that. Even making allowance for the Nazi effort to find authoritative figures in an historical past most of whose heroic intellectual figures (Goethe, Schiller, Kant) were unlikely forebears (which doesn't mean, to be sure, that they weren't invoked at times); and making allowance also for the polemical clang—the *Rausch*—of Nietzsche's prose which taken by itself (that is, minus its pervasive irony) fits the rhetorical mode of fascism, there seems something more substantive to the connection, and I offer two suggestions of what that "more" may be.

One of these proposals is straightforwardly historical. This is Nietzsche's call for the "transvaluation" or overthrow of conventional "values"—those norms (religious, moral, social) that governed the public domain and cultures of Europe. The twofold Nietzschean project here of invoking a new mode of being, a new "man" and rejecting the old, that is, the current one, would indeed later mesh with fascist ideology. But well before that, it had struck a chord in a multitude of other "radical" movements—many of them at odds with each other, most of them at odds with other sides of Nietzsche's thought, and few of them otherwise in sympathy with what would then become fascism. Steven Ascheim has enumerated the improbably large array of camp followers whose opposition to conventional norms led also to their regard for Nietzsche as a "godfather"; these diverse partisans included socialists, Marxists, antisemites, Jungians (and Jung) but also Freudians (and Freud), anarchists, feminists, Zionists, and futurists.[28] More recently, even with the benefit of hindsight that now includes the fascist past, claims have been entered of his paternity by postmodernists and democratic liberals (whatever else they have to say about each other).[29]

This widespread, superficially indiscriminate enthusiasm does not, however, answer the question of what factors *more specific* than the attack on conventional norms explain the affinity to him in fascist advocates and apologists—an affinity that in the end was more sustained and enduring than that of any of the other groups mentioned. Here it seems to me an explanation does emerge— from a connection that forcibly joined the two conditions of the Fascist Minimum cited earlier. What occurred there, on this interpretation, is a conceptual sleight of hand recognizable in "informal" logic as the "Fallacy of Composition": attributing a quality or qualities of individuals to the group of which the individuals are members. This logical misstep, in its political migration, turns out to shape a harsh reality—and one can readily see why. Nietzsche's "aristocratic radicalism" is, as has been argued here, fundamentally individualistic: it is the power of the individual, in will and ability, that stands at the principle's center. But power is itself a mass noun; and as it evokes the association of collective or group power as superceding or "overpowering" the individual, it becomes an easy, albeit unwarranted, step to ascribe the individual predicate of power to the group—with group power (in the event, the power of the state) then usurping the role of the individual.

This scenario of a forced connection, I would emphasize, is more than only a "thought experiment" or imaginary construct. Specific advocates of Nietzsche in the name of German nationalism, including figures early in the twentieth century like Werner Sombart and, during the Nazi regime, the philosopher Alfred Bäumler, openly describe the deliberate effort required—and undertaken—to force the interpretation of Nietzsche through this transposition from power in the individual to power in the state. (That effort, Bäumler ingenuously notes, was "difficult but necessary.") The outcome of the process could not, in any event, be doubted: the Nietzsche of fascism would *have* to accord significant authority to the state—at the very least as consistent with whatever else he advocated. But, quite simply, it is a consistency absent in Nietzsche himself.

I do not wish to claim too much for this interpretive reconstruction that may itself be something of a misinterpretation. But the fact that fascism saw in Nietzsche a kindred spirit is beyond dispute—and if one asks how that could occur, given Nietzsche's antagonism to the necessary conditions of fascism as stated above, this is the *kind* of explanation, if not the one itself, that is required. To be sure, even if for the sake of argument we were to accept this account, it would not yet solve a still more fundamental problem in the thesis being posed. For if we do accept this historical reconstruction, the question appears in fuller force than ever of how Nietzsche himself can be held responsible. Why should *he* be blamed for his readers' logical blunders or, more simply, for their tendentious reasoning? Surely if they are responsible for anything at all, it would extend to this part of their "misinterpretation."

But there is, I suggest, a gap between logic and rhetoric, and it is in this space that the charge of responsibility gains its purchase here. It is not only that at the center of Nietzsche's social critique was a theory of how political power evolved (his genealogy)—but that he also recognized that groups which thought in terms of collective rather than individual power, in the mystification of group will and spirit, would—as they already had during his lifetime—see in the conception of power that he advanced a justification for their own collective, not individual use of that quality. He was as much aware of this as he was aware more generally of the easy—subtle, subterranean, glib—transition effected when individuals, failing to find sufficient capacity in themselves, join together to assert their combined force: this is the basis of his critique of the bourgeois society in which he lived, a comfortably outfitted version of the slave morality from which it emerged. (If you wish to know, he asks, "which of them has won for the present, Rome or Judea?" there can be no doubt: "Consider to whom one bows down in Rome itself today.")[30]

What we find, then, is Nietzsche in opposition to certain essential features of the fascism that would follow him historically, aware of the elements of his own thought that might be appropriated in support of them—and yet willing to take the risk. Not, as I have emphasized, blindly and without speaking out: his many anti-nationalist statements demonstrate this, as do his many anti-antisemitic statements that are of a piece, after all, with his anti-nationalistic declarations. To defend the post-enlightenment Jewish culture in Europe and specifically in Germany as Nietzsche did in the face of then current antisemitism was already both to recognize and contest the proto-fascism of the antisemitic chorus known well to Nietzsche through his acquaintance with the Bayreuth circle around Wagner.

What more, one might then ask, could Nietzsche have done than he did? I have not even considered here the readerly equivalent of "caveat emptor" (I suppose it would be "caveat lector") that absolves the seller (and so, in the case of interpretation, the author) of all product liability. Isn't reading, after all, even more than "buying," a purely voluntary act? In assigning responsibility to the author in this transaction, even if only "up to a point," would it not be to propose the establishment of an agency that would test books for their effects, much as the national FDA does in the United States when it takes responsibility for testing foods and drugs? But no. Only assume that words or books—ideas—do indeed have consequences (social, psychological, historical), and then, quite apart from any institutional arrangements based on it, the question of the role and extent of the author's responsibility becomes undeniable.

What, however, does this mean in practice? Is Nietzsche responsible for not anticipating the rise of Mussolini and Hitler and their fascist states—or more modestly, for the use they or their followers made of him in those settings? But already in his own lifetime, we have seen, he was aware not only of the conflicting appropriations of his work but of its appropriation by partisans with whom he found himself seriously at odds and whom he attacked again and again.

Nietzsche himself labels *The Genealogy of Morals* a *streitschrift*—a polemic—and thus a representation in his own hand of what he took to be a declaration of war against the world of known values. In choosing the means, we know (and he certainly knew) that we also choose the end. Aware, then, of the risk—and yet preferring the risk because of what it entailed: that is, the responsibility of each self, each reader, to create himself, to make of himself the individual of whom Nietzsche spoke. And willing to risk that even if it also nourished the possibility of abuse—a possibility that was later realized as he himself had, and should have, anticipated. His was not only a case like that of the manufacturer of a product that unexpectedly turns out to be dangerous to its user—although even for this, the charge of negligence can at times be sustained; but that knowing *something* of the danger threatened, weighing it against the possible benefits of writing as and what he did, he chose to stay the course. What more would be required than this to invite (and for Nietzsche to accept) a judgment of responsibility? Not (at least not directly) for what the fascists *did* on the basis of their misinterpretations, and not for their own contribution to the misinterpretation itself when they took the step from privileging the individual to privileging the group and then the state—but for his own, more limited side of the process which if it was not decisive was not negligible either. It amounted to failing to build a fence around what he did mean so as to separate it from what he did not—and evidently refusing to do this, because to do so would in his view have diminished the force of what he did mean for those who interpreted him correctly.

In sum: Nietzsche accepted the risk of misinterpretation, in sufficient if not full knowledge—and was willing to chance the consequences of misinterpretation (and so too, of their consequences). He was willing, in other words, to have views ascribed to him that ran counter to those he held because of the challenge he wished to pose in doing so; it was for the reader to decide in the face of Nietzsche's attack on him of how to respond—with Nietzsche unwilling to hedge that attack by qualifications beyond the limited ones he provided even if by doing this, an outcome closer to his own view would have been more assured. The hedging and qualifications required to do this would themselves have conduced to another outcome—the weakening or diminution of what he *was* affirming.

Would Nietzsche have persisted in this commitment had he been able to survey the European landscape on 8 May 1945, at the end of the bitter World War II in Europe—with the echo of his name sounding among fragments of the carnage? We cannot know much about the answer to this question, and speculation about it will almost certainly feed the impulse of interpretation that remakes authors in their interpreters' image. We *can*, however (and in the moralizing terms introduced here, ought to) ask ourselves what *we* would have had Nietzsche do differently, knowing what we do about those who, as has been claimed, misinterpreted his words. (This question would be pertinent even if one denies his responsibility for the misinterpretation, but especially, of course, if one accepts it.)

Would our response to this question be to urge Nietzsche to turn down the volume (the *Rausch*) of his writing a notch? *Two* notches? Should he have bequeathed, instead of the quasi-posthumous *Will to Power*, a more sober Last Will in which he set everything straight—perhaps like the Spinoza whom he admired beyond all other philosophers, laid out in *more geometrico*? Should he have added disclaimers to his books, stating, for example, that he did not really mean to replace the political tyranny of a slavish majority with the tyranny of a brutish minority? It should be obvious that the larger the number of such proposals we accept, the closer we come to concluding that it would have been better if Nietzsche, quite simply, had not been Nietzsche. To be sure, some readers of Nietzsche would be willing to say just this—and Nietzsche or not, almost everybody would be able to identify *some* writer whose name might be inserted into the general form of that extreme judgment: the literary counterpart of capital punishment. But to do this for (that is, *against*) Nietzsche? Even the Nietzsche who, if he was not a fascist or advocate of fascism, unapologetically extolled violence as a political means and explicitly rejected the Enlightenment ideals of human equality as grounded on individual rights?

We frequently hold people accountable for actions (or inactions) without willing them (the people) to be quite other than they are. Admittedly, in such cases, the restraints on our judgment depend on mitigating factors in the actions judged or their consequences (including as possibilities among these, I have been claiming, writing and *its* consequences). A well-known essay on a topic related to the history of fascism was titled (and argued—convincingly, in my view) "No Hitler, No Holocaust."[31] Nobody, to my knowledge, has gone so far as to assert "No Nietzsche, No Fascism" or anything close to it, and for good reason: the complex material and ideological factors involved in the rise of twentieth-century totalitarianism (and fascism within that category) surely extend beyond the actions or will of any single individual, certainly those of any single philosopher (or even any group of them). Even within the domain of likely contributory causes, furthermore, writings and their interpretation, and even their misinterpretation, justifiably acquire a certain benefit of clergy because of the freedom that even the most fanatical or dogmatic writing nonetheless leaves for the reader in the text; there is unquestionably a totalitarian or fascist style in writing—but even that has not yet found a way to vanquish the space between text and reader; that is, to so dominate interpretation as to leave the text without a voice of its own. But as a pardon to Nietzsche, more than to any other author, should not be based on his status as a cultural monument, neither should it (or need it) rely on a general amnesty extended to all writing. The principle that remains can only say that every text should be read—and judged—for itself. To leave Nietzsche as Nietzsche, furthermore, would not nullify his responsibility for his misinterpretation or the weight and culpability which that responsibility brings with it—any more than it absolves authors in general of responsibility for their misinterpretations (if only up to a point). Indeed, the crux of the argument presented here has been that this responsibility of the author extends exactly as far as does the author's authority. Including Nietzsche's fascism, for instance.

Afterword
Philosophy and/of the Holocaust

To inquire about the contributions of philosophy and philosophers to thinking about the Holocaust or, more academically, to Holocaust Studies, is both to ask and to leave a question. The fact is that those contributions have by any measurement been few and sparse, and if the reasons and explanations for this seem evident, they are also discouraging insofar as they reflect on contemporary philosophy and the life of its mind. A more heartening and practical question might focus on the *potential* role or contribution of philosophy to thinking about the Holocaust—but the innocence, even naivete, of that formulation as it views philosophy and the Holocaust in isolation from each other only underscores the marginal role philosophy has so far had—or more damning, has attempted to have—in addressing the other.

That this past role *has* been marginal seems indisputable—not in the sense that philosophical issues have not been raised or discussed in writings about the Holocaust, but that when they have appeared, it has been mainly in the contexts of historical, literary, or theological analysis, shaped there by authors whose interests and methods were grounded in those fields rather than in philosophy. These other perspectives may, of course, be "philosophical" in emphasis, and it is indeed a longstanding question within philosophy itself as to whether it has a subject matter or method *apart* from those articulated in other, more explicitly defined and restricted disciplines. But it also seems clear that "professional" philosophers—applying that term as we otherwise recognize "professional" historians or literary scholars—have contributed relatively little, in quantity or significance, to Holocaust Studies in its now more than half-century history. It is impossible to know what or how much philosophers might have contributed that they did not—or what they may yet do, notwithstanding the record so far. But if philosophy has in the past illuminated historical events—ranging from the details of everyday life to more singular events of war and peace—there is no reason to suppose that it would not have or may not yet add a useful voice to studies of the Holocaust. I would also suggest that when the neglect that I have alleged in relation to the Holocaust is viewed in the context of the indifference or even antagonism in much contemporary philosophy to the relevance of history *as such* for philosophical inquiry, the loss to philosophy becomes clearer still.

I propose to say something more about these two assertions—the claim of philosophy's marginal presence in Holocaust Studies and the loss this has represented on both sides, for Holocaust Studies *and* for philosophy—before suggesting an explanation for them and then, in conclusion, citing a number of potential contributions that philosophy may yet make to the study of the Holocaust. That is, if philosophy can bring itself and its practitioners to the point— and, of course, if what they bring in the way of contribution finds a reception. That transaction, after all, requires *two* participants, and the responsibility of philosophy to speak joins a responsibility on the part of an audience to listen. Assuming, of course, that philosophy has something relevant to say.

First, then, on philosophy's (heretofore) marginal presence. If we are not to bog down in fruitless, and endless, discussion of what should be recognized as a *philosophical* account or contribution, the only practical criterion seems an ostensive definition; that is, a definition constituted by naming formally designated philosophers or professors of philosophy (not quite the same, to be sure) who have written within the "universe of discourse" of Holocaust Studies. Again, the conclusion that emerges from the composition of this list seems unmistakable: that given the scope and resources of Holocaust Studies as a field, a notably small part of it represents the work of philosophers. It is true that Karl Jaspers published a brief book titled *The Question of German Guilt* in the early post-war years (1946), and that Jean-Paul Sartre published his also brief *Anti-Semite and Jew* at about the same time. But the former, an important marker at the time, was a summary account of issues that would resonate without much further word from Jaspers himself, and Sartre's essay was extrapolated from his earlier *Being and Nothingness* with—by his own admission—only slight attention to the substantive factors implicated in the history of antisemitism or of the "Jewish Question" or the character of Nazism itself. Also in the subsequent "post-Holocaust" period, philosophers who are cited, or better, *re*-cited in the literature of Holocaust Studies, remain scarce; that a list of them can be ventured at all is itself indicative of this. So, for a first pass, in alphabetical order and mingling ideologies and nationalities: Theodor Adorno, Giorgio Agamben, Zvi Bar-on, Emil Fackenheim, Alain Finkelkraut, Jürgen Habermas, Philip Hallie, Hans Jonas, Steven Katz, Sarah Kofman, Emmanuel Levinas, Alan Milchman and Alan Rosenberg, Michael Morgan, Susan Nieman, Gillian Rose, Joan Ringelheim, Nathan Rotenstreich, John Roth, Leo Strauss, Lawrence Thomas, Elisabeth Young-Bruehl, Michael Zimmerman (analphabetically, I would list my own name here as well).

Obviously, other figures appear on the periphery of this circle, some of them large indeed: Hannah Arendt, for example, whose own explicit rejection of the title *philosopher* might itself justify her inclusion even without the more substantial reasons there are for including her. Jacques Derrida has circled the edges of the Holocaust from a number of directions. A small "Society for the Study of Holocaust and Genocide," founded by Alan Rosenberg, convenes regularly at sessions of the American Philosophical Association—and a diverse group of mainly French and American philosophers who had not otherwise addressed issues bearing on the Holocaust have found in the Nazi history of Martin Heidegger an occasion for considering the character of National Socialism more generally as they assert or deny the relation between Heidegger's biography and his theoretical work. These have included, in the United States, Richard Rorty, Tom Rockmore, and Hans Sluga; and in France, Victor Farias, Jean-François Lyotard, and Phillipe Lacoue-Labarthe.

These may seem a not insignificant number, and they include prominent names. But it also needs to be said that the Holocaust has been a minor theme for many even of these figures, and one consequence of this is that few of them or of the positions associated with them have made their way into the canon of Holocaust Studies in its still provisional but nonetheless recognizable form. (Such a "short list" seems to me reducible to Adorno, Arendt, Fackenheim, and Habermas.) I know that additional or alternate candidates for these lists will occur to readers—but even if the compilation offered here were expanded, the order of magnitude would remain essentially unchanged, and its limited extent thus underscores the characterization of philosophy as marginal to the general field of Holocaust Studies. Certainly the role there of philosophy has been off-center—matching on those margins the place that the Holocaust has occupied in philosophical thinking itself.

The questions then remain "Why? How is this consistent pattern of mutual exclusion to be understood—and what does it promise for the future?" Obviously, if the marginality or indifference or professional dissonance were understood as intrinsic or necessary, marking the limits of any possible connection between philosophy and the Holocaust, the future would necessarily be much like the past, with the philosophical analysis of the Holocaust then permanently sparse. I do not believe, however, that this need be the case. For the following reasons.

Even in its own brief history, the field that has come to be known as Holocaust Studies followed an evolutionary pattern that is still very much in process. Raul Hilberg's *The Destruction of the European Jews* was published in 1961; and although certain scholarly studies of the Holocaust had appeared previously (e.g., Leon Poliakov's *Brevaire de haine la IIIe Reich et les Juifs* [Paris, 1951] and Gerald Reitlinger's *The Final Solution: The Attempt to Exterminate the Jews of Europe* [London, 1953]), Hilberg's book proved foundational in the construction of the field of Holocaust Studies. It was no accident that this initiating

moment should be a work in history (and historiography). In scholarly terms—
in moral terms as well—the very first question impelled by the enormity of
the Holocaust would, *of course*, be historical; that is, the question of what
happened—then extending laterally to how, and finally venturing vertically to
the more speculative "why." Thus began a dominant historical discourse, with
history as a discipline continuing to hold center stage even in the constantly
expanding circumference of Holocaust Studies—with little dissent from other
disciplinary perspectives to either the persistence or the warrant of that centrality. If ever it was necessary to have the facts of the matter fully and accurately gathered, surely that would hold for this event; even to judge its moral
weight clearly depended first on questions taking the elementary form of who
did what to whom: when, where, and how.

On the other hand and in sharp contrast: When Hegel wrote that "The owl
of Minerva begins to fly only with the falling of the dusk" [Preface to *The
Philosophy of Right*], he evidently intended his use of a gentle metaphor to
assert—not gently at all—that in *its* relation to the ongoing rush of history,
philosophy would always and only appear late in the day. And this, not by
choice or as a matter of style, but by necessity; that is, the need of reflection or
reason to have something present before it in order to be able to set its own
activity in motion. If this lag was for Hegel an intrinsic requirement for philosophical reflection in its "take" on everyday circumstance, furthermore, that
condition would be all the more pressing for complex and extraordinary historical events, of which the Holocaust is obviously one. Undoubtedly, other
modes of analysis or reflection are also characteristically "later"—deferred
from the flow of immediate experience. Historical writing itself is subject to
this, as events require the passage of time before resolving themselves into
even provisional historical causes or effects. But even allowing for a more widespread lag of this sort between act and word, it seems still undeniable that the
primary figure or trope in the first stage of what would later become Holocaust
Studies was, and by right should have been, historical. That priority, furthermore, has and is likely to continue, not only in contrast to philosophy but also
in relation to psychology or sociology, to literary criticism and even to the
more rapidly increasing interest and emphasis on artistic representation (in fiction, films, etc.). All of these, whether they acknowledge it or not, remain
nonetheless dependent on the grist that passes first through the mill of history:
the facts of the Holocaust that are still, constantly, virtually every day, coming
to light. (Consider how much valuable, and new, information has surfaced recently about such rudimentary matters as the role of the Wehrmacht in the
"Final Solution" or the roles played in the Nazi war effort of the "neutral"
nations, or the involvement in the Nazi project of multinational corporations
and banking.)

To grant all this, however, is not to preclude shifts of direction in or around
the center of historical reference; and it is here, it seems to me, that a basis

appears for suggesting what philosophy might have contributed before this—but did not—to an understanding of the Holocaust. Perhaps still more relevant for present purposes, we may also point in anticipation to aspects of the Holocaust that seem to invite philosophical inquiry and that left untouched as they have been, disclose lacunae in some of the even standard accounts or narratives of the Holocaust, including those of historians. Admittedly, certain institutional factors that have before this contributed to obstructing this prospect—from the sides of both philosophy and history—are unlikely simply to disappear. For its part, contemporary philosophy, especially in its dominant Anglo-American tendency, has been notably a- or anti-historical, even in respect to its own history, let alone in addressing "external" historical events. There has been some movement recently to counteract this prejudice—directly, in addressing the figures and concepts of philosophy's past in relation to their historical contexts; indirectly, through efforts in "applied philosophy" as in bioethics and the philosophy of law that have drawn philosophers (now sometimes appointed to medical or law faculties) into contemporary history in ways that would have seemed improbable a few decades ago. Even here, however, I suggest that there is danger, both from the outside and internally: of the mistaken attribution to philosophers, because they speak *about* ethical principles and values, of special expertise in practical moral judgment; that is, in assessing (let alone in making) ethical decisions. In any event, even taking account of the potentially fruitful connections between philosophy and the "*alltäglich*" world, the general claim remains largely unshaken: that contemporary philosophy has yet to overcome its estrangement from history. The dominance in the twentieth century of the model of philosophy as a form of science, with the latter's focus on the present for its means as well as for its ends, has carried over into the new century. And if some of the optimism in twentieth-century philosophical projects that idealized for philosophy the model of scientific discourse has faded, the principal motifs and methods have not yet changed radically enough to redirect philosophical attention to the process or even to the philosophy of history; one has only to examine current bibliographies in philosophy or the programs of current philosophical conferences to see this disproportion.

From the other side, the writing of history has not been notably receptive to philosophy, even when the historical discourse could have benefited from connections between the two. This wariness no doubt reflects to some extent a sense of territoriality: history as the primary mode of discourse in Holocaust Studies would feel entitled to address relevant conceptual questions also when those extend beyond its own customary limits. Although the philosophy of history—reflection on the conditions of historical explanation, the nature of the relationship between description and interpretation and then between them and evaluation—comes close to the center of writing history (including of course the history of the Holocaust), historians themselves can hardly be faulted for not considering those topics apart from their appearance as ingredi-

0.1

ent in their work. Thus, historians have only *presumed* on such issues, understandably pleading the urgency of getting on with the task of unearthing and assembling data, and in any event resistant to what philosophers might have to say about the theoretical frameworks in which those data are set. Even in the recognizably boundary issues of moral judgment, historians—no doubt because the moral questions posed by the Holocaust are so deeply embedded in its history—have at times simply assumed moral authority: an analogue in my view to the assumption of authority on moral issues by professional "ethicists" among philosophers. The marginality of philosophy in Holocaust Studies has thus reflected an alliance of complementary imbalances: an unduly purist or restrictive self-image on the part of philosophy that complements, on the other side, a too generous or ambitious view of its reach and expertise by history itself.

It may be objected that this account is a historical hypothesis in its own right (or wrong); in any event that also if we accept it for the sake of argument, it says little about what philosophy can in fact contribute to Holocaust Studies even in general terms, let alone by illuminating specific angles of vision. Here, let me for the moment conflate what philosophy might have contributed in the past but did not, with the prospect of its future; thus, I outline a number of issues central to Holocaust Studies that also involve substantive considerations of continuing philosophical importance. Again, I do not mean to claim that philosophy has or should have special authority, let alone a monopoly, in addressing such issues—but rather that by joining its efforts to those coming from other modes of discourse, philosophy can add substantially to their understanding. I mention four such topics out of a larger number of possibilities —all four no doubt familiar but still perplexing, contested, and most of all recurrent in the context of Holocaust Studies.

1. The Concept of Genocide: When Winston Churchill, in a speech about the unfolding Holocaust (late in 1942) dramatically asserted that "We are in the presence of a crime that has no name," he heralded an issue that continues to this day, one which the coining of the term *genocide* two years after Churchill's speech did something but not enough to resolve.[1] The 1948 UN Convention on Genocide, however important symbolically, left virtually all the basic questions about the structural and moral character of genocide unsettled: the definition of the groups and types of action to which the term is applicable; the role of intention in those actions; the place of genocide in moral history. That *genocide* as a term has since its first appearance become an all-purpose epithet, in common usage designating the most heinous crime to which a name has been given, only reinforces the need for elaborating its analysis, as the term and concept no doubt apply paradigmatically not only to the Holocaust but in their occurrences elsewhere as well. Both for this analysis and for its obverse side—that is, the implied assertion of group *rights* as violated by genocide (rights analogous to and yet arguably distinct from individual rights)—moral and legal philosophers have increasingly focused attention on the concepts and practices involved. And if their work on these issues is still exploratory, anyone familiar with that work will, I believe, recognize its usefulness for understanding the concept of genocide in principle as well as in its specific bearing on the Holocaust (for one small but contentious matter, on the "Uniqueness Question," concerned with the claim of uniqueness ascribed to the Holocaust).

2. *Corporate and Individual Intentions:* Although the heat of conflict surrounding the Intentionalist and Functionalist interpretations of the "Final Solution" and the related *Historikerstreit* has diminished, the conceptual issues in those disagreements have arguably remained unsettled. What emerged from those discussions is a large middle ground occupied jointly by what might be called "intentional functionalists" and "functional intentionalists," with other smaller groups still remaining at the far ends of the spectrum—an outcome that, however, seems to me the result of practical compromise rather than conceptual clarification. It is, I believe, a matter of record that a common assumption by all parties to this dispute supposed that what intentions *are*—whether for individuals or corporately; that is, for groups—is self-evident, requiring little or no systematic analysis. That a great deal of attention had been paid specifically to the concept of intention and its complexities in twentieth-century philosophy (both in phenomenology and in linguistic philosophy) never, so far as I am aware, entered the discussion. Would such reference have made a difference to analyses which simply assumed that they involved questions of fact, not theory? Perhaps, perhaps not, and it may now be too late to determine this. What we do know is that the issue of how to ascribe responsibility within the bounds of the Holocaust—the extent and nature of responsibility on the parts of individuals and groups, and the differentiated relation of such responsibility to intentional or non-intentional acts—is very much alive in the retrospective assessment of the events constituting the Holocaust. Few commentators, whether philosophers *or* historians, would defend the claim that where there is no intention, there is no responsibility. But this makes it all the more imperative to consider how and to what extent intentions are legitimately found or ascribed to individuals or to groups, and then, too, of what the moral varieties are of non- or extra-intentional acts.

3. *Classical Ethics:* Whether an event with the dimensions of the Holocaust entails revision in considering the nature of ethical values or decision-making as such, is itself a pertinent question. Even if that possibility is rejected, furthermore, the status of the classical—standard—ethical questions as they bear on the Holocaust will still be informative, perhaps also innovative, in respect both to those standard questions and to the Holocaust itself. Beginning with such concrete and immediate issues of judgment as the status of punishment and reparation, revenge and forgiveness, the relation between causes and moral reasons, such analysis eventually makes its way to the "Question of Evil" that has long bedeviled the Western religious and rationalist tradition—how evil can

subsist in a just or divinely ordered world. A specific and more concrete variant of the latter arises in respect to the Holocaust perpetrators in the question of whether evil or wrongdoing can be knowingly willed or chosen. For even the undoubted role of bureaucratic processes in the Holocaust does not preclude a role for consciousness or decision-making, and the specific question cannot be avoided, then, of whether Nazi actions were undertaken in the belief of a good to be realized—or with the agents' own consciousness of wrongdoing. The historical issues here are inextricable from the philosophical one of whether the latter framework is indeed an option—an ostensibly empirical question that has too rarely in the history of philosophy been addressed empirically. *Do* or *can* people do wrong knowing that it *is* wrong? The philosophical history of this question has relied more on obiter dicta than on argument; so far as the issue is open to evidence at all, it seems clear that aspects of the Holocaust may prove an important source of such evidence. And then, too: the Holocaust by its extremity suggests a parallel to "stress tests" in engineering or medicine: whatever warrant may be found for practice or theory in the context of such an event would, everything else being equal, apply a fortiori in less extreme conditions. Or *would* it? The question of how—or more importantly, whether—ethical practice in extreme situations bears on ethical decisions in everyday (non-extreme) life has been left largely untouched in Holocaust narratives; surely this would be a natural and important point of contact between philosophy and those narratives.

4. Holocaust Representation: I use this phrase as a catchall for designating a variety of forms of expression related to the Holocaust and the proportionately large number of issues they engender: from the function—or desirability—of Holocaust memorials and museums, to disputes over artistic depictions of events or figures from the Holocaust (the issue of the relation between form and content in fiction, poetry, and films of the Holocaust); to the more general problem of the connection (or as it may be, disjunction) between historical and (so-called) imaginative representations of the Holocaust. And once again: problems like the relation of fictionality to truth, the comparison (or connection) between art and aesthetic values, on the one hand, and ethical values, on the other—not only what can but what *ought* to be represented; the social or political function of art more generally—these all have long and continuing philosophical genealogies. To be sure, such philosophical accounts have rarely settled the issues addressed, but even at their slightest, they have brought sharply into focus the alternative lines of argument around them and what the choices among the alternatives involve. "Art for Art's Sake" has had its Holocaust advocates as it has also had its critics—and if the Holocaust seems an unlikely venue for the presence of that view, one has only to look at the range and variety of artistic representations of the Holocaust to see how that association has been made. Here, too, the question that philosophical aesthetics has largely neglected—of the possible or necessary *limits* of artistic representation—becomes unavoidable: a contribution, if it could be put in this way, from the Holocaust as a subject to philosophical inquiry.

Again, I claim no special privilege for philosophy in considering the issues assembled under these four rubrics. I noted earlier something approaching a consensus that philosophy remains dependent, to a greater or lesser extent, on provisions supplied by other of the "humane" and natural sciences. But the converse relation also holds, in the need of practice for theoretical and conceptual frameworks—frameworks that, as the history of ideas has demonstrated, are never immaculately conceived and thus require constant monitoring, whether as invoked by philosophers or anyone else. We do well here, it seems to me, to recall Kant's severe warning about the interdependence of the empirical and the theoretical: "Concepts without percepts are empty; percepts without concepts are blind." And if philosophy, past and present, has often seemed more repetitive than progressive, at times following (or leading) the questions it considers into blind alleys, it has also advanced on them in the broad context—by its very formulation—of a general understanding of reality and of human nature within it. None of this gives philosophers as such privileged access to the topics mentioned; but it brings them at least even with other investigators who, too often, deploy such general frameworks without acknowledging or, at times, recognizing their archaeology: the layers of meaning and contestation from which they come.

Admittedly, at least one serious, probably intrinsic danger threatens this prospect: the defect of its quality. This is the risk that the abstractive impulse of philosophy will express itself at the price of obscuring historical particularity; specifically, that it may come to present the Holocaust as no more than one of a large number of historical events, all of them subsumable under common and so indistinct denominators. The threat of this flight to abstraction is constant for philosophical reflection, and the central figures in philosophy's history, from Plato to Spinoza to Kant and Hegel, have been notable in good measure just insofar as they have *not* fallen victim to it; objections to which their *conceptions* of history are open stand quite apart from the close and intense refraction of historical experience in their thinking. At any rate, philosophy is certainly not alone in facing such characteristic pitfalls, the danger of what Hannah Arendt in a different context called "professional deformation." Whatever this threat amounts to, furthermore, it seems to me outweighed by the gaps that would be—I have suggested, have been—left by the absence of philosophy, whether that absence was caused by its own hand or that of others or, as I have suggested, by the harmful common cause the discipline of philosophy has made in this respect with the discipline of history.

I mean thus to propose that philosophy, in addressing the Holocaust on its own reflective grounds, may contribute innovative understanding—innovative even in respect to apparently straightforward historical questions and still more for comprehending historical understanding as such—at the same time that its focus on that complex and all-too-concrete event may enable philosophy to see more deeply into itself. Hegel, in a letter of 1805, wrote to his correspondent Johann Heinrich Voss, "I should like to say of my aspirations that I shall try to teach philosophy to speak German." However we judge this aspiration of Hegel's (or his success in realizing it), there should be little disagreement about the value for both philosophy and history if the Holocaust could teach philosophy to "speak history." And, of course, if the historians and other readers of philosophy would then listen.

NOTES

1. THE NAZI AS CRIMINAL

1. Ernst Nolte, *Marxism, Fascism, Cold War* (Atlantic Highlands, N.J.: Humanities Press, 1982); and François Furet, *Fascism and Communism*, trans. T. Todorov (Lincoln: University of Nebraska Press, 2000).

2. Joachim Fest, *The Face of the Third Reich*, trans. Michael Bullock (New York: Pantheon, 1970), pp. 108–109.

3. Cf., e.g., Henry Friedlander, *The Origins of Nazi Genocide: From Euthanasia to the Final Solution* (Chapel Hill: University of North Carolina Press, 1995); Michael Burleigh, *Death and Deliverance: Euthanasia in Germany 1900–1945* (Cambridge: Cambridge University Press, 1994).

4. Mark Mazower, *Inside Hitler's Greece* (New Haven, Conn.: Yale University Press, 1993), pp. 149–50. Numerous civilian massacres by the Germans in Greece are also on record, e.g., at Komeno and Distomo (Mazower, pp. 195–97, 210–15).

5. David T. Zabecki, ed., *World War II in Europe* (New York: Garland, 1999), p. 42.

6. Cf. Rolf-Dieter Muller and Gerd R. Ueberschar, *Hitler's War in the East, 1941–1945*, trans. Bruce D. Little (Providence, R.I.: Berghahn Books, 1997), pp. 213–18; also Christian Zentner and Friedemann Bedürftig, eds., *Encyclopedia of the Third Reich* (New York: Da Capo Press, 1997), pp. 728–30.

7. Cf. *Germany and the Second World War*, vol. V, Research Institute for Military History (Oxford: Clarendon Press, 2003), pp. 1071–90.

8. See on the issue of Nazi goals, e.g., Gerhard Weinberg, *The Foreign Policy of Hitler's Germany* (Chicago: University of Chicago Press, 1980), pp. 18–28; Ian Kershaw, *Hitler, 1936–45: Nemesis* (New York: W. W. Norton, 2000), p. 517. (Kershaw finds in Hitler's planning "the vaguest notion" of a "socialist revolution.")

9. *Between Friends: The Correspondence of Hannah Arendt and Mary McCarthy, 1949–1975*, ed. Carol Brightman (New York: Harcourt Brace, 1995), 20 September 1963.

10. *The Nazi Doctors* (New York: Basic Books, 1986), p. 63.

11. Primo Levi, *The Drowned and the Saved*, trans. Raymond Rosenthal (New York: Summit, 1988), Ch. VI.

12. Gitta Sereny, *Into That Darkness: From Mercy Killing to Mass Murder* (New York: McGraw-Hill, 1974).

2. FORGIVENESS, REVENGE, AND THE LIMITS OF HOLOCAUST JUSTICE

1. There have, of course, been scattered accounts of Holocaust revenge, fictional and non-fictional, but these have usually been fragmentary themselves and in some cases historically questionable. In any event, there has been, so far as I have been able to discover, no systematic consideration of the topic. Cf., e.g., John Sack, *An Eye for an Eye* (New York: Basic Books, 1993), and a brief reference in I. F. Stone, *Underground to*

Palestine (New York: Pantheon, 1978), p. 101. For a quasi-fictional account of revenge killings by the Jewish Brigade in Northern Italy at the end of the War, see Hanoch Bartov, *Brigade*, trans. David Segal (London: Macdonald & Co., 1968); see also Aharon Appelfeld, *Iron Tracks*, trans. Jeffrey Green (New York: Schocken, 1998). Survivor testimony also includes occasional references to revenge, although again, less frequently than might be expected; see, e.g., Aaron S., HVT-1533 (New Haven, Conn.: Fortunoff Archives, 1991); Yitzhak A., HVT-4103 (New Haven, Conn.: Fortunoff Archives, 2001). For analyses of revenge more generally, see, e.g., Martha Minow, *Between Vengeance and Forgiveness: Facing History after Genocide and Mass Violence* (Boston: Beacon Press, 1998), and Peter French, *The Virtues of Vengeance* (Lawrence: University of Kansas Press, 2001).

2. For a fuller account, see Dina Porat, *Me'ever le-gishmi: Parashat Hayav shel Aba Kovner* [Hebrew] (Tel Aviv: Am Oved, 2000); cf. also Berel Lang, "Holocaust-Memory and -Revenge," in *The Future of the Holocaust: Between History and Memory* (Ithaca, N.Y.: Cornell University Press, 1999).

3. On the general concept of forgiveness, see, e.g., Martin Golding, "Forgiveness and Regret," *Philosophical Forum* 16 (1984): 121–37; Jeffrie G. Murphy and Jean Hampton, *Forgiveness and Mercy* (New York: Cambridge University Press, 1988); Joram Graf Haber, *Forgiveness* (Savage, Md.: Roman and Littlefield, 1991); Berel Lang, "Forgiveness," *American Philosophical Quarterly* 31 (1994): 105–17.

4. Simon Wiesenthal, *The Sunflower* (New York: Schocken, 1976).

5. Daniel Jonah Goldhagen, *Hitler's Willing Executioners: Ordinary Germans and the Holocaust* (New York: Knopf, 1996).

6. An unusual point at which the issues of forgiveness and revenge converge appears in the Post-Holocaust aphorism (variously attributed) that "The Germans will never forgive the Jews for Auschwitz." The *Post*-Holocaust pogroms against the Jews in Poland (the largest of them in Kielce) although motivated also economically, almost certainly had this residue as part of their motivation.

7. Primo Levi, *Collected Poems*, trans. Ruth Feldman and Brian Swann (Boston: Faber & Faber, 1988).

3. EVIL, SUFFERING, AND THE HOLOCAUST

1. *The Book of Theodicy*, trans. and with a commentary by L. E. Goodman (New Haven, Conn.: Yale University Press, 1988).

2. See G. E. Moore, *Principia Ethica* (Cambridge: Cambridge University Press, 1903); see also, for a later summary, William Frankena, *Ethics* (Englewood Cliffs, N.J.: Prentice-Hall, 1963). Plato's *Theaetetus* remains a locus classicus for both the presentation and disputation of this view.

3. That societies invariably find gradations among acts of wrongdoing and their related punishments has passed largely unnoticed in the widespread search for "cultural universals."

4. See on this comparison Helmut Dubiel and Gabriel Motzkin, eds., *The Lesser Evil* (London: Routledge, 2004).

5. Susan Neiman sees Rousseau as "historicizing" evil—but she seems here to be speaking about the history of the individual agent (even as in a social context), not the

structural history of evil through its acts. Cf. *Evil in Modern Thought* (Princeton, N.J.: Princeton University Press, 2002), pp. 36–46.

6. See, for a variety of examples, Arthur A. Cohen, *The Tremendum: A Theological Intepretation of the Holocaust* (New York: Crossroads, 1981), p. 21; Emil Fackenheim, "Leo Baeck and Other Jewish Thinkers in Dark Times," *Judaism* 51 (2002): 288; Irving Greenberg, *Living in the Image of God* (Northvale, N.J.: Jason Aronson, 1998), p. 234. In his 2002 Nobel Prize speech, Imre Kertesz speaks of the "break" caused by the Holocaust, with Auschwitz "the end point of a great adventure"; *PMLA* 118 (2003): 607.

7. As, for example, in such books (and titles) as Sara Horowitz, *Voicing the Void* (Albany: SUNY Press, 1997); Andy Leak and George Paizis, eds., *The Holocaust and the Text: Speaking the Unspeakable* (London: Macmillan, 1999); George Steiner, *Language and Silence* (New York: Atheneum, 1967).

8. Consider, as one of many possible examples, the statement by Werner Hamacher: "We do not just write 'after Auschwitz.' There is no historical or experiential 'after' to an absolute trauma. The continuum being disrupted, any attempt to restore it would be a vain act of denegation. . . . This 'history' cannot enter into history. It deranges all dates and destroys the ways to understand them." Werner Hamacher, Neil Hertz, and Thomas Keenan, eds., *On Paul de Man's Wartime Journalism* (Lincoln: University of Nebraska Press, 1989), pp. 458–59. Cf. also John Rawls, on "after Auschwitz": *The Law of Peoples* (Cambridge, Mass.: Harvard University Press, 1999), p. 20.

9. Alan Mintz, *Hurban: Responses to Jewish Catastrophe in Hebrew Literature* (New York: Columbia University Press, 1984), p. 98. See also Jacob Katz, *Tradition and Crisis*, trans. Dov Bernard Cooperman (New York: New York University Press, 1993): "The essential attitude toward tradition did not change" (p. 184).

10. In the range of possible "moral" consequences, see, for example, Yisroel Yuval's controversial suggestion, as part of that aftermath, of a possible causal connection between suicidal martyrdom (including the killing of their children by Jewish parents) and the medieval emergence of the blood libel ("Ha'Nakam v'Haklalah" (Hebrew), *Zion* 58 (1993): 33–90.

11. Cf. Primo Levi, *The Drowned and the Saved*, trans. Raymond Rosenthal (New York: Summit, 1988). On the claim of Holocaust uniqueness, cf. especially Steven T. Katz, *The Holocaust in Historical Perspective*, vol. 1 (New York: Oxford University Press, 1994). Katz's arguments for the *historical* uniqueness of the Holocaust leave unaddressed the question of what, if any, moral or philosophical implications would follow even if that *were* the case.

12. Eliezer Berkovitz, *Faith after the Holocaust* (New York: Ktav, 1973), pp. 90, 98.

13. I would relate this to a question that seems to me indicated for "uniqueness" claims for the Holocaust quite apart from the issue of their historical basis; that question would ask what difference it makes if the Holocaust *is* unique—or more bluntly, "So what?" Cf. Berel Lang, *The Future of the Holocaust* (Ithaca, N.Y.: Cornell University Press, 1999), pp. 77–91.

14. G. W. Leibniz, *Theodicy: Essays on the Goodness of God, the Freedom of Man, and the Origin of Evil*, trans. E. M. Huggard (New Haven, Conn.: Yale University Press, 1952).

15. Maimonides, *Guide of the Perplexed*, 3:17, trans. S. Pines (Chicago: University of

186

Chicago Press, 1963), p. 469. Maimonides distinguishes his own position from this communal and traditional one—although *how much* difference his own formulation entails is arguable (cf. *Guide*, III, 51 [p. 625]).

16. Shabbath 55a. Cited by Maimonides, ibid., p. 470.

17. The Art Scroll prayer book comments on this statement: "This is a cardinal principle of Jewish faith. History is not haphazard. Israel's exile and centuries-long distress is a result of its sins." *The Art Scroll Siddur,* trans. Nosson Scherman (Brooklyn: Mesorah, 1984), p. 678.

18. Eliezer Berkovitz, *Faith after the Holocaust,* p. 94. See also, e.g., Amos Funkenstein, "Theological Responses to the Holocaust," in *Perceptions of Jewish History* (Berkeley: University of California Press, 1993), p. 311.

19. Teitlebaum and Wasserman as cited in Yosef Roth, "The Jewish Fate and the Holocaust," in *I Will be Sanctified: Religious Responses to the Holocaust,* ed. Yehezkel Fogel (Northvale, N.J.: Jason Aronson, 1952), pp. 58–59.

20. Reported in the *New York Times,* 7 August 2001.

21. For other examples (and analysis) of the "punishment–reward" view in Orthodox and Haredi sources, cf. especially the writings of Gershon Greenberg—e.g., "Orthodox Jewish Thought in the Wake of the Holocaust," in *In God's Name: Genocide and Religion in the Twentieth Century,* ed. Omer Bartov and Phyllis Mack (New York: Berghahn), and "Jewish Religious Thought in the Wake of the Catastrophe," in *Thinking in the Shadow of Hell,* ed. Jacques B. Doukhan (Berrien Springs, Mich.: Andrews University Press, 2002).

22. Ignaz Maybaum openly affirms this (admittedly, as a rhetorical question): "Would it shock you if I were to imitate . . . [Isaiah's] prophetic style and formulate the phrase 'Hitler, my [God's] servant'?" Cf. *Ignaz Maybaum: A Reader,* ed. Nicholas De Lange (New York: Berghahn Books, 2001), p. 165.

23. Berkovitz, *Faith after the Holocaust,* p. 105.

24. "The Face of God: Thoughts on the Holocaust," in B. H. Rosenberg and F. Heuman, eds., *Theological and Halakhic Reflections on the Holocaust* (Hoboken: Ktav, 1999), pp. 191–92.

25. Berkovitz, *Faith after the Holocaust,* pp. 105, 107.

26. Maimonides preempts this explanatory effort in favor of the literalist view of punishment and reward: "It is clear that *we* [emphasis added] are the cause of this *'hiding of the face,'* and we are the agents of this separation. . . . If, however, his God is within him, no evil at all will befall him." Maimonides, *Guide,* p. 626.

27. *Sanhedrin,* 101a.

28. Cited in Arthur Green, *The Tormented Master* (University: University of Alabama Press, 1977), p. 175.

29. "Kol Dodi Dofek," trans. L. Kaplan, in B. H. Rosenberg and F. Heuman, eds., *Theological and Halakhic Reflections on the Holocaust,* p. 56. The value posited would presumably hold also for people who did not survive their suffering; in any event, the statement is presumably not a prediction about human behavior, since no evidence (here or elsewhere) suggests that suffering typically *has* the effects described.

30. David Weiss Halivni offers an intriguing variation on this thesis in his application of the concept of "*Tsimtsum*" ["*contraction*"] to the question of God's presence. See "Prayer in the Shoah," *Judaism* 50 (2001): 268–91. There are differences that Halivni emphasizes between "*Tsimtsum*" and "*Hester Panim*"—but a common element in their

logical structures holds that at some historical moments, divine non-intervention, no matter how severe the context, is preferable to intervention. Eliezer Schweid argues that since free choice does not *require* "*Hester Panim,*" this line of explanation as a whole seems either redundant or beside the point. Cf. *Wrestling until Daybreak: Searching for Meaning in Thinking about the Holocaust* (Lanham, Md.: University Press of America, 1994), p. 390.

31. Hugh Rice, *God and Goodness* (New York: Oxford University Press, 2000), p. 92.

32. Emmanuel Levinas, *Entre Nous: Thinking-of-the-Other,* trans. Michael B. Smith and Barbara Harshav (New York: Columbia University Press, 1998), p. 241.

33. Arthur A. Cohen and Paul Mendes-Flohr, eds., *Contemporary Jewish Religious Thought* (New York: Scribners, 1987), p. 945.

34. Berkowitz, *Faith after the Holocaust,* p. 128.

35. Richard Rubenstein, *After Auschwitz* (Indianapolis: Bobbs-Merrill, 1966); cf. also *The Cunning of History: The Holocaust and the American Future* (New York: Harper, 1978). For a fuller account of Rubenstein and especially of Emil Fackenheim, see Michael Morgan, *Beyond Auschwitz: Post-Holocaust Jewish Thought in America* (New York: Oxford University Press, 2001).

36. E.g., Thomas J. J. Altizer and William Hamilton, *Radical Theology and the Death of God* (Indianapolis: Bobbs-Merrill, 1966); Harvey Cox, *The Secular City* (New York: Macmillan, 1965); William Hamilton, *The New Essence of Christianity* (New York: Associated Books, 1965).

37. Richard Rubenstein, *The Age of Triage: Fear and Hope in an Overcrowded World* (Boston: Beacon Press, 1983).

38. Hans Jonas, "The Concept of God after Auschwitz: A Jewish Voice," in Lawrence Vogel, ed., *Mortality and Morality: A Search for God after Auschwitz* (Evanston, Ill.: Northwestern University Press, 1996), p. 140.

39. See, e.g., Emil Fackenheim, *Quest for Past and Future* (Bloomington: Indiana University Press, 1968), Ch. 1.

40. See, e.g., Michael Wyschogrod, "Faith and the Holocaust," *Judaism* 20 (1971): 250.

41. Emil Fackenheim, "Leo Baeck and Other Jewish Thinkers in Dark Times," *Judaism* 51 (2002): 288. For earlier and fuller accounts of the Commandment, see *God's Presence in History: Jewish Affirmations and Philosophical Reflections* (New York: New York University Press, 1970), pp. 70ff; and *The Jewish Return into History* (New York: Schocken, 1978), pp. 27–29.

42. Irving Greenberg who speaks of the Holocaust as a breach in the Covenant—to be repaired thereafter only by a new, "Voluntary Covenant"—articulates a "principle" (not, as he conceives it, a law) with some of the force of Fackenheim's commandment: "No statement, theological or otherwise, should be made that would not be credible in the presence of burning children." In Eva Fleischner, ed., *Auschwitz: Beginning of a New Era* (New York: Ktav, 1977), p. 22. See also "Voluntary Covenant," in *Perspectives* (New York: National Jewish Resource Center, 1982).

43. Arthur A. Cohen, *The Tremendum: A Theological Interpretation of the Holocaust* (New York: Crossroads, 1981), p. 8.

44. *Eichmann in Jerusalem: A Report on the Banality of Evil* (New York: Viking, 1963).

45. See on Arendt's relation to Jewish sources, Richard Bernstein, *Hannah Arendt and the Jewish Question* (Cambridge, Mass.: MIT Press, 1994), pp. 6–13.

46. Letter dated 24 July 1963, in *The Jew as Pariah,* ed. Ron H. Feldman (New York: Grove, 1978), p. 251. Arendt elaborates on this view in the opening pages of *The Life of the Mind* (New York: Harcourt, Brace, and Jovanovich, 1978). Richard Bernstein (idem.) emphasizes the vagary in Arendt's distinction between "judgment" and "thinking"; an arguably more basic issue is justification for the power that Arendt ascribes to thinking—apart from the question of its relation to judging.

47. *The Origins of Totalitarianism* (New York: Harcourt, Brace, and Jovanovich, 1951).

4. COMPARATIVE EVIL

1. Plutarch, *The Lives of the Grecians and Romans,* Great Books, vol. XIV (Chicago: Britannica, 1952), p. 70.

2. So, for example, Kant in *The Metaphysics of Morals:* "Whatever undeserved evil you inflict upon another within the people, that you inflict upon yourself." Trans. Mary Gregor (Cambridge: Cambridge University Press, 1996), pp. 105–106.

3. *The Differend: Phrases in Dispute,* trans. G. van den Abbeele (Minneapolis: University of Minnesota Press, 1983), p. 56.

5. THE GRAMMAR OF ANTISEMITISM

1. Senator Jadwiga Stolarska, in the Polish Senate, September 13, 2001. Cited in Anna Bikont, "Seen from Jedwabne," *Yad Vashem Studies* XXX (2002): 8.

2. The specific occasion noted here was a book review by Tony Judt in *The New Republic* (27 October 1997) of Norman Davies, *Europe: A History* (Oxford: Oxford University Press, 1996).

6. THE UNSPEAKABLE VS. THE TESTIMONIAL

1. See, e.g., *Act and Idea in the Nazi Genocide* (Syracuse: Syracuse University Press, 2003), Ch. 6; *Holocaust Representation: Art within the Limits of History and Ethics* (Baltimore: Johns Hopkins University Press, 2000), Chs. 2 and 3.

2. Andy Leak and George Paizis, eds., *The Holocaust and the Text: Speaking the Unspeakable* (London: Macmillan, 1999).

3. Roger Gottlieb, ed., *Thinking the Unthinkable* (Mahwah, N.J.: Paulist Press, 1990).

4. Sara Horowitz, *Voicing the Void* (Albany: SUNY Press, 1997).

5. Daniel Jonah Goldhagen, *Hitler's Willing Executioners: Ordinary Germans and the Holocaust* (New York: Knopf, 1996), esp. Ch. XVI.

6. Lawrence Langer, *Holocaust Testimonies* (New Haven, Conn.: Yale University Press, 1991).

7. Henry Greenspan, "Imagining Survivors: Testimony and the Rise of Holocaust Consciousness," in H. Flanzbaum, ed., *The Americanization of the Holocaust* (Baltimore: Johns Hopkins University Press, 1999), p. 59.

8. Elie Wiesel, "Looking Back," in Peter Hayes, ed., *Lessons and Legacies III* (Evanston, Ill: Northwestern University Press, 1999), p. 15.

9. Similarly, Dori Laub considers the testimony of a witness who claimed to have

seen four crematoria chimneys blown up in the revolt at Auschwitz—when the histori-cal evidence shows that only one was, thus that the witness *could* not have seen what was claimed. Laub uses the concept of the "unimaginable" context to distinguish such tes-timony from the historical evidence. Cf. Shoshana Felman and Dori Laub, *Testimony* (New York: Routledge, 1992), pp. 59–60.

10. Agamben makes the important point—more important because once said, so obvious—that in one of its two meanings, testimony is intrinsically partial, *non*-objective: the words of a participant in an event, rather than (as in its second meaning) the words of a "neutral" observer. Cf. Giorgio Agamben, *Remnants of Auschwitz*, trans. Daniel Heller-Roazen (New York: Zone Press, 1999), p. 17.

11. This sense of contingency holds—in my view, even more intensely—for the ex-traordinary example of Herman Kruk, the Vilna diarist, who evidently wrote the last pages of his diary in a camp only hours before he was killed and with the "knowledge" beforehand of that imminent end.

12. Evidence of such revision does not seem to have made any difference in the re-ception of the most widely read Holocaust diary, of Anne Frank—but because there are other, external reasons for that difference, the example is not, in my view, counter-evidence.

13. Jacques Derrida, "A Self-Unsealing Poetic Text: Poetics and Politics of Witness-ing," in Michael Clark, ed., *Revenge of the Aesthetic* (Berkeley: University of California Press, 2000).

14. *Camera Lucida*, trans. Richard Howard (New York: Hill & Wang, 1981).

15. Cathy Caruth, *Unclaimed Experience: Trauma, Narrative, and History* (Baltimore: Johns Hopkins University Press, 1996); Dominick LaCapra, *Representing the Holocaust: History, Theory, Trauma* (Ithaca, N.Y.: Cornell University Press, 1994).

16. Venturing into what is at best "pop-etymology": The German *"Traum"* ("Dream") has no connection with the Greek root of *"trauma"*—but is it so implausible to suggest that, through Freud, a connection has been reinforced between the two?

17. See, e.g., Leslie Morris and Jack Zipes, eds., *Unlikely History: The Changing German-Jewish Symbiosis, 1945–2000* (New York: Palgrave, 2000).

18. This need not exclude the possibility of properties or events that are "unspeak-able," but the basis here would, it seems to me, go beyond psychology. The name of God, for example, is sacred in the Hebrew Bible—not to be uttered except by the High Priest inside the Temple, and then only in the performance of a specific rite.

7. UNDOING CERTAIN MISCHIEVOUS QUESTIONS ABOUT THE HOLOCAUST

1. This question has had more than only "popular" currency. Two important (al-beit quite different) scholarly formulations of it appear in Raul Hilberg, *The Destruction of the European Jews* (New York: Holmes & Meier, 1985), and *The Politics of Memory* (Chicago: Ivan Dee, 1996); and Hannah Arendt, *Eichmann in Jerusalem: A Report on the Banality of Evil* (New York: Viking, 1963).

2. For summaries and analyses of Jewish resistance, see, e.g., Reuben Ainsztein, *Jewish Resistance in Nazi-Occupied Eastern Europe* (New York: Harper & Row, 1974);

Yitzhak Arad, *Belżec, Sobibor, Treblinka* (Bloomington: Indiana University Press, 1987); Yehuda Bauer, *A History of the Holocaust* (New York: Franklin Watts, 1982); Dov Levin, *Fighting Back* (New York: Holmes & Meier, 1985); Leni Yachil, *The Holocaust: The Fate of European Jewry* (New York: Oxford University Press, 1990).

3. For a concise account (and additional references) to the status of Soviet prisoners of war, see the entry on "Soviet Prisoners of War" by Christian Streit, in *Encyclopedia of the Holocaust* (New York: Macmillan, 1990), pp. 1192–95.

4. On these three massacres (respectively), see Vojtech Mastny, *The Czechs under Nazi Rule* (New York: Columbia University Press, 1971); H. R. Kedward, *Occupied France* (Oxford: Blackwell, 1985); Mark Mazower, *Inside Hitler's Greece* (New Haven, Conn.: Yale University Press, 1995).

5. On the claim of such a "defect," see Nechama Tec, "Jewish Resistance: Facts, Omissions, and Distortions" (Washington, D.C.: United States Holocaust Memorial Museum, 1997).

6. For a sampling of accounts of resistance to Nazi occupiers by other groups, see, e.g., S. Okecki, *Polish Resistance Movements in Poland and Abroad, 1939–1945* (Warsaw: PWN, 1987); J. Schunadeke and P. Steinbach, eds., *Der Widerstand gegen den National-sozialismus* (Munchen: Piper, 1984); Maria de Blasio Wilhelm, *The Other Italy* (New York: Norton, 1988).

7. Such explanations become even more mischievous when they are presented as historically or empirically grounded. A notable recent example of this is the concept of "eliminationist antisemitism" proposed by Daniel Goldhagen as a tenet acted on in common by Germans during the Nazi period. Cf. Daniel Jonah Goldhagen, *Hitler's Willing Executioners: Ordinary Germans and the Holocaust* (New York: Knopf, 1996).

8. On Nazi Party membership figures, see Michael Kater, *The Nazi Party: A Social Profile of Members and Leaders, 1919–1945* (Cambridge, Mass.: Harvard University Press, 1983).

9. Christopher Browning, *Ordinary Men: Reserve Battalion 101 and the Final Solution in Poland* (New York: HarperCollins, 1992). Admittedly, the sample on which Browning bases his analysis and conclusions is small and in certain respects atypical—but it is just by the accumulation of such samples that any conclusions at all about this matter can be reached. (See also, for a broader sampling of "ordinary" Germans, Eric Johnson, *The Nazi Terror: Gestapo, Jews and Ordinary Germans* (London: John Murray, 1999); and Robert Gellately, *Backing Hitler* (New York: Oxford University Press, 2001).

10. For fuller development of this point, see Berel Lang, *The Future of the Holocaust: Between History and Memory* (Ithaca, N.Y.: Cornell University Press, 1999), Ch. 8.

11. Tim Cole, *Selling the Holocaust: From Auschwitz to Schindler—How History Is Bought, Packaged, and Sold* (New York: Routledge, 1999); and Norman Finkelstein, *The Holocaust Industry: Reflections on the Exploitation of Jewish Suffering* (New York: Verso, 2000). A more sophisticated version of the same line of argument (and open to the same objections) appears in Peter Novick, *The Holocaust in American Life* (Boston: Houghton Mifflin, 1999) which is discussed in the present volume in Chapter 10.

12. See, for three examples of this formulation (out of many possible ones), the essays by Hans Kellner, Wulf Kansteiner, and Robert Braun in *History and Theory* 33 (1994): 127–97; cf. also a response to them in Berel Lang, *Holocaust Representation: Art*

within the Limits of History and Ethics (Baltimore: Johns Hopkins University Press, 2000), Ch. 5.

8. FROM THE PARTICULAR TO THE UNIVERSAL, AND FORWARD

1. On the issue of linguistic representation in relation to the Holocaust, see especially Victor Klemperer, *The Language of the Third Reich*, trans. Martin Brady (New York: Continuum, 2002). Cf. also George Steiner, *Language and Silence* (New York: Atheneum, 1964); James Young, *Writing and Rewriting the Holocaust* (Bloomington: Indiana University Press, 1988); Berel Lang, "Language and Genocide," in *Act and Idea in the Nazi Genocide* (Syracuse: Syracuse University Press, 2003). On Holocaust representation more generally, see Saul Friedländer, ed., *Probing the Limits of Representation* (Cambridge, Mass.: Harvard University Press, 1992); Dominick LaCapra, *Representing the Holocaust* (Ithaca, N.Y.: Cornell University Press, 1994); Berel Lang, *Holocaust Representation: Art within the Limits of History and Ethics* (Baltimore: Johns Hopkins University Press, 2001).

2. See on the issue of use of the phrase *the Holocaust*, Giorgio Agamben, *Remnants of Auschwitz*, trans. Daniel Heller-Roazen (New York: Zone Books, 1999), pp. 26–31.

3. The narrower definition of "Who is a Jew?" in the Nuremberg Laws in effect superceded the "Aryan Paragraph" that had been part of the Civil Service Law of 7 April 1933 and that was soon applied in excluding Jews from other professions than just the Civil Service. To be sure, the Nuremberg Laws were also more severe than the Aryan Paragraph insofar as they excluded Jews from citizenship and not only from certain professions. See on this shift the account of the Nuremberg Laws in Christian Zentner and Friedemann Bedürftig, eds., *Encyclopedia of the Third Reich* (New York: Da Capo Press, 1997.

4. Ian Kershaw's summary of an address by Hitler in Munich on 24 February 1944, celebrating the anniversary of the announcement of the Party Program in 1920. Cf. Ian Kershaw, *Hitler: 1936–1945* (New York: Norton, 2000), pp. 624–25. The Luftwaffe project of developing the "New York Bomber" was intended to be more than only a rhetorical flourish.

5. Primo Levi, *Survival in Auschwitz*, trans. Stuart Woolf (New York: Collier, 1961), p. 98.

6. Recounted in E. Thomas Wood and Stanislaw M. Jankowski, *Karski: How One Man Tried to Stop the Holocaust* (New York: Wiley & Sons, 1994).

7. For a sustained literary account of "surprise" in the context of deportations and the camps, see Imre Kertesz, *Fateless*, trans. Christopher C. Wilson and Katharina M. Wilson (Evanston, Ill.: Northwestern University Press, 1992).

8. *Survival in Auschwitz*, pp. 24–25.

9. OSKAR ROSENFELD AND HISTORIOGRAPHIC REALISM (IN SEX, SHIT, AND STATUS)

1. Hayden V. White, *Metahistory: The Historical Imagination in Nineteenth Century Europe* (Baltimore: Johns Hopkins University Press, 1974).

2. As, for example, his inclusion of "singular existential propositions" as a ground

for historical narrative. Cf. "Historical Narrative and the Emplotment of Truth," in Saul Friedlander, *Probing the Limits of Representation* (Cambridge, Mass.: Harvard University Press, 1992), p. 38.

3. Cf., e.g., Hayden V. White, *Figural Realism: Studies in the Mimesis Effect* (Baltimore: Johns Hopkins University Press, 1999), Chs. 1, 2, 4.

4. Oskar Rosenfeld, *In the Beginning Was the Ghetto: 890 Days in Lodz*, ed. and with an introduction by Hanno Loewy, trans. Brigitte M. Goldstein (Evanston, Ill.: Northwestern University Press, 2002). Oskar Rosenfeld (b., Moravia, 1884, d. Birkenau, 1944) received a doctorate in literature from the University of Vienna in 1908, and after that remained in Vienna, working as a journalist, novelist, and translator, among other things engaged with Zionism in its earliest years. After the *Anschluss* in 1938, he fled to Prague; he was deported from there to Lodz in November 1941 where, after a half year, he found work in the Lodz archive and began to contribute to what became the Lodz "Chronicle" (see Lucjan Dobroszycki, ed., *The Chronicle of the Lodz Ghetto 1941–1944* [New Haven, Conn.: Yale University Press, 1984]). Rosenfeld himself kept a private diary in addition to his contributions to the *Chronicle;* of twenty-one notebooks, nineteen survived, and are in the collection of Yad VaShem. The volume edited by Hanno Loewy, which is cited here, consists of selections from those notebooks. Rosenfeld was deported from Lodz to Auschwitz in August 1944. The first entry in his notebooks is dated 17 February 1942; the last entry is dated 28 July 1944.

5. Except, of course, in the vacuous sense of acknowledgement for the slightest spatio-temporal difference among objects or events.

6. *The Warsaw Diaries of Adam Czerniakov*, ed. Raul Hilberg, Stanislaw Staron, and Josef Kermisz (New York: Stein and Day, 1979); Etty Hillesum, *An Interrupted Life: The Diaries of Etty Hillesum*, trans. Arno Pomerans (New York: Pantheon, 1983).

7. Cf., e.g., Oskar Rosenfeld, *Die Vierte Galerie: Ein Wiener Roman* (Vienna: Hugo Heller Verlag, 1910) and *Tage und Nachte* (Leipzig: Ilfverlag, 1920)—the latter a collection of six novellas.

8. Berel Lang, *Holocaust Representation: Art within the Limits of History and Ethics* (Baltimore: Johns Hopkins University Press, 2000), Ch. 1.

9. Victor Klemperer, *The Language of the Third Reich*, trans. Martin Brady (New York: Continuum, 2002), pp. 285–86.

10. Raul Hilberg, *The Politics of Memory* (Chicago: Ivan Dee, 1996), pp. 46, 85–88.

11. For a recent account that addresses part of the issue of sex in the camps, see Jonathan C. Friedman, *Speaking the Unspeakable* (Lanham, Md.: University Press of America, 2002), Ch. 3.

12. Almost alone, Terrence Des Pres, in his notable book, *The Survivor* (New York: Oxford University Press, 1976), includes a chapter on "Excrement" in the camps.

10. LACHRYMOSE WITHOUT TEARS

1. New York: Cambridge University Press, 1988.

2. Boston: Houghton Mifflin, 1999.

3. Norman Finkelstein, *The Holocaust Industry: Reflection on the Exploitation of Jewish Suffering* (New York: Verso, 2000).

4. In a heavily documented book, the expression Novick cites here as representative of American debate—"truly holocaustal or merely genocidal"—goes unattributed to

even one source, let alone to many. No doubt the locution appeared in the debate (what, after all, did not?)—but was it really at the focus of the debate (as compared, e.g., to the question of which American interests were really at stake)? It is worth noting that Novick does not consider even as a possibility that the occurrence of the debate itself had a good deal to do with the *presence* of the Holocaust in public memory.

11. "NOT ENOUGH" VS. "PLENTY"

1. See Susan Zuccotti, *Under His Very Windows: The Vatican and the Holocaust in Italy* (New Haven, Conn.: Yale University Press, 2000), and Ronald J. Rychlak, *Hitler, the War, and the Pope* (Columbia, Mo.: Genesis Press, 2000). For other views in this far-flung debate, see, for examples, James Carroll, *Constantine's Sword: The Church and the Jews* (Boston: Houghton Mifflin, 2001); John Cornwell, *Hitler's Pope: The Secret Life of Pius XII* (New York: Viking, 1999); Daniel Jonah Goldhagen, *A Moral Reckoning: The Role of the Catholic Church in the Holocaust* (New York: Alfred A. Knopf, 2002); Carol Rittner and John K. Roth, eds., *Pope Pius XII and the Holocaust* (New York: Continuum, 2002).

2. Cited in Saul Friedländer, *Pius XII and the Third Reich*, trans. C. Fullman (New York: Knopf, 1966), pp. 207–208.

12. THE EVIL IN GENOCIDE

1. Raphael Lemkin, *Axis Rule in Occupied Europe* (Washington, D.C.: Carnegie Endowment for International Peace, 1944).

2. The charge of genocide was not formally part of the charges brought at Nuremberg. Arguably the first appearances of the charge in formal juridical argument occurred in Poland, in discussions and judgments rendered by the Supreme National Tribunal. Cf. the trials of Amon Leopold Goeth (1946) and Rudolf Hoess (1947), summarized in *Law Reports of Trials of War Criminals,* vol. VII (London: Published for the United Nations War Crimes Commission, 1948). (I am indebted to Raul Hilberg for this reference.) Cf. also on the history of genocide, Samantha Powers, *"A Problem from Hell": America and the Age of Genocide* (New York: Basic Books, 2002). On the evolution of the UN Convention on the Prevention and Punishment of the Crime of Genocide, cf. especially William A. Schabas, *Genocide in International Law: The Crime of Crimes* (Cambridge: Cambridge University Press, 2000).

3. Cf., e.g., Richard Tuck, *Natural Rights Theory* (Cambridge: Cambridge University Press, 1976).

4. In its verdict of 2 September 1998, the UN Tribunal for Rwanda identified under this heading the systematic rape of Tutsi women by the Hutu as a genocidal act, although the wording of the verdict suggested the possibility that rape might also be considered an independent modality of genocide.

5. Certain implications concerning this parallel seem unavoidable—since during the more than twenty-year struggle in the United States Senate to win confirmation from the U.S. of the UN Genocide Convention, the Endangered Species Act (1977) passed without dissent and on its first presentation.

6. See Hannah Arendt, *Eichmann in Jerusalem: A Report on the Banality of Evil* (New York: Viking, 1963), especially the Epilogue.

13. MISINTERPRETATION AS THE AUTHOR'S RESPONSIBILITY

1. Always a possibility, one supposes, once the a priori thesis is discounted that not to have a politics is already to have one (this claim, even if not true a priori, might nonetheless be warranted in particular historical circumstances). See for the contention that Nietzsche does not have a politics, Tracy B. Strong, "Nietzsche's Political Misappropriation," in Bernd Magnus and Kathleen M. Higgins, eds., *The Cambridge Companion to Nietzsche* (Cambridge: Cambridge University Press, 1996), pp. 119–47.

2. And are cited here for the purpose of flogging a by no means dead horse. So, a serious literary critic writing in a recent issue of a serious literary journal: "I'm for getting rid of interpretation altogether. Banning it. Anyone caught interpreting will be made an associate dean. I'm also against texts. We would be better off without them. They simply are no fun. . . . They spoil the party. Like a cousin of mine who is ubiquitous and terrible at parties. . . . [A text] has no will, no power, no being beyond what we can make of it. And we can make of it what we will." James Kincaid, "What Do We Owe Texts?" *Critical Inquiry* 25 (1999): 762–63.

3. See, for example, Arthur C. Danto, *Nietzsche as Philosopher* (New York: Macmillan, 1965), Ch. 1.

4. "On Truth and Lies in the Extra-Moral Sense," trans. Daniel Breazeale, in *Truth and Philosophy: Selections from Nietzsche's Notebooks of the 1870s* (Atlantic Highlands, N.J.: Humanities Press, 1979), p. 84.

5. *The Genealogy of Morals*, trans. Walter Kaufman and R. J. Hollingdale. (New York: Vintage, 1989), p. 77.

6. *Aus dem Nachlass der achtzigerjahre*, *Werke*, III, p. 903.

7. Benito Mussolini, "The Doctrine of Fascism," in Adrian Lyttelton, ed., *Italian Fascisms* (New York: Harper, 1973), pp. 42–49.

8. Walter Z. Laqueur, *Fascism* (Oxford: Oxford University Press, 1996), p. 25.

9. This specific disagreement is, of course, linked to the general question of the extent to which ideas or ideology affect large-scale historical events. As there has been no consensus on the answer to the larger question, its particular instances are also invariably contested; I propose in this connection only that the question should always be put in "triangulated" form, and with alternatives of a different "kind"; that is, not to what extent (e.g.) Nietzsche was responsible for the rise of Nazism or fascism—but in terms of the comparative consequences that ensued from Nietzsche's writings, on the one hand, and (e.g.) the Treaty of Versailles after World War I, on the other. The argument might well continue—but the proportions would then be clearly different.

10. See, e.g., Benito Mussolini, "La Filosofia del Forza" (1908), in *Omnia Opera*, vol. 1 (Firenze: La Fenice, 1951), pp. 174–84; "La Volonta di Potenza" (4 January 1930), in *Omnia Opera*, vol. 35 (Firenze: La Fenice, 1962), pp. 90–96.

11. To be sure, there is the oddity in this that for Nietzsche, the *resistance* to his work, insofar as that manifested itself in public neglect, would itself be evidence of a correct understanding: *of course*, the readers (and culture) he was so vehemently attacking would wish to bury him in silence and poverty—but only insofar as they understood him to be attacking them.

12. Letter to Franz Overbeck, 24 March 1887, in *Selected Letters of Friedrich Nietzsche*, ed. and trans. Christopher Middleton (Cambridge, Mass.: Hackett, 1996), p. 264.

13. *Beyond Good and Evil*, trans. R. J. Hollingdale (New York: Penguin, 1973), p. 181.

14. "The Case of Wagner," in *Ecce Homo*, trans. Walter Kaufman (New York: Vintage, 1966).

15. *Zarathustra*, "Of the New Gods."

16. Ibid.

17. Early draft of "The Use and Abuse of History," cited in Geoffrey Hartman, *The Fateful Question of Culture* (New York: Columbia University Press, 1997), pp. 6–7.

18. *Beyond Good and Evil*, trans. R. J. Hollingdale (New York: Penguin, 1973), p. 156.

19. Ibid., p. 57.

20. Ibid., p. 126.

21. *The Will to Power*, p. 86.

22. Letter to Georg Brandes, 2 December 1887, in *Selected Letters of Friedrich Nietzsche*, p. 279.

23. Yirmiyahu Yovel, *Dark Riddle: Hegel, Nietzsche, and the Jews* (University Park: Penn State Press, 1998), Chs. 7–10.

24. *Beyond Good and Evil*, p. 112.

25. *Zarathustra*, "Of War and Warriors."

26. *The Will to Power*, p. 389.

27. See, e.g., Charles Larmore, "Nietzsche's Legacy," in *The Morals of Modernity* (Cambridge: Cambridge University Press, 1996).

28. Steven Ascheim, *The Nietzsche Legacy in Germany, 1890–1990* (Berkeley: University of California Press, 1992), pp. 60–69.

29. So, for example, Richard Rorty, "The Priority of Democracy to Philosophy," in *Objectivity, Relativism, and Truth* (Cambridge: Cambridge University Press, 1991); Lawrence Hatab, *A Nietzschean Defense of Democracy: An Experiment in Postmodern Politics* (Chicago: Open Court, 1995).

30. *The Genealogy of Morals*, First Essay, Section 16.

31. Milton Himmelfarb, "No Hitler, No Holocaust," *Commentary* 76 (1984): 37–43.

AFTERWORD

1. Churchill's reference was to Nazi persecution of the Polish population as such.

INDEX

Index

BEREL LANG is Professor of Humanities at Trinity College in Hartford, Connecticut. He is author of, among other books, *Act and Idea in the Nazi Genocide; Holocaust Representation: Art within the Limits of History and Ethics;* and *The Future of the Holocaust: Between History and Memory.*